Real Estate Business and Investment Opportunities

Real Estate Business and Investment Opportunities

The Complete Guide to Starting a High-Profit Business

Bryan C. Wittenmyer

www.infoleverage.com
PO Box 13246
Reading, PA 19612

Disclaimer

This book is designed to provide accurate and reliable information with regard to the subject matter presented. It is offered with the understanding that the publisher and author is not engaged in rendering legal, accounting, or other professional service. If legal advice or other expert assistence is required, the services of a competent professional person should be retained.

Before launching any business or investment program, consult with a qualified attorney as to the legality and safety of the endeavor. Investments and businesses do have risks. You could lose money. The author and publisher specifically disclaim any liability, loss, or risk, personal or otherwise, incurred as a consequence, directly or indirectly, of the use or application of any ideas or investments discussed in this book.

Published by InfoLeverage
PO Box 13246, Reading PA 13246
www.infoleverage.com
ISBN 0-9644380-2-X
Printed in the United States of America
Produced with assistance from Griffith Publishing Consultants
Cover design by Prevario

Contents

Dedicated to my father who
gave me the real estate "talk" so
many years ago

Foreword

You're probably a lot like me. You have spent hours in bookstores gazing at all of the books in the busines section looking for the perfect opportunity to build an exciting business, career, or investment program. You are hoping that among all those pages of ink and eye-catching covers there will be some breakthrough opportunities that can change your life. Believe me, I have researched countless opportunities, and some are simply a waste of energy and time.

At some point your search has brought you to the real estate section or you've watched late-night infomercials with the real estate gurus for the hundredth time. Real estate investing is a fascinating world at first glance, and the more we consider it, the more we are intrigued by it. Real estate is simply alluring.

Real estate is a true wealth builder, a maker of jobs, industries, and a magnet for capital. Real estate is more than just land, and it is more than just buildings. It is an industry around which virtually the whole economy revolves. I encourage looking beyond the stereotypical landlord as the only option to a real estate business or investment opportunity (although income property—rentals—can be an awesome business!). This is only one of many options available. The opportunities presented in real estate vary as much as one person to the next. There are plenty of opportunities in real estate to fit each of your different personalities, goals and skills. This book is an incredible resource to help you determine which opportunity in real estate is for you and your lifestyle. You may be looking to own a few houses to create the income you need for retirement or you may have large ambitions of becoming a fulltime investor like myself.

If there was ever a perfect time to consider real estate investing, that time is upon us. The collapse in high-tech stocks was the first hit to the markets, followed by the outrageous terror assaults on our nation. More recently, we had the fall of energy giant Enron and the lack of honesty in many of the firms that audit financial statements of the publicly traded companies. The latest bad news is of brokerage firms themselves being investigated because of their buy recommendations for stocks of companies on the brink of insolvency. I can only predict that the woes of the bulls and bears will continue.

As the stock markets have struggled, real estate has maintained a slow and steady appreciation, and increases in rental rates, despite the ups and downs of Wall Street. Investors are looking for an alternative. Many are clearly looking for security, somewhere to invest their money in something tangible like real estate. To us that use OPM (other people's money) to invest in exchange for a good return for their investment, we are finding more and more partners with capital to invest. After all, bond and savings account investors are finding rates so low that their after inflation yeilds are almost nil. Real estate is becoming more and more attractive for all types of investors, active or passive. I fully expect the real estate market to rise considerably over the next five years as investors look to real estate as the vehicle of choice. Why not get involved in real estate now?

No matter what type of investor or entrepreneur you would like to become, real estate has an opportunity for you. You can start a new service business helping to serve this massive industry, become a housing tycoon in your own right, or just own a few units to pay for your children's college education. Whatever your goals or aspirations, there is a niche market waiting for you to take advantage of it.

Is real estate a get-rich quick opportunity? Yes and no. A friend of mine went from $15,000 to $750,000 in three years by applying only one of the techniques described by Bryan. Does he have a special talent allowing him to succeed so quickly? Only his willingness and passion to apply the strategies within this book. Others will be content to build their business at a slower pace. The rate at which you succeed is limited only by your level of passion and desire as well as your work habits and your ability to apply these principles to your business.

Bryan has again provided us with the informational leverage that we need in order to claim our portion of the real estate opportunity. He explains virtually every aspect of real estate investing, even some that are new to me. I was overwhelmed the first time I received a book written by Bryan. He compiles and includes an incredible amount of information in each of his books. It always results in a dog-eared book within reach of my desk. I constantly refer to them until I loan them out. For obvious reasons, the books are never returned.

Well, maybe you'll end up in the same place I am. I choose real estate investing over all the other opportunities. No other opportunity offers you the ability to create wealth and enjoy an incredible lifestyle. Becoming a real estate entrepreneur, you'll be able to gain control over your life and future. I truly believe that anyone who will apply the strategies contained in this book, will obtain financial freedom. I can only hope that you utilize the resources and knowledge that Bryan offers you in this new book.

To your success,

Matt Scott
DealmakersCafe.com

"Drive thy business or it will drive thee."

—Ben Franklin

"Real estate cannot be lost or stolen, nor can it be carried away. Purchased with common sense, paid for in full, and managed with reasonable care, it is about the safest investment in the world."

—Franklin D. Roosevelt
1882-1945

"For what shall it profit a man, if he shall gain the whole world, and lose his own soul?"

—Jesus   Mark 8:36

The High Profit World of Real Estate

People start their own businesses for a multitude of reasons. The main reasons usually are to better their income and increase the amount of personal direction and freedom in their lives. If you want more income and a better lifestyle, then you have found the right book. This unique book presents literally scores of proven real estate business models, investments, and ideas that will help you start a new business or improve the current business you may be operating. Best of all, you will learn how to operate a business or start real estate investing with very little cash. You won't need a lot of capital, but you must have a high level of enthusiasm and persistence to build one of these businesses.

Why Real Estate? You will notice throughout this book that I say "high-profit real estate." Why? Few businesses or investments can match the profit potential of real estate. In fact, I can't think of a single industry that offers the small entrepreneur as much opportunity as real estate. Besides being fertile soil for entrepreneurs, real estate offers a safe haven for investors and their capital. Real estate is a "hard asset." While the value of questionable stocks or bonds can virtually plummet overnight, buildings, land and houses aren't going anywhere. Real estate is fixed and immovable.

Real estate is considerably more stable than other vehicles because real estate is **tangible.** Stock, bonds, and insurance (and even cash currency) assets are intangible—really paper assets. With paper assets values are far more volatile and susceptible to fraud and governmental devaluation (inflation). Real property, on the other hand, is touchable, visitable, provable. That's precisely why it's called REAL estate!

When you compare the real estate industry (home ownership, investments, real estate service businesses) as a whole, you will find

1

that building a business around this industry is a great opportunity. Generally speaking, real estate is more secure, more productive, and more profitable than other investment venues. Consider this: Real estate is safer than the stock market, because typical values rise and fall at rates of less than 10 percent annually. Real estate is safer than the commodities futures market because it is infinitely more stable. Real estate is safer than the bond market because rising interest rates devalue bonds due to inflation, while real estate values rise with inflation, and they also rise with low interest rates. The big secret is that low interest rates increase real estate prices, because people can buy more property for lower payments, which creates more demand and market activity.

When we compare real estate against other tangible assets like artwork, antiques, numismatics (coins), other collectibles, or precious metals, we find that although they have some similar qualities as tangible objects, there are two major drawbacks. First, collectibles generally do not produce income (rent, interest rate, or dividend payment). Therefore, they are an unproductive asset, not generating cash flow. Second, collectibles are products people often want but don't actually need. In times of crisis or economic downturns, many collectibles are difficult to sell. Combine this with the fact that they do not produce an income stream, and the case for owning them becomes less appealing. Keep in mind that the federal government confiscated all privately owned gold (except numismatic coins) during the Depression of the 1930s. The bottom line: real estate is an asset of utility.

Lastly, when we compare real estate (investments) to the myriad of small businesses opportunities we again find that real estate is safer. Most small businesses don't make it past the initial five-year period of infancy. Real estate (land), on the other hand, has been around for thousands of years. When properly maintained, houses and other buildings will last for hundreds of years. Another point worth considering is that the foreclosure rate of real estate loans is considerably less than 10 percent, while the business failure rate is closer to 50 percent. I know this isn't really an apples for apples comparison of vehicles (property versus businesses), but I think the historical and utilitarian comparison is valuable to consider. Note: While I believe real property is a better investment than the others mentioned above, I'm not saying that you shouldn't own any investments besides real estate. With the right expertise, stocks, bonds, antiques, coins, and precious metals, should be considered if you want some diversification in your portfolio.

Being involved in the real estate investment and business industry, I can vouch for the wide range of opportunities awaiting the industrious but cash-poor entrepreneur. As you will see, there are dozens of high-profit opportunities awaiting you. This book doesn't offer just a few ideas for starting a business or investment program. No, it is stuffed with ideas. Your biggest problem after reading it won't be a lack of ideas—just the opposite; there are so many exciting ways to make money in real estate that you'll find it tough to pick just one!

Real estate has a business or investment opportunity waiting for you whether or not you feel that you have a lot of skills or capital. You can choose from a wide range of opportunities that will fit your skills and temperament. If you are a detail-oriented, paperwork person, there are opportunities for you. If you are more of a handy, fix-anything person, there are opportunities for you. If you are a people person, if you are an organizer and manager type of person, there are opportunities for you. Whatever your personal blend of talents, skills, and capital, this book has a high profit business for investment opportunity waiting for you!

High Profit. You can earn many different forms of profit in real estate businesses or investments, including rents, consulting fees, capital gains, commissions, product sales, asset management fees, interest income, and other fees from services. In this book we cover a full spectrum of real estate businesses and investments that will generate nearly every conceivable type of profits. **Rentals, property flipping, consulting, property management, mortgage brokering, property maintenance services, publishing, mobile homes, paper investments, land deals, and a host of other opportunities are explained in these pages along with dozens of helpful resources to help you achieve your goals.**

This book goes into detail on the best ways to make money from real estate starting with very little cash. Many of the opportunities are businesses, particularly service businesses, and some are investment opportunities. Whatever the case, I have geared this book towards opportunities that require minimal cash (less than $10,000) and minimal education and licensing, although some opportunities may require all of the above. For example, this book does not cover real estate appraisal, since in most states bona fide appraisal work requires extensive course work, testing, and licenses. On the other hand, I extensively cover buying and selling real estate, landlording, investor services, mortgage brokering, and many, many other opportunities that can typically be operated with minimal cash and licensing!

Profit Potential.
From my many years of being involved in real estate opportunities I can say with confidence that the potential is really up to you. I have met folks making $10,000 a year from a real estate venture and I have met others making closer to the big one-million dollar mark. As in most businesses, the potential is more based on you than on the actual business.

People often ask me if a particular business or investment is a "good" one to get involved with. In most cases, the answer should be in the form of a series of questions: Are you a highly ambitious person? Are you a persistent, determined, efficient, hard working, enthusiastic person? Are you a self-starter? Are you willing to fail along the way and consider it as a learning process rather than validation of who you are? Are you willing to continually educate yourself about your business or investments? If the person can answer yes to most of these questions, then yes, the business or investment is "good." In my business travels I have seen ordinary people build unusually good businesses from seemingly lowly services. For instance, I know one family that has made a small fortune selling French fries at sporting events with small trailer concession stands. Their product is simply fresh cut potatoes, deep-fried in oil. Sounds pretty simple to me. Making money doesn't have to be complicated.

While making money can be simple, keep in mind that very few businesses or investments are easy. In fact, from my years of entrepreneuring, I have yet to find an easy way to make money! Unfortunately, you need hard work to make businesses successful. Businesses must be worked—yes, like a job—in many cases to prosper. Forget some of the trendy nonsense which suggests you can make a lot of money without wearisome work.

Also, ALL businesses have problems that at times make the owners want to throw up their hands in disgust. Any talk about making money being easy, fast, or no-risk is total foolishness. Can you make a lot of money in real estate? Yes, you certainly can. This book will show you how. In addition, this book will provide abundant resources to further your real estate education and research.

Real Estate is Everywhere. Real estate is profitable for many reasons. First, you must remember that virtually everything we consider valuable is real property. There is more real estate in the world than all of the other "stuff" (personal property) that is ownable. It's safe to say that 90 percent of all property is real property, not personal. And as we know, most personal property depreciates. Let me repeat that: **Most personal property depreciates! Land appreciates.** Remember, the land New York City is built on was purchased from the American Indians for $24 and a few muskets! So that's some serious land appreciation. Today you can't even park in downtown Manhattan for $24. Think about it. You spend every minute of the day walking, driving or sitting on real estate—it might be land, houses, apartments, commercial buildings, or roads, but it is all real estate.

Because real estate is such a supreme part of life and the economy, billions of dollars of services and capital are needed to sustain it. You can take advantage of this by creating a service business or investment program to get your piece of this enormous pie. If you can't find a business or investment opportunity in this industry then you either don't like real estate (this is okay, too) or you need to really examine whether being in business is the right choice for you.

People Will Always Need Shelter. I heard a successful landlord explain that he didn't get upset with the thought of economic recessions or depressions because no matter what state the economy was in people always need a roof over their head. (He owns a lot of lower and middle income housing.)

He figures that rich folks facing tough times will need his middle income housing if things get rough, and lower income folks will need his middle class housing if the economy gets great! It's a fact. Folks will always need place to call home!

No matter how bad the economy gets, recession or even a desperate depression, people will always need a place to sleep. From birth until death everyone will either be a tenant or a property owner. Folks, that isn't good news—that is great news! Real estate is a product everyone wants and needs.

Shelter is one of the few indispensable needs. Because it is such a giant need, consumers need all of the supporting services and businesses that revolve around this industry. This creates a tidal wave of demand for services and investment products from smart entrepreneurs such as you. Wall Street and the stock market might shut down during a market free-fall (trading circuit breakers kick in when the market declines more than 500 points in a session), but the real estate industry will never shut down or cease to exist. Opportunities may expand and contract within segments of the industry, but as one door closes, another opens.

Pillar of the Economy. Because of the sweeping size of this industry, real estate is one of the main pillars of the economy. Think about it. All building, remodeling and development revolves around real estate. Next, think about all of the natural resources and labor that go into building, remodeling, and development. Here is a brief list of trades and professions that are needed to support the real estate industry: bankers, builders, architects, plumbers, real estate brokers, lawyers, landscapers, electricians. Next, consider all of the appliances, carpeting, and other durable goods that go inside real estate, and you see that there is a huge segment of the population working to service real property.

The multiplicity of trades and products builds diversification into real estate. In order for real estate values to decline rapidly, user demand would have to decrease dramatically while materials and labor also deflate. Unlikely. By starting a business or investment program in real estate you have more protection because of all of the diversification in the industry. The bottom line is that real estate is less volatile and therefore safer. Since real estate is so critical to the economy, the marketplace greatly rewards those entrepreneurs who create businesses and invest in it! This book is about getting your share of this money!

Land Cannot Be Manufactured. Another major reason real estate has been so stable and securely profitable is that the supply is limited. You can manufacture all forms of durable goods, but you can't create more land. Whenever you have a resource where the supply is fixed combined with a growing demand (population increases) you have rising prices. As the population of the nation (and the world) increases, you naturally have a rising demand for housing, shopping centers, industrial centers, and offices. And, once again, because we all use real estate every single day for both working and living, the real estate industry needs businesses to service, sell, finance, manage, and maintain it. The larger an industry and the more consumer demand for it, the more money there is to be made from it.

A good example of this is the projected population growth of the United States. The governmental estimates are somewhere in the area of 50 to 75 million new citizens in the next fifty years. Although much of this demand will be met through new construction, some of it will be handled from renovating and redeveloping the existing housing stock—rents and values will continue to climb.

> **"So far as we can see with any certainty, the quality of value has longer and more consistently attached to the ownership of land than to any other valuable thing. Everywhere, in all time, among all peoples, the possession of land is the basis of aristocracy, the foundation of great fortunes, the source of power. Those who own the land must be masters of the rest. Land can exist without labor, but labor cannot exist without land."**
> **—Henry George (1839-1897)**

Park Your Money. There is a myth that says more millionaires have made their money from real estate than from any other source. This myth comes from an old saying from steel industry magnate Andrew Carnegie in the early 1900s. While there is a grain of truth to this, the facts show that most millionaires have made their wealth from some sort of entrepreneurial business or professional occupation. Research by *Forbes* magazine and Dr. Thomas Stanley support the fact that most millionaires have made their fortunes from a business, not from the stock market or real estate investments.

It is true that there is more capital stored in real estate than in all other types of assets or investments. Capitalists generally make their money in various businesses and then dump or store it in real estate assets. There is far more wealth in real estate than in cash currency in all of the nation's banks. There is also more total wealth in real estate than in the stock market. The point is, real estate is a colossal storehouse of wealth, which needs people like you to service it. You can profit by tapping the multiplicity of profit centers like: rentals, management, marketing, consulting, financing, sales, title searching, bad debt recovery, inspections, foreclosure REO cleanup, maintenance, mortgage brokering, etc. Again, the huge nature of the market creates lucrative opportunities.

I don't want to be misunderstood on this point about real estate producing more millionaires than any other field. It is true that you can create a tremendous amount of wealth from real estate investments. In fact, I have met countless people who have created a net worth exceeding a million dollars from real property investments. In many cases these folks own apartment buildings, houses, farms, land, or commercial properties. I just want to make it clear that while real estate is the king of all investments (compared to, say, stocks or bonds), we need to be careful not to exaggerate the case for real estate.

Service Businesses and Investments. Real estate offers unique opportunities because a large portion of the businesses needed to serve the market are service businesses. **The advantage of a service business is that you usually do not need a lot of cash to start and operate them.** These opportunities require more time and specialized knowledge than operating cash. Time you have—knowledge and skills you can learn.

The other major business opportunities are what I call investment opportunities. These require larger amounts of capital than do service businesses, but I cover them in this book because real estate is the easiest of assets for investors to buy with leverage (borrowed money). **In fact, some of the best opportunities in real estate are investment properties that can be operated full or part-time from your home office.**

Buying and selling houses, landlording, and other real estate investments all require larger amounts of capital, but they are the best assets to buy and manage with a limited bank account. In fact, these are among my favorite business opportunities for cash-poor entrepreneurs! As much as many people dislike rental properties, I can tell you there are few businesses or investments that will provide the ultimate, long-term freedom rental property can offer.

Try to borrow money to buy a business and you will quickly find that bankers do not like to loan money for business start-ups! Bankers know the failure rate is high among business start-ups. Bankers also do not know how to value the price of a business since much of what is being sold is the so-called "goodwill" portion of the business. Goodwill is an intangible "asset" which represents the value of the company name, customer following, future business potential, etc. Because it is not concrete, it is hard to value. The bottom line: bankers do not like to lend money for business start-ups or existing business purchases. But, and this is critically important, bankers do lend money to buy real estate with very little problem! You can buy real estate investments far easier than you can buy a business. Yet, real estate income properties perform like a business and can even provide many advantages standard businesses do not!

Investment Tax Advantages. Real estate investments (property held for rental) are typically taxed more favorably than regular employment or business income since the income is classified as investment income.

Investment income is taxed of course, but in most cases you do not pay self-employment tax (Social Security) which can be a huge saving since the self-employment tax is about 15 percent. Regular wage income or business income requires you pay anywhere from 7-15 percent Social Security tax on top of all the other taxes like federal, state, and local. Rents generally are considered investment income and therefore, are typically exempt from the self-employment taxes. Tax laws change and sometimes are complex, so make sure you speak to a tax professional.

Depreciation and Capital Gains. Two other tax advantages of real estate investments are the favorable depreciation write-off and low capital gains tax rates. Depreciation is where the tax code allows you to take what are called "paper" losses, which can shelter other income. This basically allows you to shelter some of your cash flow without paying tax since the income is shown as a loss on paper since in theory the building is wearing out and losing value (depreciating). While buildings can and do lose value from wear and tear, in most cases buildings actually increase in value when the land, location and other factors are considered.

Capital gains are a special tax treatment for profits generated from the sale of an investment that was held on a long-term basis.

These laws change from time to time, but the point to remember is that if the asset qualifies as a true investment, you have a major tax saving on the profit generated from a sale of the asset. While the actual capital gains tax rates change periodically, the fact that capital gains are treated with low rates almost never changes.

So you can see, numerous tax advantages to real estate investment will ultimately improve your cash flow and return on investment. This is just another reason to seriously consider a real estate investment opportunity!

Passive Income. Real estate investment opportunities often produce what we call passive cash flow. Passive cash flow is income that comes in month after month, year after year without requiring your active involvement. In many cases after you have the property fixed up and on-line with a tenant or buyer, the income comes in with minimal work over a fairly long period of time. In addition, once the asset becomes free and clear, you get to keep all of the money previously paid out to the mortgage lender. Your cash flow will increase without any additional effort on your part. Well-bought properties become annuities, providing steady income for years into the future with minimal work.

No Need to Quit Your Job. Real estate offers many opportunities that can be worked as a part-time venture. There's no need to sacrifice your current security until you're good and ready. Real estate investments (rentals) work especially well as a part-time endeavor. Most businesses require you to quit your day job, but real estate offers plenty of solid, part-time opportunities.

Better Lifestyle. Because most real estate businesses and investments can be conducted from a home office without fixed office hours or employees, they offer an extremely flexible lifestyle. You can customize your own work schedule and lifestyle.

At this point, I hope I have you fired up for a real estate business or investment opportunity where you can take advantage of all the good things real estate has going for it! I have no doubt that there is at least one or two great opportunities that are perfectly suited for you within this book. Let's keep rolling!

What You Will Learn from this Book

Here is an overview of what you can expect to learn from this book.

Chapter 2 will cover how to start and run a high-profit business without a lot of cash. This is critical information, since most businesses fail because they run out of operating capital. Most of these concepts and ideas are proven methods that have been field tested by entrepreneurs who didn't have a lot of cash when they got started. This chapter will guide you in making wise business expenditures and investments.

Chapter 3 is an explanation of the new extreme business model. This chapter will tell you the newest cutting edge strategies for surviving and prospering under the highly competitive business environment of the future. You can throw out many of the old methods of running a business because times have changed, and frankly, business and investing is difficult. This chapter, like chapter 2, will show you how to run a lean and mean, street-smart business operation.

Chapters 4 to 14 is where the truly fun stuff comes. In these chapters we explain the best opportunities in real estate today—the opportunities that can be started with very little cash. We cover dozens of business opportunities, cash flow ideas, profit centers, and investments.

This section literally is a smorgasbord of cash-flow generators. You are sure to get plenty of ideas that you can try in your existing investments or business. You name it, we cover it: Buying and selling houses, apartment preparation services, property management, marketing consulting, creating high-yield notes and contracts, cash-flow landlording, real estate sales, title searching, rooming houses, lease-purchasing, mortgage brokering, land sales money machines, real estate judgment recovery, investor services, apartment building efficiency consulting, home inspections, FSBO consulting, discounted paper, mobile homes, and many more ideas. Best of all, I provide resources where you can get further information and contacts about your field of interest.

Chapter 15 covers the much under estimated importance of selecting the right company name. The name you select will help you present the image you want to portray to the public. We will also give you samples of names to avoid like the plague. You must read this chapter.

Chapter 16 covers scores of street-smart business tips, strategies, concepts, and rules to run your business by. This is a multi-topic cornucopia of business wisdom, observations, and ideas to help you run your business shrewdly and profitably. This chapter is priceless informational leverage.

Chapter 17 is an explanation of the main entities in which to run your business and investments through. It will clear up some of the myths and misinformation about corporations and sole proprietorships. Brief, but good.

Chapter 18 covers marketing tactics and strategies that you absolutely must use if you want your real estate venture to succeed. Business at its core is marketing. It is the way you present and position your company to the marketplace. I will give you a full plate of ideas and concepts to help you dominate your marketplace within the specialized field you select. You will learn why you should never outsource your marketing to an outsider—you must be in charge of this part of the company.

Chapter 19 is my list and explanation of 10 stupid things business owners do to mess up their business. It's amazing how good people mess up good businesses and investments by doing foolish things. Here we cover in depth 10 things that can doom your business life. Many a good business or investment portfolio has been sunk by loose practices like absentee management, the boredom syndrome, daily work deficits, fast riches mindset, lending money, and too soon a rich lifestyle. This chapter also includes my concluding remarks and a few words of parting advice followed by an appendix and contact information.

So there you have it. I have presented the case for why real estate is a great field to start a business opportunity with very little start-up cash. It is a huge area with opportunities unmatched in diversity and profit. It will always be a high demand field with room for flexible and hungry entrepreneurs. The tax laws are favorable to the investment side of real estate, and people will always need housing whether the economy is strong or weak.

Real estate is especially attractive in two areas—service businesses that require low-cash to start, and investments where you can safely leverage your way into an asset and have others pay the debt service with you making a profit to boot. Without question, real estate is a great industry. A high-profit industry where folks like you can make a nice living on your own terms! Literally billions of dollars are there for the taking. You can get your share of the profits providing services or housing to folks who not only want them, but need them.

What you are reading is in essence like sitting down for a few days and picking the brain of a real estate entrepreneur who has spent literally thousands of hours investing, studying, researching, and networking in the real estate world. Over the years I have met and exchanged ideas with hundreds of other investors and business people who have shared what they are doing to make money in real estate. This combined with my own diverse experiences from buying, selling, renting, and consulting will serve you well as you read this work.

How to Start a High-Profit Real Estate Business with Very Little Cash

In this chapter we explain in detail how to start and operate a business using very little start-up capital. First we cover the unique concepts you will need to effectively get a business up and running using only a minimal amount of cash. Next, we go into precise detail on the step-by-step rules and ideas on how to keep a business running successfully with only a few thousand dollars of working capital.

We explain the new way to play the business game based on concepts borrowed from the military, the virtual economy of the internet, and the new thinking coming from street-fighting entrepreneurs who are gutting it out in the real trenches of the business world.

A good portion of this chapter covers the new strategic smallness theory. We unpack and explain how to run a ruthlessly lean and mean operation that is not top heavy with payroll but totally equipped to generate cash flow from one employee, namely you, and a team of contract workers.

This chapter along with the next one will give you all of the tools and concepts to start and operate a successful business or investment with a bare-bones amount of cash. Let's not spend any more time on introductions. Let's get into some stimulating information on how to start and operate a real estate service or investment business.

The Two Solutions to Your Problem. Your problem is not unique, you like most business people, do not have a lot of excess cash sitting around to start and operate a business with. The facts are that very few people have a lot of idle cash sitting in the bank. Even most successful business people do not have a lot of cash at their disposal—it's tied up in their home, lifestyle, inventory, or being used to service their debts and payroll. Everyone is looking for ways to make money without having to invest a lot of money.

Real estate offers you two giant opportunities to make money without a lot of cash in the bank. Your time yes, cash no. Opportunity number one is what we call a service business. This is where you specialize in providing some sort of needed service for people who either do not have the time or do not have the skills needed to get the work done. You, the self-employed specialist, have the knowledge and time to get the job done quicker and cheaper then the person could have without you. Life is too complicated and busy for most people to handle all of the problems associated with buying and owing real estate.

Service businesses are ideal because they typically require knowledge, skills, and time—not large inventories, payrolls, and storefronts. In essence, *you* are the product *and* the service. In many cases, you will be effectively leveraging the assets of your customers. You won't necessarily have to own real estate because you will be feeding off your client's assets—ethically.

Since service businesses don't manufacture products, you have a major advantage of being able to conduct business without all of the capital-intensive equipment and personnel that is usually part of producing a product. You are the product they are buying, not a big storefront or fancy office.

In case you have been sleeping under a rock the last fifteen or twenty years, the economy has shifted from an industrial based economy to more service and information based industries. Cars, furniture, appliances, and other "durable" goods are still being manufactured as much or more than ever. The change is that more dollars as a percent of the economy is being created in service type industries. Karl Albrecht and Ron Zemke in their book, *Service America,* call these new businesses, "Help Me" businesses. Help me do my taxes, help me manage my rental property, help me with my legal problem, help me with my cooking, help me find a house, help me with my investments, and the list goes on and on.

Opportunity Number Two. The second great opportunity to make money with very little starting cash is in real estate investments. This branch of opportunities can be worked alone or in combination with another job or business you might be working. Depending on the investment area you select, this kind of opportunity can be more passive, making it a perfect compliment to your current line of work. In other words, this might be perfect for those of you who want to continue working your present job or business. In fact, the vast majority of real estate investments are complimentary, and not the sole source of income for their owner.

Maximum Leverage. Just as many service businesses allow you to "use" the assets of other people to make your profits, investments allow you to use good old OPM, other people's money, to buy your properties. In fact, I can think of no other business or asset (stocks, coins, etc.) that can be as easily acquired with so little of your own cash as can real estate. You cannot buy stocks or bonds with owner financing, but you can sure buy houses and apartments whereby the seller will hold all or part of the financing for you! If the owner will not finance the property for you, an abundance of banks and lending institutions will consider your proposal. It's a fact: commercial lenders like lending against real estate because they have solid collateral that can be repossessed and sold if you don't pay! Banks love real estate because collateral values are easy to determine, and the value is stable.

We've all heard about buying properties with no money down. Although some of this is hype, this happens every day, in every county of America. Properties are bought and sold where the buyer didn't use any of their own cash. The term "no money down" is really a misnomer. Money is being paid down at closing, it's just some form of OPM ("other people's money"—either a bank's money or owner financing) or a combination of the two. Another example is when you buy properties where you just "assume" or take over the old financing with no money down. Again, this happens all the time with knowledgeable investors who know how to buy from highly motivated and desperate sellers!

Investment Options. There are plenty of investment business models from which to choose. We will review and explain the best ones for cash-poor investors and entrepreneurs. Opportunities include single family houses, multi-unit apartments, rooming houses, mobile home parks, low-income rentals, lease options, and storage space rentals.

Buy/Sell Investments. The second type of investment businesses are what I call buy/sell investments where you acquire or control building with some form of leverage and the resell or "broker" the properties to others. These are less passive and typically require more time than does the income property approach. These models are more like businesses than investments. Opportunities like: rehabbing rundown houses and apartment buildings for resale, buying and selling houses on installment contracts, lease options, wholesaling deals to investors (buy low, sell low), flipping option contracts, and land sales.

So there you have it. We have reviewed the two main types of business models we will be discussing in this book: Service Businesses and Investments.

What Very Little Cash Means. At this point I need to define what very little cash means to me. After all, to some people $2,000 is a LOT of cash; to others $25,000 is not a lot of cash. I believe a reasonable definition of very little cash is anywhere from $2,000 to $10,000 at your disposal ready to put into a business or investment. You will need some startup cash on hand, but don't worry if you are broke; you just will need to get a couple thousand pulled together. If that is an impossible task, then perhaps you need to rethink your spending or current work habits. Let's face it, $2,000 is not a lot of money. **Note:** Some opportunities in this book can be started with NO cash investment.

Secondly, as stated earlier, many investment type opportunities can be acquired using various forms of leverage via owner financing, bank loans, taking over existing payments, or master leasing the asset. These opportunities may require large amount of capital ($15,000 to $100,000), but this can effectively be handled with prudent borrowing (mortgages) involving minimal amounts of cash on your part.

The Guerrilla Operator. Many of the principles discussed in this chapter fall under the category of guerilla strategies for doing business. Before we explore the precise ideas behind being a guerilla operator, let me explain where this whole concept was adapted from.

We have all been brainwashed that big organizations, whatever form they be, governmental, military, or business, are better than small organizations. Generally speaking this was true. The operative word here is was. You see, in the past, big companies, big armies, and big governments were the way you dominated your world. Things have changed. Small, or shall I say, strategic small-ness is in vogue. Why? Because it works.

Let's take armies for example. The modern day military model has begun to change. Why? Terrorism. You see, all the bright minds working in the world's various military institutions are completely bewildered with how to handle terrorism. The problem is, How does a slow-moving bureaucratic army handle an agile enemy that is virtually impossible to pin down and keeps moving?

These small bands of guerrilla terrorists wreak havoc against enemy nations because they are small, fast moving, and nearly impossible to strike back at back. Combine the guerrilla army's strategic smallness with their low-budget, but lethal weapons, and you have one nasty enemy that is hard to beat. When large armies try to fight guerrilla armies they usually find that they are simply outfoxed by the sheer nimbleness and invisibility of the their oppo-nent. One writer likened it to trying to hit houseflies with a sledge-hammer!

Along with being extremely agile, these terrorist groups use extreme weapons that are highly effective, but incredibly cheap to make. For example, a typical terrorist bomb probably can be built for less than $10,000, while modern armies use missiles that cost upwards of a hundred thousand dollars to manufacture. The world's most powerful nations are extremely troubled by these small mer-cenary groups. They don't know how to fight them.

The terrorist analogy fits well in the business world. You can build a highly competitive business or investment program with a modest amount of cash and a large amount of creativity. Your guerrilla operation can run rings around your slow, lumbering competitors.

The same thing has begun with the virtual world of the Inter-net. Big businesses are perplexed with how to handle these small companies that out service, out price, out speed, and out maneuver them! For example, there's the case of Matt Drudge and his Internet site **www.drudgereport.com.** Several years ago, this one-man show was unheard of in the media. He started a little company that monitored the world's news agencies for fast breaking news reports and then posted the link with a headline on his site. The viewer then could click the headline and it would bring up the blockbuster story. The stories are typically unusual or dramatic in nature. He's not so much a journalist as he is an organizer and researcher of fast breaking news stories around the world. The advantage for the news seeker is they only need to visit one web site for the day's hottest breaking news stories.

These days Drudge gets over two million hits per day. The astounding thing is this one-man web site is operated from a spare room in his condo! Talk about low budget! The mainstream media are completely perplexed as to how to drive this much traffic to their own web sites operated by countless employees from big expensive offices in New York City! Small is in, big is out.

In business we can take these strategic-smallness concepts and apply and adapt them to our business. Clearly, we don't condone the horrific acts of terrorist groups, but we can plainly see how building a strategically small company can be better than a top-heavy, high-overhead company.

The balance of this chapter will give you plenty of idea and concepts you can use when building and structuring your business for maximum profit with a bare bones overhead.

Part-Time Bridge to Full-Time.
Many people think that when it comes to starting a business they must quit their regular job. In many cases this is a bad idea, at least until you've learned the business and have gotten things rolling smoothly with your new venture. I believe most people should use the bridge technique. The bridge technique is where you retain your current source of income and do the start-up business or investment as a part-time opportunity. Most of us have a fairly high fixed cost of living (house and car payments etc.) and this can get tricky to maintain when starting and learning a new business. But with this method you work your business part-time as if it were a second job. This will help stabilize your income and reduce your risk of failure.

Many of the investment opportunities discussed in this book are perfect for the bridge because they require only a handful of hours per week to maintain after you get them up and running. This way you maintain your current cash flow from your other job or business while building your income from the investments.

Stepping Stones.
Many of the real estate entrepreneurs I meet are quick to want to quit their jobs to do real estate full-time. They begin to hate their jobs because that's not where their passion is. If you find yourself in this situation you need to view your cur-

rent job or employment not as the horrible enslavement that you feel it is, but rather as a powerful stepping-stone that will help you build a rock solid foundation towards a possible full-time real estate business.

You see, from my experience and observation, many folks that go full time, quitting their job cold turkey, end up having extreme cash shortages because they end up eating most of their revenues from their real estate business to live on.

Many times it pays to be patient, building your foundation, knowledge, and revenue first. Learn before you leap. Many investors quit their jobs before they have the capital and full knowledge they need to succeed long term. Remember a paycheck from a job isn't necessarily a bad thing—having the extra cash flow and verifiable income will make you more bankable and help fund your living expenses while you build your part-time business and investments.

Ultimate Objective. I'm not saying you shouldn't do any of these businesses full-time. What I'm saying is you want to be careful before you up and quit your current employment to seek out the new venture. If your spouse has a strong income, this is a real advantage since the steady income will help your cash flow while you build the business. Learn as much as you can—do business, develop a track record, then consider if you want—full-time entrepreneuring. Now let's jump right into strategy!

Rules, Tips, and Strategy for Low-Cash Start-Ups

No Employees. The first rule for starting and operating a business with very little cash is—no employees. Payroll is the biggest expense most businesses have. Right from the start you eliminate this expense by not having employees in your company. You should be a sole operator. Payroll is a giant fixed expense that you must avoid.

You will need people, you can't do everything yourself, but these workers do not have to be on your payroll as a fixed expense. In the next chapter, we will explain the best way to find and hire independent contractors to handle all the work you cannot handle yourself.

There are two primary reasons you don't want to hire employees. The first, as mentioned, is the payroll factor. This is especially important in the early months and years of a business; cash is your limited commodity—you must conserve it. In business, you often wear multiple hats. Typically there are many small jobs that need to be handled, but the total workload doesn't justify hiring an extra person to perform those tasks. In many cases, you will have more time than cash, therefore, in the early stages do it yourself.

The second reason to avoid employees is the governmental regulations. Being a sole operator is pretty cut and dry from a tax and legal standpoint, but when it comes to hiring actual employees you enter a swamp of tax and employment regulations. We will explain more in the next chapter on how to handle this in a simple and very cost effective way.

No Storefront or Office. Next to payroll, the second biggest expense business owners have is paying for rented office or storefront space. Jungle fighter entrepreneurs do not want this monkey on their back—no rented offices. Renting office space may seem like a neat idea and may help you feel like you are a more legitimate business person, but paying a monthly payment each month is the last thing most of us should consider.

The solution of course is to operate a home office. Again this doesn't seem as romantic as having your own office, but it will help keep your expenses down. It's a whole lot more convenient, too!

Why do people think they need a fancy office to conduct business? Today, most business is conducted over the phone, fax, or email. Why do you need an office down in the high rent district? You don't. And we'll explain in the next chapter several great ideas for getting around the occasional times when you need to meet folks in a professional setting.

With all of the low-cost technology today, you can operate a low-profile office in an extra room in your current living quarters. No one even has to know since you won't be meeting clients there. We will explain several clever strategies about this in the next chapter.

No Partners. A big part of my philosophy is being a sole operator. Partnerships in my opinion are not a good business model because you have two mouths to feed, not one. Also, there are problems equitably dividing the workload and sharing the profits. The reality is we want a partner because we are a little scared about taking on the new venture alone—we want someone to hold our hand and be there to reassure us. In many cases, entrepreneuring is a lonely endeavor, another reason many of us seek out partners. We want camaraderie. But what small benefits you gain with a partner will be cancelled out by the many negatives of having a partner.

I'm not saying partnerships never work. I have seen a few that seemed to work well, but I still believe you should avoid them. It's rare to find two people who work equally hard with equal talent and who actually get along with each other on a long-term basis. If the partners do not work equally hard with equal talents and skill, one of the two will begin to resent the other partner for not pulling their weight!

Partnerships are often formed out of a preexisting friendship. Friendships do not typically make good spawning grounds for business partners. In many cases, people create partnerships without really knowing the work habits or business acumen of the other party. They just know the other guy makes a good friend.

I really don't believe you need to share your great business ideas and profits with friends or partners. Creating a partnership creates a whole new set of problems when running a business or investment. When you run the show yourself, you don't need anyone else's approval to spend money or take extra cash out of the business! There's no dispute over money, time worked, expenditures, cash advances, or the future direction of the business.

Invest in Communications. I believe in what I call Strategic Cheapness. This is the idea that in many areas of operating our business we will be selectively cheap. One area where I believe you should NOT be cheap is the area of communications.

Investing in good technology will pay you back many fold in additional business. You see, in today's business environment you must be accessible to consumers at all times. This means having an effective telephone, fax, voice mail, e-mail, and cell phone. These tools are probably the most important tools in your entrepreneurial toolbox.

With the price of technology dropping almost monthly, these tools are affordable for even the low-budget, start up business. You should be able to be outfitted with the newest tools for under $400 for everything. In fact, many of these are available from the local phone service for a low-monthly fee and no money down.

Service businesses don't need a storefront because the customer will only be speaking to you from the phone, at least initially. Your number-one goal should be to make it easy for your customer to reach you and get answers to their problems on the phone!

A telephone or a cell phone is going to be your number one way to conduct business. It is an extremely cheap way to transact business. Your second line of tools will be your voice mail, e-mail, and fax. You will be open for business 24 hours per day with these tools! Next chapter, we will go into cutting edge ways to use these tools in place of having employees and staff!

No Inventory. If you are going to start and operate a successful business with very little operating capital, you want to avoid inventory. Inventory ties up capital. In most of the service type businesses covered in this book there is no inventory needed. You are the product. Your knowledge, skills, time, and problem solving solutions are your inventory!

In those cases where your business needs some sort of inventory, try to work a pay-as-sold (consignment) arrangement or work with suppliers that will ship on demand. Just in time inventories work for billion dollar car manufactures, it will work for you too! Another option is to use drop shipping where you handle just the sales and paperwork with your product supplier drop shipping the order from his or her location to your customer.

Another effective way is to use OPA (other people's assets). In this model, your business doesn't need to own the assets it uses in trade; OPA will work equally well. For example, you don't need to own real estate to make money. You just have to be able to profit, ethically, of course, off your client's assets. This is leverage plain and simple. Big business has been doing this for years—banks broker loans with their customers' money; stockbrokers trade stocks they don't own; real estate brokers buy and sell their clients' property. You don't need to own the asset, just the ability to control and use it.

You Don't Need to be Fancy. You need to be highly personable, effective, reliable, enthusiastic, honest, punctual, appreciative, solution oriented, fast, industrious, and hard working, but you don't have to be fancy.

The point I am making is once again you are the product. You are selling your time, knowledge, energy, solutions, and ideas. You are the company, not some fancy office filled with expensive furniture. People are buying you.

A few years back I worked with a top producer at a real estate company who made around $250,000 per year selling real estate as a realtor. He was the top agent for several years. The amazing thing I learned from my friend Don was you don't need a fancy setting—you need a desk and a phone.

While many in the company had a fancy office with expensive decorating and office furniture, Don had the most lowly office I think I have ever seen. You see, all Don needed to sell millions of dollars worth of real estate was a basic desk, filing cabinet, telephone, voice mail, cell phone, and a trash can. I am not exaggerating—this guy was ultra-basic. BUT, he was a master at handling people, and he was an action-oriented person who was always moving!

Hack Away Expenses. If you want to succeed starting with very little cash you must ruthlessly weed out waste in your company. This means watching all of your expenses for waste and nonproductive spending. "Lean and mean" certainly is a cliché, but it describes how you must operate.

I do not mean being a miser, but you must monitor all spending. There are two parts to profit making—revenue and expenses. You must minimize the expense portion of your business to the bare essentials. For start-up entrepreneurs this means you probably won't be joining the chamber of commerce or the local country club!

Money Saving Resources. If you make long distance calls the absolute lowest cost and easiest plan in the nation seems to be from **www.onesuite.com.** Check these folks out if you like saving outrageous amounts of money.

Another resource for you tightwad entrepreneurs is the free business cards available from **www.vistaprint.com.** This company offers a variety of printing products, and their way to get to know you is their free business card offer. The cards are not cheap looking!

This reminds me of the story I saw on television explaining how the late founder of Airborne Express, a man worth about $400 million, still went down to the supermarket to buy chicken when it went on sale for 28 cents per pound! Thrift has always been a mark of a successful businessperson.

A good example of weeding out all excess spending is my own father in his business. I have seen him year after year looking for ways to operate his business for less money. For example, he changes Visa or MasterCard processors about every two years because he finds another company that will do it for a smaller percentage fee. He changes long distance service about every year because he finds companies that will provide the same service for less. He changes banks about every two years because one will raise its fees while another one will handle the business checking totally free. He scrutinizes every bill that comes through the office looking for overcharges and mistakes. He gets three insurance companies to bid on his insurance coverage for his various businesses every year. The point is, he takes all expenses seriously, because he realizes that the long-term health of the company is dependent upon low expenses.

You are the Marketing Specialist. Many people believe that you should hire an advertising agency to handle the marketing of your company. I totally disagree with this thinking. I believe that as entrepreneurs the total focus of our company should be marketing. Simply put, you should be your own marketing guru.

Business is Marketing. Marketing is business. These two words are really interchangeable. Marketing is the sum total of everything we do to get customers to buy our products and services. Next to being fully competent at your primary business craft, you need to become fully competent at marketing.

Marketing is more than advertising. It is the following plus a whole lot more: your name, logo, dress, presentation, niche market you service, price, speed of service, guarantee, terms of payment, advertising, brochures and cards, free consultations, advice, the way you answer the phone, how organized you appear, your unique offers, your promptness, and countless other things that show the customer why you are the best solution to their needs. You see, marketing really is the nuts and bolts of attracting, servicing, and keeping customers.

Since marketing really is the guts of a business, you cannot afford to pass this off to someone else. You need to run the marketing show.

Being your own marketing expert will not only make your company wildly successful, it will save your precious capital in needless fees which can be plowed back into your business. Buy lots of books on marketing, but save your money by not hiring advertising agencies or marketing consultants.

Conservative Lifestyle. This point is very simple: in the early years of your business or investing live well below your income. Many people don't realize that to grow your investments and business you must funnel a lot of money back into your business to keep it growing. Cash flow from a business isn't always predictable, so you must keep liquid cash around to handle the ups and downs. Many new entrepreneurs who find early success fail to realize that just because business was great for the last few months doesn't mean it will be great a year from now.

I know this point very well. For over ten years I lived cautiously and conservatively with my finances so I could build my business. This point is all the more important if you are starting a business with less than $10,000 in the bank.

Build Capital with Sweat Equity. If you do not have a lot of capital then you probably have time and energy. Your job being a low-budget startup artist will be to convert your time and energy into capital. Capital is the stuff that drives a business—business fuel.

Thousands of immigrants do this every year. We have all seen them: folks that come to this country with very little cash but plenty of ambition. These folks work like dogs for countless hours, even at low wages, to build a pile of cash. Eventually many of them buy or start a business.

If you are cash poor, you, too, will have to pay your dues by converting your time into capital by doing even some low wage work for yourself. Why pay someone else to do labor type work when you probably have more time than money? Eventually you will be able to hire most of this work out, but don't do so not too soon or you will run out of operating capital.

Go Heavy on Image and Marketing. I think I've fully inculcated you on going low budget when it comes to things like fixtures, furniture, and other expenses that do not produce prof-

its. Where you should spend money is on polishing you, the primary product of your company.

You need to do two things: drive customers to your phone lines with powerful marketing, and create the image—or shall we say the illusion—of the company that you are. You need a crowd of eager customers, and you need to present your company as powerfully as you can by conveying the right image.

We will cover image in more detail in forthcoming chapters, but for starters let me just say image cannot be created by going cheap on things like business cards, stationery, logo design, company name, your phone system, voice mail, and your personal appearance. These things can all boost your perceived value in the mind of your clients and customers. Think I'm overrating this? Do you think lawyers could get away billing $150 per hour dressed in old blue jeans and sneakers?

Along with image, you need to invest plenty of resources (not always cash) into your marketing. Do not go too cheap here! You must attract enough customers to make your business's cash flow. We will spend a whole chapter on marketing, so don't worry. I'll arm you for the fight.

Don't Buy Until You Need It. There's a tendency among many of us start-up entrepreneurs to feel we can't start doing business until we have everything we need or until we have every single piece of knowledge about the subject. Don't let this trip you up. Get started with the resources you have and then buy additional things as you need them. Better yet, rent the tools or services you need when you need them. Renting makes sense at times because it enables you to conserve capital.

You need to get some money rolling in first by getting out and doing some business. You do not have to wait until everything is perfect.

Many times we stock up and buy things before we really need them. Sometimes our needs change or we find out that we really didn't need what we bought. We end up wasting precious cash flow on something that we may not even need or use until many months down the road.

Ask yourself these things before you spend money: Can I rent the tool or machine from a rental center for my short-term use? Can I trade a friend or acquaintance for something in exchange of my use? Do I really have to have it now? Is there anywhere I can get this same item for free? Can I purchase a used one or a recondi-tioned one? Can I pay a fee and use the product or services of another company, such as a business center like Staples, Office Max, or Kinko's? Can I outsource the job to someone else? If I buy this now, will I use it within the next sixty days?

Looking back on my business life I can clearly see some major buying blunders when I have bought stuff thinking I would later end up using it but didn't. Sometimes I was buying something on sale and couldn't pass up the bargain even though I didn't need it at that point. Other times I have bought things when it would have made better sense not to tie up my cash but to rent the item for a day or two when needed. For example, many years ago when I was starting out I spent about $1,200 on a fancy copier. Looking back I really didn't have a lot of extra cash and should not have wasted that much money on a copier I hardly used. I should not have tied up my money when I could have paid another business or print shop for the use of their copier when needed.

Mother Necessity. The old saying, "Necessity is the mother of invention" is exactly on target. If you are starting out with very little capital you will eventually be faced with a cash crisis. This happens even with older established businesses. When this hap-pens, you must use your imagination and creative thinking to find alternate ways of doing business.

People who start businesses with large amounts of cash are frequently at a disadvantage because they don't enter the new ven-ture with much creativity or a mindset of cash conservation. When they have a problem or need, they just throw money at the problem rather than find alternative solutions. Before they know it, they've spent all their dough. If you aren't flush with money you will need to be more resourceful, clever, and most importantly harder work-ing to make it.

When you are up against a wall with your business you must "invent" yourself out of the problem. For example, several years ago I was renovating a house that I had bought at auction. This place was dilapidated, and I bought it at a salvage price. As I rehabbed it, my cash was extremely tight. I noticed a few blocks away a demolition contractor was preparing an area of a group of houses for demolition. I walked over and talked with him. He explained that the funeral home across the street had bought the homes to tear down for more parking. I asked him if I could walk through them. To my surprise we found lots of good building materials including doors, carpeting, handrails, water heaters, vinyl windows, electrical panels and other valuable items. I paid him cash to pull out various fixtures and doors that I was able to recycle into my building. It worked great. The bottom line: I saved hundreds of dollars by being creative. I was forced to do this because I was working on an extremely tight budget! Do you see from this example how you can think yourself out of your limitations or problems? As they say, you must think outside of the "box."

Concept Summary. Be a guerrilla operator using your own business agility to move fast and seize opportunities. Be extremely frugal with your cash. Do not hire employees—outsource or do it yourself. No rented office space—work from a spare room at home. Nothing fancy—avoid spending money on frills and fluff that won't directly affect the profitability of the business. Be a tightwad—keep a sharp eye on all expenses—competitively shop price. Do invest in good technology and communication systems like voicemail, cell phone, fax, phone systems. Do invest in image stuff like professional business cards, brochures, and a company name. Work long hours to convert your time to capital and equity. Start part-time to learn and build then consider your options. Strategic smallness theory—small means low overhead and low fixed costs.

The New Extreme Business Model

In this chapter I will explain how to run a business based on the hottest cutting edge strategies and concepts that will enable you to out maneuver and out think your competitors. Many of these ideas and concepts are extreme, but that is exactly what cash poor entrepreneurs need in order to survive and advance in business.

I will explain why you must adapt and change your way of thinking or you will be doomed in this new economy. I will then give you dozens of tips and ideas to help you build your new business machine. If you already have a business, I will provide you a full plate of information to help you retool your existing business.

This chapter is so critically important that I ask you not to skip it or quickly breeze through it. Let's not fool ourselves, business is hard, brutal is not too strong of a word. The facts are that most new businesses do not survive more than five years. Therefore, you must exploit every useful tool and piece information I provide you.

Why Change? The business paradigm (model) has changed from companies being large and very physical to small and virtual. You cannot afford to run a business using old economic templates and technology.

You must change because things are changing. There is a strong tide of change, and you must be pliable and flexible. Businesses that are stiff and rigid will be smashed against the jagged rocks along the economic shoreline.

The Forces of Change. There are four major forces driving change in today's economic world. These factors will help you understand the strategy that I will be laying out for operating a business and real estate investments.

Complexity. The world is becoming more complicated every year. As the world becomes more complicated, life and work become more complex. Running a business isn't the simple thing it was in the early 1900s. Today, the average entrepreneur almost needs to be a lawyer to keep out of trouble with lawsuit-happy consumers and an absurd level of legal regulations.

A basic example of things becoming more complex would be television news broadcasts. A few decades ago one would have three major network newscasts around the dinner hour. Now we have 24-hour world news, sports news, 30-minute headline news, business news, network evening news, political news, 24-hour weather news, *ad nausea.*

Another area to further prove the point is taxation. In the early 1900s the tax laws were all contained in a few compact volumes. Today, the tax code is some 20,000 voluminous pages long, which nobody fully understands.

We have a world where the average consumer is dealing with more laws, more choices of products, and a much higher level of technology and complexity in consumer products. Not only that, but consumers are more educated than ever before and therefore demand knowledgeable experts to help them.

Fierce Competition. Years ago there many business owners enjoyed a monopoly in their town or city. If you talk to a cross section of business owners or professionals today, you will find one common theme: Their particular business is fiercely competitive.

With the new borderless economy, the world has become much more competitive. Think about all the little stores across America that sell some sort of merchandise. Who is their competition? Sam's Club or Wal-Mart. These two companies offer some of the toughest competition for small merchants in America. Wal-Mart's wide array of products and low prices make a brutal combination. Not only do business people have to compete against heartless competitors like Wal-Mart and Home Depot, but they must also compete against a throng of small business owners all fighting for market share. It's not that these guys are as tough on price competition as the big guys, but just that the sheer number of competitors all fighting for the same consumer can be difficult.

Today's entrepreneur must compete not only against giant competitors, but they also go against Internet competitors across the nation and globe. The overall level of competition has never been greater.

Expensive World. Years ago employing someone was pretty much cut and dried. The employee would work a set number of hours each week and at the week's end the employer would pay the worker for his or her time. Yes, there were some taxes to be accounted for and withheld, but basically the process was routine. Today the process is not only complicated, it is also expensive.

Due to a multitude of factors ranging from workers' compensation to Social Security to health insurance, the employment process is expensive. These costs trickle through the economy and makes everything else expensive. Labor is the biggest expense most businesses incur.

A host of other factors affect costs in business, but the main thing to realize is that the world, generally speaking, is getting more costly to live in and do business in (rising real estate and energy prices being a major contributor).

I Want it Yesterday. A major force in today's society is the public's demand for getting their needs met immediately. We see this trend in all most all facets of our culture. Everything from FedEx to the proliferation of fast food restaurants proves this phenomenon.

This condition seems to be multi-factorial in that there is no single reason for its development. Here are a few reasons that seem to drive this: people are working more hours to support and ever-increasing lifestyle and debt-load, therefore, they have less free time. People have so many choices (shopping, cable TV, Internet, restaurants) in the marketplace competing for their time, therefore, consumers are almost on a stimulus overload. Thirdly (and this is a big one), in this free market economy, businesses continually outdo each other by offering consumers better and better service, price, speed, and options, in order to gain a competitive edge in the marketplace. The bottom line: Consumers have become like spoiled brats. Good old instant gratification!

These forces or trends in society force businesses to change the way they operate. The grand total is an environment that is more complicated, expensive, competitive, and demanding. You must adapt and modify your marketing and customer service methods in order to remain a serious player.

The New Expense Paradigm. The principle that I'm about to explain is the foundation for all of the other concepts in this chapter. You want to pay strict attention to this new business model.

All businesses incur expenses. Expenses are either fixed or variable in nature. (**Note:** technically there is a third type called semi-variable expenses). Fixed expenses are those expenses that don't change much from month to month. They remain steady regardless of the amount of business you conduct. If you have a two-year lease on an office, this would be an example of a fixed expense; your monthly cost remains fixed whether you have $100 in sales or $5,000 in sales.

Variable expenses are those that change with the amount of business you conduct. Commissioned sales people are a perfect example of a variable expense. If sales are $100 that month you might incur a $10 commission expense. If sales are $5,000 you might incur $500 in commission expense.

Fixed expenses tend to be better during high volumes of business since higher sales lower the percentage of the expense in relation to the gross sales a business does. Simply put, high sales dilute fixed expenses.

Businesses, especially new businesses, do best with a variable cost structure because variable costs are safer and more manageable!

The Rule: Structure your business with variable costs, not fixed.

Even though high variable costs can begin to work against you as sales rise, many entrepreneurs still like them because they protect the business during the slowdowns that every business experiences. As business slows, so do your expenses. Variable expenses are easier to budget since they are tied to something else happening. You know that if X happens you must pay Y.

The New Payroll Paradigm. As I explained in Chapter 2, you must avoid employees in your real estate business or investments. There are a multitude of reasons for avoiding employees, but the root of the problem is one of expenses. Employees are one of those fixed expenses that must be paid whether or not you have sales and whether or not they perform! In essence, they are a liability.

A host of other tricky problems are associated with employees on your payroll. Governmental regulations are onerous when it comes to actually employing people as true employees. Now don't get me wrong, I'm not saying these problems are completely unmanageable. What I'm saying is that employees create a lot of extra legal obligations and work. In many cases you will need to be paying workers' compensation insurance, social security taxes, unemployment taxes, and taking care of other legal and accounting chores related to personnel management.

At this point it's critical that I explain something about people. People are more valuable than anything else to help you make more money. You and I need people. We cannot do it all, even as a one-person company. You will need to focus on what you are skilled at, and not try to what you either hate or are lousy at. But, keep in mind, in the earlier months or years or your business, you will be wearing many hats with many job descriptions.

The Rule: Outsource work to self-employed specialists who are independent contractors.

Since you and I need people in order for us to succeed in business, we must find a ways to get jobs done without creating a fixed cost, nine to five payroll. The trend among many savvy business people is the use of independent contractors. Independent contractors do two big things for us: it creates a variable cost expense, where we only pay for services performed, and in most cases, it eliminates the burden of various accounting and tax withholdings, i.e., social security/insurance, etc.

There are more and more people becoming self-employed specialists who work not for one company, but many. These folks usually have a specialty service they perform at highly competitive rates. Since they are in their own business, they handle their own taxes and insurance.

These independent contractors gain the ability to set their own hours and be their own boss. Plus, being self-employed, they have more ability to create a higher income than if working a fixed salary position.

You win because you have fewer fixed expenses and less paperwork, tax withholding and accounting. You also gain someone who probably far more motivated to get the job done quickly and efficiently. Lastly, the self-employed specialist typically has the tools and knowledge to get the job done better and faster than you could do yourself.

How To Find Self-Employed Specialist. The best way to learn who is available for self-employed specialist work is to run small classified ads in the newspaper. You can also try the yellow pages, word of mouth referrals from other business people, and, of course, the internet.

Many of the people who respond to your ads may not consider themselves to be owners of a business. In that case you will need to explain how you want to be billed and how you will pay them. Look for individuals who seem positive, enthusiastic, and who have some prior experience.

In my real estate business I always ask the people if they have tools and transportation. I then ask a series of questions to see exactly what construction tools they own. I can determine if they are experienced repair people or just a clumsy amateur who needs on the job training.

Important Note: The IRS has important rules and guidelines as to what constitutes an independent contractor. These rules and laws change so be sure to check with an accountant or attorney to protect yourself from any surprises.

Basic Guidelines for Establishing an Independent Contractor Relationship. They must be able to set their own hours. They should have other customers they service. They should use some of their own tools or equipment. They should provide a formal bill. They should sign a statement for you explaining that they understand they are an independent contractor and are responsible for paying their own withholding taxes and insurance.

Fully Exploiting Technology. One of the biggest reason businesses have been prospering so much these last few decades

has been due to all the low-cost technology. Technology makes most jobs quicker, easier, and cheaper.

One of the biggest advantages of investing in good technology tools is that technology replaces staff! Read that again—TECHNOLOGY REPLACES STAFF. If we fax a document, do we need an office clerk to type a letter, apply postage, and run it to the post office? No, we just take ten seconds and fax it. If we have a call-forwarded cell phone in our possession at all times do we need a secretary to answer the phone and take a message? If we have 24-hour voice mail do we need an answering service? If we have voice recognition typing software do we need office staff to type a letter for us? Do you see how we can replace people with tools?

The Rule: Invest in good tools and good technology. One of the biggest reasons you will be able to operate from a spare room in your home is that cheap technology can outfit your office with tools that only large corporations could afford twenty years ago.

For about $1,500 you can outfit your office with all the tools you will need to get a nice business or serious investment program started. Although you certainly won't need all of these do run a business, for this price you can own a good starter package of technology tools. Your package should include low priced basic copier, fax machine, digital answering machine or voice mail system, cell or digital wireless phone, a separate phone line for business, a computer, a printer, and an office software package like Microsoft Office. Start with the above tools and gradually add a few more high tech-options that I will explain shortly.

The Accessibility Rule: The easier you make it for customers to contact you and get

immediate answers, the more business you will do.

There's no doubt about it, if customers can't reach you quickly and easily, they will call someone else. Answering machines or voice mail are acceptable for a backup during weekends or late evening hours, but you should not rely on them as a gatekeeper for your business. **Whatever you do, don't make it hard for your customers to do business with you.** The customers of the twenty-first century will not wait around for you—they will call your competitors.

The Rule: Your telephone is the lowest cost, highest profit tool in your office. As a service entrepreneur you need this tool just as much as a carpenter needs a hammer. Do not screen calls with an answering machine. Pick up the phone and greet your customer. Every time that phone rings it is an opportunity to make money.

Tip: Get a cell phone and keep it with you whenever you leave the office. Set up call forwarding with the phone company so when you leave your office all calls get forwarded to your phone. This is especially important in the early years of a business when you cannot afford to lose any customers.

Tip: make sure your cell phone has a voice mail program that will capture those few calls that you won't be able to answer—explain in your message that all calls will be returned within 30-60 minutes.

More Advanced Tools. If you end up conducting most of your business over the phone like I hope you will, consider investing in some more advanced tools after your business starts generating income. If you spend more than an hour or two on the phone per day you probably should buy a hands-free telephone headset. There are a variety of models available, so spend several hours comparing before you invest the two or three hundred dollars the better models sell for. For a great catalog of headsets and other advanced phones to make communications easier, contact HelloDirect in San Jose, California at 800.444.3556 and ask for their great catalog or visit their internet site at **www.hellodirect.com.**

There are several other more advanced tools you might consider after your business starts making a good profit. An advanced call center controlled by a sophisticated telephone system or your computer will enable you to capture calls 24-hours per day and perhaps even be a automated order taker. This system might be created mainly as a late evening information center where you could advertise 24-hour free information via recorded messages. For example:

Landlords: make more profit, guaranteed. We will show you how to cut costs and raise revenue for a 2-to-1 return on investment. Call 800-777-7777. Informative message 24 hours.

There are several systems and options available, so I highly recommend you thoroughly investigate before you invest. Look for a system or software that is user friendly.

You may also want to consider other tools such as a fax machine with automated batch fax capabilities to handle mass faxing to your phone list, also known as fax broadcasting. (This need may be best served with a computerized fax system that you run from your regular computer). A wireless email sender and receiver like the Palm Pilot system, a laptop computer with Internet modem used in conjunction with a cell phone, and a compact fax machine with a cell phone connection for faxing from an automobile or when you are away from the office can all enhance your ability to communicate with your clients. Another tool that could be valuable to you is voice recognition software that makes your computer type what you dictate without having to pay an office clerk to do your typing. Two programs in this category are IBM's ViaVoice and Dragon Systems' Naturally Speaking.

If you find you're using a lot of postage for direct mail or sending packages you may consider using an on-line postage systems that works with the U.S. postal system. Companies like **www.e-stamp.com** or **www.stamps.com** will give you the details of how you can keep from running to the post office for buying postage. An ordinary postage meter from a provider such as Pitney Bowes can be a major time-saver as well, and you can add more postage with a few clicks on the keyboard.

Keep in mind that many of these more advanced technology options are for those who have gotten their business up and running. Do not spend your precious start-up dollars on these tools. Invest instead on basic tools like the fax, small copier, voice mail, cell phone, and computer.

Specialized Field Software. After you have established

an investment or service business focused around a specialized field of real estate, I highly recommend that you buy specialized software to automate your business. For example, if you were a professional landlord you would eventually want to invest in property management software that will automate everything from printing late notices to tracking expenses per unit!

Scores of real estate software packages are tailor made to specific specialties within the real estate business. One company that sells a large variety of real estate related software is Z-Law Software, Inc., at 800.526.5588. Or you can click up their web address at **www.z-law.com** for a terrific site!

Note: If your cash position is extremely tight, you only need a home phone and a small office area to get started investing or running a small business. Do not think you have to buy a bunch of office stuff before you get started. Many of us think everything must be perfect before we start; this is just a subtle form of procrastination. When you need a copier or fax, you can go to any of the business centers and pay a few dollars to use their equipment.

Repair and Renovation Tools. Depending on the type

of real estate opportunities you decide to get involved in you may need to purchase additional tools for repairing and renovating real estate. Later in this book we will discuss which opportunities will require these tools.

Many folks complain that they are lousy at fixing things or handling anything related to construction. I can personally attest to this because I used to believe that you were either mechanically inclined or you were not. Let me share what I discovered.

Seventy-five percent of the problems are caused because we try to do a job without the correct tools. Having the right tool is most of the battle. The rest of the battle is just having some knowledge and practice. The truth is you can learn to repair and renovate real estate just like you learned to read or write—it is a learnable skill.

The Rule: If you are involved in the more physical part of owning or managing real estate, definitely buy a good stock of tools. Tools like a high powered cordless screw driver/drill, reciprocating saw, circular saw, various hand tools, pipe wrenches, cutters, small torch, shop vacuum, airless power paint sprayer, pressure washer, wrecking bar, etc.

Rather than buy these all at once, consider a plan where you buy one good tool per month, starting with the most critical tools first, then acquire the higher priced, but less used tools later. Also, keep in mind you can always rent tools like power paint sprayers for about $30 per day. Even after all the years I've been in real estate, I still rent some of my tools rather than buy them.

The Home Office Trend. As mentioned in Chapter 2, the home office is an ideal place to operate your business. With all of the low-cost office equipment, there's very little reason to rent some high priced office, especially since much of your business can be conducted over the phone or out in the field.

There have been whole books written on how to work from your own home office, but the key points can be boiled down to this: no office rent or mortgage payments are being paid because you work from living space already being paid as your regular housing expenses. No commuting saves time, fuel, traffic hassles, and automobile depreciation. The sum total of these benefits is that a home office saves money.

Where to Meet Clients and Prospects. There are times when a home office will not be suitable, especially if you need to meet clients and prospects in person. Meeting a lot of people in your home for business has many drawbacks like security, privacy, legal, or image issues. The last thing you want to do is have a bunch of strangers knowing where you live, plus there are legal issues such as zoning to be considered.

Extreme Office Leverage. As a bootstrapping entrepreneur we need to get maximum leverage from our resources. Some of the greatest resources can be those people we already know and do business with. Bankers, title companies, accountants, and lawyers usually have traditional offices that are furnished with beautiful furniture and conference rooms. For those times when you need to meet clients in person, have an arrangement with one of your contacts to use their office. This can be arranged on a per use fee basis (good old variable expense) or maybe they won't charge you anything if you use their regular services or send them a lot of referral business! Also, keep in mind many hotels have small office suites they rent out for meetings. These rooms are often equipped with copiers, phones, fax machines, and internet service.

A secondary solution that is even easier and cheaper is just to meet your client (seller, buyer, tenant, customer) at a local diner or coffee shop. I often use this technique when I meet with tenants to sign leases! It works, and the rent is the cost of a few cups of coffee and the tip.

I hope you can see the beauty of this technique in leveraging the assets of other people for very little dollars. Wouldn't it be better to pay a business associate $25 for a couple hours to use a conference room than to pay $600 to $700 per month for your own fancy office? This changes your expense from an on-going fixed expense to an occasional low variable cost! Great stuff!

Do you think if you did a lot of business with the local title company they would mind if you used a conference room a couple times per month? Would they mind if you occasionally brought pizza or sandwiches in as a nice way of thanking them for your occasional use of the room? If you give them plenty of business or refer other clients who buy their services, you should have no problem as long as you don't abuse them by wearing out your welcome.

Low Profile Office.

If you operate a home-based business you need to be aware that local bureaucrats may not like you operating a business from your residence. They may say it is a violation of certain zoning laws related to doing business in a residential area.

I believe you can avoid most of these problems if you take several steps. First, do not hang any signs on your apartment or house advertising your business. Second, avoid manufacturing products at the residence or receiving frequent trucking shipments of products to your home. Third, avoid a lot of customers (clients) from coming and going to your home office—meet them elsewhere as suggested above. Fourth, keep a general low-profile approach to the office you have in your home by not blabbing it to everyone you meet.

Note: For those in more rural areas these issues typically are not a problem, since zoning is favorable to privacy and personal freedom. But, whatever your situation, you may be wise to get legal advice from a sharp attorney. Lawyers are great for finding loopholes in laws.

With the huge new trend of people telecommuting with computers and fax machines, it's really difficult to see a major problem if you mainly use your home office as a communication center (phone, fax, computer) for your business. (Besides, we all transact business from our homes every time we pickup the phone and order something with a credit card.) The operative words for a home-based business would be—low profile.

They Are Not Customers.

With your new business or investments, you should rethink the way you view "customers." The new business model of the twenty-first century views these valuable people not as customers but as *clients*.

Typically we don't view regular customers as clients. We view clients as people who get professional help from accountants, lawyers, plastic surgeons, business consultants, and other professionals. "Client" implies more class and respect than the term, "customer."

Client comes from the Latin word *cliens*, meaning follower, dependent, or one who bends for another. It implies submission on the part of the client. The funny thing is it seems as though we can charge clients more than we can charge customers. Customers won't pay $100 per hour, but clients will!

Many businesses that normally have customers have begun calling them clients. This is a new trend that I'll explain shortly.

The Rule: Start calling the people you do business with clients. It may feel a little funny, but you will get use to it. It's amazing how it creates a subtle change in the way we view the customer. A client is someone we need to advise and protect. In addition, when you treat clients like they are under your careful guardianship and protection you will find your referrals will increase.

Twenty-first Century Salesman. We all are sales people to some degree or another. I don't care if you are a landscaper or a cosmetic surgeon, you are selling your services, and that makes you a form of a salesperson. Well, sales people are out and consultants are in.

The Rule: You are not a salesman— you are a CONSULTANT. The new way is advising clients (not customers, remember?), not twisting someone's arm into buying something! Consultants advise, inform, protect, caution, motivate, educate, and gently persuade their clients to make wise decisions to purchase a product or service! Powerful.

The terms "salespeople" or "salesman" often convey someone who is looking to make a big commission and doesn't care about the customer. The general public views salespeople as selfish liars, and as with some stereotypes, there is some truth to the image.

The new consultant-advisor concept is a much nicer image. Again, you are there to help and advise them into making a beneficial purchase, and kindly educate and inform them. It's a softer, less manipulative image.

The new term for this process is "consultative selling." The method revolves around forming a protective relationship with the client/buyer. This may involve some initial smaller profits since everything will center around what's best for the client, not the salesperson. But in the long run, you will make more money because you will be building a long-term relationship that will pay you fees for years to come. (**Note:** you earn fees, not commissions.) Referrals are a big key here because when you begin putting your client's interests first they will see that you are their advisor and not a greedy "salesman." This will generate substantial referral business from others wanting the same treatment.

Choose Your Craft. In this new world of complexity and fierce competition, you have to be top-notch at servicing clients. This means being knowledgeable and efficient at getting their needs met. Today's consumers are incredibly knowledgeable, demanding, impatient, and disloyal. If you are going to maintain their business, you need to be several steps ahead of them.

The Rule: Become a specialist within a specific niche market in real estate.

Many years ago there were a lot of what were called general stores. These were stores that had most of the general items that people needed in their life. While this general store business model made sense in a more simple time, they clearly don't today.

Today the world is filled with specialty stores that carry a broad line of products within a very narrow segment of the market. Specialization is happening everywhere. In clothing you have stores for kids, stores for teenagers, stores for larger sized women, big and tall stores for men, stores for wedding clothing, and on and on. In medicine you see fewer general practice physicians and more specialists. The same thing is happening in the legal profession. Because the consumer base is so large and society is so complex we need to specialize to become experts. People are attracted to experts who know their business.

The real estate world has also grown increasingly complex. The days of the small mom and pop landlord are almost over. Life is not as simple as it once was. As the saying goes, "It takes a Philadelphia lawyer to understand the maze of laws and regulations." This isn't to say you will only make money doing one service or type of investing, but it does mean you will need to really learn and master a segment of the vast real estate industry. In this field it is not a good idea to try to be a generalist.

Build a Business Within a Business. This strategy
is slowing gaining popularity in business circles. Here's the concept: rather than start a business from ground zero with virtually no customers and no cash flow, you work as an independent business within another established business.

Both parties can be a winner with this arrangement. Here's why. The bigger, more established business gains because they hire you as a consultant/contractor to do some facet of their work without all of the corresponding baggage of being an employee. You, being self-employed, should work harder and perform a better job since you have more at stake. They typically will pay you on a performance basis, which ultimately will benefit them, since it won't cost them anything if you stand around drinking coffee. You gain because with just one or two large clients you have an immediate cash flow along with the freedom to work for yourself.

If you are having a difficult time conceptualizing this, consider this example. A licensed salesperson working for a broker company is really just a business within a business arrangement. The agent salesperson is an independent contractor who works out of the office of the broker based on some kind of split fee arrangement. In reality the agent is self-employed even though technically he or she works for the ABC Brokerage Co. The agent pays for his own automobile, advertising, and cell phone expenses. The company in effect has an employee who only gets compensated when they perform, thereby creating a variable expense arrangement.

The agent wins by having the autonomy of being self-employed and the capacity to earn whatever income he or she chooses. The company wins by paying sales fees only when sales occur without the tax withholding/legal liability of an employee/employer relationship.

There are two ways you may be able to use this strategy. One, go to your existing employer and explain the benefits of allowing you to work as your own separate company within their company. You might actually chart out on paper all the benefits the company gains. The second way is to consider a company that you don't currently work for and offer them your services on a contract basis. Thoroughly explain the advantages they gain while anticipating any objections they might present.

This strategy may offer advantages to both parties with very little off-setting disadvantages. Furthermore, it allows you a seamless transition from being an employee to being self-employed. (**Note:** do not sign a restrictive covenant whereby you promise not to compete against them if you ever leave their association. Do not sign away your right to make a living.)

Co-opetition, the New Buzzword. Years ago business was more of a loner's sport where businesses aggressively fought one another for market share. Today the newest concept is co-opetition.

The Rule: Don't compete, cooperate. Co-opetition is where businesses form short-term partnerships or alliances in a certain segment of their business in order to work together rather than fight each other.

We all have seen this at work although we may not have recognized it. The local mini-mart sells gasoline, but inside their building is another franchise selling pizza or tacos. Or, the advertisements where you see two different companies being promoted in the same commercial.

Years ago my grandfather was in the appliance business. For his highly competitive business he would buy, literally, train car loads of appliances to get the best pricing. Effective, but outdated. Today, appliance dealers join together with other appliance dealers to buy large quantities as a single buyer. This type of arrangement is called a buying group or buying cooperative. Without this cooperation small businesses would be buried by the large chain stores.

Think of ways in your real estate investing or business that you cooperate rather than compete with your competitors. Avoid outright partnerships, but consider ways to work together to profit both of you. (**Note:** be cautious in your spirit of cooperation not to offer or give away any of your proprietary trade secrets!)

Client Centered, Not Company Centered. In this new highly competitive environment you must make sure all of your marketing and service methods are client/customer centered, and not company centered.

Banks are notorious for feckless company-centered ads. Recently one of the largest banks in my area ran a promotion with the main message being—"Come to the rock...blah, blah, blah." My question is—Who cares? Ads like this don't give consumers specific benefits or advantages that they will garner by patronizing the business.

Consumers are bombarded with advertising and marketing messages with everyone shouting they are the BEST or WE HAVE THE LOWEST PRICE. This doesn't mean anything to people any more. It all gets discounted and filtered out. You need to give specific facts and illustrations to sell customers with your marketing. General statements are almost worthless.

A simple example of this is a yellow page ad I read. The merchant's ad read—$100 Cold Cash On the Spot if Our Price is Not The Best Deal You Find." While this particular merchant may or may not honor their bold proposition, it illustrates how to put meat on the bones of a vague sales claim that we have the lowest prices.

In your marketing, forget all the dumb stuff that tells how "great" you are, and deal only in customer advantages and benefits.

The New Power. Economists tell us that society has fundamentally changed from being an industrial economy to an information or communications economy. There are two important facts you need to know about this change.

The Rule. Informational leverage is the lowest cost, most powerful form of leverage you can acquire as a small business. You will need to continually update and upgrade your knowledge within your field to maximize your profits and work. Ideas are like gold nuggets. The more ideas and knowledge you acquire, the more power you have.

Based on my own business and investments I can vouch for the power of information. It always amazes me how little tips I pick up here and there can greatly multiply my efforts and returns without any corresponding increase of effort!

Intelligence within one's field can be gathered five main ways: from the people you network with, from the books and periodicals you read, from audio tapes programs, from courses and conferences within your field, and from your own trial and error experience.

You can make serious gains by using information as a leverage tool to multiply your efforts with little increase in effort or risk.

Performance Pay. There's nothing worse than paying people to handle a problem and not get the desired result. Performance pay is the concept of structuring your job payment based on performance rather than effort. In other words, pay people when possible on a completed job basis, rather than by the number of hours they take to do the job.

A real estate investor friend of mine used this technique whenever he had a house or apartment that needed painting. He would have the worker give him a price per room. My investor friend supplies the paint and the worker would quote him a price per room. Typically he would get rooms painted for about $30 per room.

When the job was completed he would pay the painter for the number of rooms that were completed. This was especially effective because he often used unemployed day workers who would come and go from the job scene.

Another business colleague of mine pays everyone in his business some form of incentive or performance pay. He still pays many of his people on an hourly basis since they are actual employees, but he ties incentive pay bonuses into his payroll. This works well because it rewards folks when they work harder or smarter.

Another spin-off idea is to structure things on a contingency basis. This works just like it does with a lawyer—You win my case, I pay you. If you don't prevail I owe you nothing. This concept won't be applicable all the time, but use it when feasible.

Strategic Smallness. I have explained this concept earlier, but it's worth spending a few more minutes unpacking it. Strategic smallness is the concept that smaller aggressive companies make more money than large, clumsy companies with multiple layers of employees, management, and overhead!

Don't be ashamed if you operate a small company. Large companies have bloated payrolls and amazingly small bottom line profits as a percentage of total dollars earned. You on the other hand are agile and adaptable. If a certain part of the marketplace dries up, you can adroitly switch courses finding a replacement profit center. You are not small; you are agile, adaptable, and efficient!

I'm Sorry We Can't Take Your Money. Years ago you could easily survive by just taking cash payment for your goods or services. In this new economy consumers have many other ways they pay their bills: Visa, Master Card, Discover, American Express, Check/Debit cards, and of course, regular checks.

Hot Profit Tip: Depending on the type of business you operate, consider taking other forms of payment like Visa, Master Card, and check cards.

There's no need to make this a first stage priority, but after your business is up and running smoothly, seriously consider accepting various bankcards. Many consumers today are conditioned to paying by credit card. Therefore, you are removing a possible barrier to them paying you. Personally I like paying bills the old fashioned way, but this isn't about me or you, it's about the client.

Be cautious about getting set up with Visa/Master Card merchant status since there are a lot of rip-off companies that will charge you outrageous machine leasing and processing fees. For starters your best bet may be your current bank. Keep in mind many banks do not like dealing with merchants who work from their home—they consider this a higher fraud risk. In any case, research your options on the Internet, where you will find a host of companies offering small business merchant accounts. Be exceptionally careful to seek out legitimate companies since the Internet is littered with scoundrels.

Concept Summary. Many of the old rules of business have changed because the business world in general has become more complex and competitive. You must implement new extreme business strategies in order to outmaneuver more wealthy and established business competitors. To do this begin by structuring as many variable expenses into your business as possible because you only pay expenses when a corresponding sale has been made or service has been rendered. Avoid employees because they can be a fixed cost liability—outsource to self-employed specialists instead. Invest in good technology so you can automate your business rather than hiring staff. Invest in the proper tools needed to perform a job—the proper tools save time and make everything easier. Create a small office within your residence rather than create a fixed expense liability by renting an outside office. Change your vocabulary and mindset by calling customers clients and treating them that way. You are a consultant/advisor, not a salesperson. Be highly reachable and accessible to your clients—make it easy for clients to buy from you. Be a specialist and master your field, not a generalist. Use information as your lowest-cost form of leverage—use ideas, not money. Look for ways to build co-opetition, where you build short-term alliances with other businesses that can benefit both of you. Consider broadening the type of payments you accept like the various cashless credit cards. Remember to build your company with strategic smallness in mind. Sometimes it's better to do $300,000 in sales with an overhead of $150,000, rather than do $650,000 in sales with an overhead of $500,000, because it will take a lot less work to generate the same yearend bottom line profit.

Section 2—Business Opportunity How-to Directory

How to use this section. This part of the book is where we get away from business theories and concepts and get into actual real estate business opportunities. I believe you will find this section to be one of the most interesting in the entire book, although you won't want to miss Section 3, which gets into some really exciting material with chapters on marketing and street-smart business tips.

The business opportunity chapters in this section contain dozens of business models, ideas, and profit centers. Not every idea is suitable for every person, but I guarantee there's at least one great business start-up idea for everyone. I invite you—no, I implore you—to read through all the ideas at least once, and then focus on the specific ideas that interest you.

The opportunities explained vary in length of commentary from a few paragraphs to several pages. This is due to the fact that some of the opportunities are full business models and others are just, ideas or profit centers that could be incorporated into a business. As you read, look for ideas that can be merged into one larger service, but be careful not to diffuse your effort in too many different directions—specialize as much as possible.

Related to Real Estate. As you read this book, you will notice that not every idea is one hundred percent real estate; many of the ideas are real estate related businesses that flow out of the real estate industry. To illustrate, look at the judgment recovery business. In this business you buy or option to buy court money judgments from amateur creditors and then professionally collect them yourself. Many of these judgments are secured by real estate. This business can yield profits that will utterly boggle your mind—sometimes you will end up owning the property for 20 to 50 cents on the dollar.

As stated earlier, most of the opportunities fall under the category of real estate services or real estate investments. I have focused on the best opportunities that can started with a minimum of cash. I have not covered those businesses requiring extensive licensing such as property appraisal or high-risk, high-capital ventures such as commercial real estate development.

Some of the opportunities may require a real estate or related license. You will need to continue diligence research. I will do my best to tell you which businesses require licenses, but I am not a lawyer and I am not giving you legal advice. Also, some opportunities that require a license can be operated in ways that legally bypass licensing regulations, but proceed with your own real estate legal counsel and research.

Lastly, not all of the ideas are created equal. A lot depends on your current levels of skills, ambition, knowledge, and interests. For example, being a professional landlord may be a terrible choice for some, and for others one of the most rewarding business/investment choices they will ever make.

In addition, consider the local level of competition and overall market demand. Some small towns may not have enough clients who need your services to make a living. Whatever the case, you will need to seriously and deliberately see what suits both your own interests and your own marketplace.

I have a strong bias towards real estate investment opportunities. In my mind they need to be run like a business, but typically they are more part-time in nature, allowing you to continue making a living at your regular profession or day job. These investment models can take a long time until you see the fruits, but ultimately can offer a lot of freedom and financial independence! Let's dive in!

4

Real Estate Investor Services

Somewhere between twenty to thirty percent of all real estate is owned by investors and not owner occupants. This amounts to billions upon billions of dollars in real estate. These properties range from single-family houses to huge apartment complexes. Your potential clients in the investor services business range from amateur landlords to professional investors.

These owners need help with many of the day-to-day problems and challenges of owning real estate. You, as the self-employed specialist, can be the answer to their problems and in the end, improve their property's profitability. Your fees to the owner will not be a true expense, because your skills will help the property owner make far more money with their property than they could without you.

Apartment Preparation Services. Landlords love rental property when the units are rented and the tenants are paying nicely. What most landlords hate is when tenants move and they must prepare the unit for the next tenant. This involves a multitude of chores like painting, detrashing, cleaning, and repairing. You can make a nice living by creating a company that handles these time consuming problems professionally for investors.

In your mind this may not sound very glamorous compared to other businesses, but I can tell you, few businesses can be started as easily as this one with so little cash, education, or risk. Besides, it can be a great opportunity to learn the investment business by working for other investors. Preparing rental units can be an ideal way for someone with very little real estate experience and cash to get involved in the rental industry.

Throughout this section you will also learn of additional services you can eventually add to your menu that will make you even more money! Don't let the nature of this type of business make you shy away from it, especially if you are already geared up to handle your own rental properties.

This is the type of business that you can enter and exit with very little problem. If after several years you're ready to move on to bigger and better things, you can sell your systemized company to someone else for a nice profit.

The Business Model. Whenever a tenant leaves a rental unit it begins to create negative cash flow for the property owner. In other words, the property begins to cost the owner money out of his pocket (even when an owner holds a property free and clear, there is a certain amount of negative cash flow when vacant due to property taxes, insurance, etc.).

The next problem for the owner is finding the time to get into the unit to clean, paint, and refurbish the unit for the next tenant. It's difficult for many investors to find the time and energy away from their regular job or business to clean up a used rental unit! If you have ever been in the rental business before you also know it isn't fun cleaning up after tenants who may have left the unit dirty and full of trash.

In addition, it can be a hassle for the owner to hunt down the supplies needed to prepare the unit (trash bags, paint, tools, cleaning supplies, repair parts, etc.) Even if the owner decides not to personally prepare the unit, he or she must hire out all of the jobs individually by calling a painter, cleaner, handyman, carpet cleaner, and others.

All of these factors make many landlords procrastinate getting their rental properties prepared for the next renter. Each day the house or apartment sits empty it costs the owner money. If the mortgage payment is $600 per month it costs the owner about $20 per day! In two weeks time the owner is $300 in the red! In six weeks he is $900! Do you see that?

The Big Question. If the property owner hates doing these things, why in the world would I want to do this "dirty" work? Good question.

The answer is that you are a professional. It will not be a hassle for you because you will have the tools and supplies ready to handle the job. You will be mentally prepared to get the job done because this is your main business, and you are mentally ready with all of the tools and supplies ready and waiting to attack the project with vim and vigor. This is your main focus, not a distraction, there-fore, you will have the time, attention, tools, focus, and expertise to get the job done quickly and effectively.

Secondly, you will have a *system.* You will not haphazardly be fumbling around at the job like the owner who only does this work once or twice a year! You will have a precast strategy and formula for preparing the unit rapidly and efficiently. You *will* have the time, because this *is* your business.

Let's not forget, you will be getting a check when the job is completed, whereas our owner does not get a check when he is fin-ished (there's something motivating about knowing you are getting paid for the work you are doing). Even though an owner would save money (thereby get paid) by doing it themselves, it is much more motivating when you do a job and get paid with spendable income like a nice check for a day or two of work.

Keep in mind, any job becomes easier (and more enjoyable) when we have all of the tools and supplies ready and waiting, and when we have developed the skills and systems to efficiently han-dle a job. If you do this everyday, you will have a momentum because you have broken through the learning curve. A job that might take a part-time landlord three days to finish will be done efficiently by you in one long day!

The image you want to present is one of pro-fessionalism. You are not a cleaning person or part-time painter, you are something new—a self-employed, income property specialist—helping clients maximize the return on their investment by proficiently preparing rental units with minimal down time and top rental dollars for the next rental cycle.

The Service in Detail. There are a lot of different ways you can present this service, but here are the services you should consider offering.

- ◆ Remove trash in the unit.
- ◆ Repaint or touch up paint on walls and ceiling.
- ◆ Inspect mechanical systems (basic heat, plumbing, roof check).
- ◆ Basic cleaning of kitchen and disinfect bathroom.
- ◆ Vacuum all carpets.

◆ Steam clean carpets.

◆ Change burned out light bulbs in fixtures.

◆ Service or install smoke detectors and/or batteries.

◆ Wash woodwork and baseboards.

◆ Inventory repairs needed and report to owner.

◆ Treat apartment unit with deodorizer and/or sanitizer.

◆ Clean windows.

The above services could be your basic service package. You would apply pre-set limits, of course, based on the size of the house or apartments. You can size the units by bedrooms, overall total room count, or square footage.

To illustrate, you might say your price for a 1-bedroom apartment to be prepped and detailed is $199 for a basic service package. A 2-bedroom would be $249, and a 3-bedroom would be $299. This of course would be your base package of services that you could expand with other a la carte offerings, such as the following:

Repair Services, Bug Extermination, Extra Trash Removal Beyond Set Amount, Large Item Removal (junk furniture), Lock Changes, Pet Odor Treatment, Small Room Carpet Installs, Patch Holes in Walls, Replace Toilet Guts, Property Management Advice/ Consulting, switch and outlet plate changes, eviction, and a host of other items.

Do you see all of the up-selling and cross selling that you can do to increase your profits? As this book progresses you will see numerous other profit centers and tangential services you can offer to real estate investors. If you efficiently and professionally service these owners, you will have built their confidence in you to handle other tasks, maybe even management. Do you see how you could also network with other suppliers and make referral fees and commissions? You might work an arrangement with a good handyman to sub-contract the more involved repairs for a percentage of the bill—maybe 15 percent.

Pricing and Presentation. I believe a big part of your success will be to price your basic package very competitively and get them to "taste" your service. Then after you professionally perform that service you will almost certainly be able to up-sell them expanded services and offers. You need to get them hooked on how quickly and easily you are to work with. Once confidence is garnered, begin to offer them additional solutions (within your range of competency) to the many problems you see with their building.

The Menu. Create a menu of services and their costs that you will use to price out jobs. Make the list as detailed as possible. For example:

◆ Windowpane replacement: $15 each

◆ Large trash bag: $10 each filled (after the initial limit is exceeded)

◆ Roach treatment: $25 for kitchen area, $10 per additional rooms

◆ Cat Urine Treatment: $30 per room

◆ Extra Room Painting: $80 up to a 14 x 14 room

◆ Lock change: $30 first lock, $15 second lock

◆ Lawn Mowing: $35 for small lots, $55 for larger parcel

◆ Smoke alarm: brand new and installed $15 each

◆ Dirty/broken switch plate replacement $1 each

If the owners see how easy it is to call you and have the unit ready to rent within 72 hours they will probably never go back to doing it themselves—especially if you show them that each week they wait to get around to it costs them more in lost rent than if they would have paid you to prepare the unit immediately.

Hot Profit Tip. Avoid quoting jobs by the hour. You want to be paid for efficiency and performance, not hours. People will push to know what your hourly rate is, but tell them you work by the job. After you get your own system down pat you will be completing this work far faster than other folks. Reward yourself by pricing by the job.

Additional Profit Center—New Construction Cleanup. This idea could be an easy addition to your existing apartment preparation business since it is very similar in form and would not require any additional tools. In this service business you

cleanup and prepare freshly built new construction for sale. This really is what is called job site cleanup.

Whenever a new construction project is finished being built there is a lot of general cleanup work needing to be done around the building and grounds before it can be sold or rented. This involves general construction waste cleanup (sawdust, nails, product wrappings, etc.). Your job would be to pick up the construction debris, thoroughly vacuum the unit and wipe down the kitchen and bath areas from the various construction dust and by-products. Your job also would entail exterior cleanup since contractors typically are in a big hurry and just throw their construction trash everywhere. You certainly won't get rich doing this work, but it will put food on the table if you're not busy with other work. The going price for this work is typically $200 for a smaller house and $275 for a larger one.

The Revenue Stream. After you become established and have demonstrated the quality of your work, you could begin to solicit service contracts from some of the larger landlords. This concept works by offering a stand-by service where the owner pays you a set monthly fee to handle all of his units.

If the owner has twenty units you might offer a maintenance contract for $70 per month. This will help you by providing a more steady revenue stream, and it can help the owner by enabling them to budget their expenses in a smaller, more manageable form. The whole key to selling this is to make the deal very attractive by your pricing and possibly by offering some additional perks to those who sign on to the service. Maintenance contracts are sold on everything from office copiers to refrigerators. Why not create a similar program for landlords and property owners?

Your maintenance contract would involve more repair work so make sure you have the basic skills to handle a variety of minor repairs. If you're geared up for this it can become quite profitable. There's one company in my area that has a monthly maintenance contract on a large condo property with over 1,000 units!

Note: as with most maintenance or insurance programs, you probably will need to do a pre-contract inspection in order to limit your liability towards preexisting problems or major deferred maintenance.

Marketing Strategy. The best strategy is to present yourself as a real pro at rental unit preparation, and not as a handyman service. There are several ways you can create the image of professionalism.

First, I would choose a good name for the firm. Something like LeasePro or Rent Savers or whatever sounds catchy but not goofy.

Next, I would invest about $100 in buying three or four uniforms with my company name embroidered on it. This is an excellent way to almost instantly gain a professional look. In addition, I would get some signs made for my vehicle, either the vinyl letters or magnetic signs. The uniform combined with professional signs and business stationery (cards, letterheads, invoices, marketing flyers) will give you credibility.

Another tool for gaining professionalism is a sharp looking receipt. This receipt could serve as both a receipt and a checklist showing the owner what work was performed on the property. The document would also serve as an internal checklist so you or your team don't miss anything. To give you a better idea of what I mean take a look at the receipt-checklist used by the various oil change businesses like Jiffy Lube. Your best bet is to use no carbon paper in duplicate or triplicate.

You will want to target the small to medium sized landlords who are too small to have their own full-time maintenance person or staff. After you have learned the business and have your team assembled you can begin marketing to larger property owners. At that point you want to begin marketing to the best prospects. I would use a combination of classified ads, direct mail, and bulk faxing.

Your message should clearly state your company WILL save the investor time, money, and hassle with one call shopping. Remind the investor that every day their unit sits empty it is costing them money. Show them some sample numbers and then explain that your service is essentially free compared to doing it themselves. Explain that you will have their units ready within days of their call, but they need to get booked now because you are so busy helping other investors!

Start building a database of names, addresses, and phone numbers of real estate investors in your town. For names of prospects, join a local real estate investment club. To locate a local club contact NaREIA at 888-7Na-REIA or go to **www.NaREIA.com.**

Real estate brokers and their sales people could be a rich source of leads. Go through the yellow pages and call every office and ask them for their fax number. Develop your fax list and then about every two weeks send out a 1-page fax flyer explaining your service (see marketing chapter for bulk fax info).

Consider running small advertisements in your local investment club newsletter with a coupon for $50 off the first job. You might even want to do a brief presentation at investor club meetings since these groups are always looking for people who have products or services that can help their members. You can book a 10-minute presentation at no charge in most cases. Think of that—free advertising!

Classified ads are another excellent source of leads. Consider running an ad that says something like this: Attention Landlords: vacancy kills cash flow. We professionally handle all phases of apartment preparation. Cleaning, painting, repairs, pest control, evictions. Don't let it sit empty. Call now, 555-7777.

Another variation could say: Attention Landlords: Need help with your rental units? We professionally and affordably handle all phases of rental unit preparation and maintenance. Painting, cleaning, repairs, evictions. We will save you money and headaches. Call now 555-7777.

Start tracking the For Rent ads in the newspaper by collecting the phone numbers of the advertisers. Any number of software or internet search programs they will provide you with mailing addresses and names to match the phone number. Then begin to periodically mail letters or postcards telling how you will help them save time and money. It is important to keep in mind that these mailings may take some time to start working since most of the folks advertising a property for rent have already prepped their unit. They may not call until the next vacancy—this is why you need to mail this list about every other month.

Tools and Supplies.
For starters you will want a full set of hand tools, including a cordless power screw driver/drill to handle the minor repairs you encounter. For larger repairs, you can either out-source the work, learn how to do it yourself, or have the owner handle it. Next, you will want a commercial quality vacuum, but any decent vacuum will work to get started. You will need to buy a broad array of painting tools like commercial sized rollers and pans, drop cloths, and brushes. You should invest in a basic commercial carpet steam-cleaner ($400 to $700), but if cash is tight, a low-cost, home unit will do.

Invest in quality cleaning supplies: rubber gloves, buckets, commercial detergent, contractor trash bags, a good deodorizer product, cleaning cloths, a wet mop, and a water hardness and scale remover (like Lime Away). Don't waste your time at the supermarket looking for these supplies—go to a janitorial supply house and buy high-powered products.

You should also keep in stock plenty of other fast-moving items such as paint, smoke alarms, light bulbs, outlet and switch cover plates, pest control products, spackle, light lenses and glass globes. Remember, the more prepared you are with the correct tools and supplies the faster you can be in and out of the property and on to the next billable job!

Your Company's Unique Twist. If you use your imagination, there are plenty of ancillary services you can offer your clients. Many of these have been explained throughout this book. But whatever you do, try to add your own unique signature or trademark to your services.

For example, maybe with every completed apartment preparation job you would provide the owner a bonus video documentation that would record the condition of the apartment in the event the owner ever needed to file a damage claim against the tenant. This video could be done before the cleanup, if the prior tenant damaged the unit, or it could be done after the prep job, to document how the new tenant received the unit. Whatever the case, try to build a unique value into your service.

Apartment preparation services may not be a way to make a million dollars, but it is a way to start working for yourself with very little start-up cash or skills needed!

REO (Real Estate Owned) Services Company. This is another business opportunity that is similar to apartment preparation services because you are helping investors with the ownership of their real estate. In this case, the owners are banks and financial institutions.

REO is a real estate and banking term that stands for "real estate owned." Whenever a bank or lending institution acquires real estate through foreclosure, that real estate typically gets classified as an REO and is handled through the REO department of the bank.

As you probably know, banks do not want to own real estate; they want to hold loans. But every lender in the country ends up owning some real estate because no one has a loan department with no bad loans. These bad loans must be foreclosed in order for the lender to get their money back. After the foreclosure the real estate (REO) is liquidated in order for the bank to get their cash back so they can re-lend the money elsewhere.

The problem for banks is they are not geared up to handle real estate as a commodity, especially the dirty rundown properties they often repossess. Banks are established to handle liens on real estate that are essentially paper assets.

The typical repossessed piece of real estate is not ready for the general public due to the distressed condition they end up in. The profit center for you, is to help the bank manage the more physical aspects of their foreclosure by securing the property, detrashing it, cleaning, and handling minor repairs in order to make the property saleable or rentable again. In this business your objective is to help preserve the lender's assets while at the same time help them liquidate the asset as fast as possible.

The Business Model. The REO Services Co. is a company that handles getting foreclosure properties cleaned up and secured, so the bank can preserve their assets and minimize their losses. This entails a broad range of potential services like: securing property, winterizing plumbing, boarding up windows, cutting down weeds and high grass, junk and trash removal, mechanical and physical inspection, vandalism prevention, installing no trespassing signage, cleaning, and preventing further damage from roof or plumbing leaks.

You as the self-employed specialist can handle all of these tasks for the lender who clearly is not set up to handle these distressed and rundown properties.

Five Big Ways You Help the Lender: 1) By stopping further losses from vandalism, theft, and liability issues. 2) To maximize sale price by preparing the property for sale. 3) You save the lender time and money since they are not geared up to handle real estate. 4) To handle repairs and minor renovation (yourself or contract the work out to someone else). 5) To provide one-stop shopping for the lender—they do not need to call multiple contractors.

The Typical Foreclosure. You need to know that in most cases the property coming back in a foreclosure action is neglected and abused. People who lose property in a foreclosure usually have a lot of personal problems ranging from divorce to substance abuse and problems with the police.

From my experience most foreclosure properties are full of trash and riddled with repair problems. Long, uncut grass and weeds are the norm, because the owners have either abandoned the property or just didn't care. The bottom line is that most foreclosure property is in rough condition.

You can greatly aid banks by taking over control of the property and mitigating further losses. There is a range of services that you will have to decide to offer. Some you can handle by yourself, and others you will need to "sub" out to another contractor.

Here is a list of potential services you could offer. Keep in mind that you could act as a manager and sub-contract much of this work out, although the more work you handle, the more money you will make.

Padlock doors, board up windows, cut weeds and grass, turn utilities on or off, stop roof leaks, mitigate plumbing leaks, winterize pipes, exterminate bugs, fill bags of trash or order a dumpster, general cleaning, fast paint job, inventory damages, repair select damages, post signs on building, install temporary fence around larger commercial buildings (portable fence rentals are best), evict squatters, and handle anything else that will solve the lender's problems.

Additional Profit Centers. If you are a licensed real estate agent you could act as a manager for many of the above tasks while at the same time selling the property. This way you will have two profit centers, preparing the unit for resale, and actually selling the property. **Note:** most of the above activities do not require a real estate license, except the actual selling of the building as an agent for the lender.

Most lenders like to sell properties "as is." This saves them from investing even more cash into the property—which, in their mind, is often throwing good money after bad. What you might consider as part of your service is a consultation on which repairs to make in order to maximize the sale price. Then, either by yourself or with a contract worker, you can have the repairs and sprucing up done, and charge the lender for the work.

Marketing Strategy. Your first task is to gather the names of all the banks, savings and loans, and finance companies in your marketplace. Next, you will need the specific department address and names of the people who handle the REO property. Then begin a marketing campaign based on direct mail, faxes, and one-on-one phone calls to the department. Explain as clearly as possible all of the services you offer.

Tip: Do not over look government agencies that end up owning real estate through loan defaults or abandonment. For example, all FHA and VA guaranteed loans that go into foreclosures, ultimately end up back in their custody.

I must dampen your enthusiasm by letting you know that many of these lenders may already be using another service. Your goal is to continue marketing to these people so when their regular service fails to perform you are the next one they will call. Consider doing some favors for the lender, possibly at no charge, just to get your foot in the door.

Realtors are another source of leads for handling this property. Many times banks have their favorite realtor managing the property. If this is the case, let the agent know you are not after his or her brokerage business, but that you can help them by handling the cleanup and resale preparation.

Let the agent know that you also can perform the same duties on other properties not owned by banks—like estate property. Estate property is often full of old furniture, trash, and debris, and needs to be prepped for sale.

Tools and Skills. You will need many of the same tools as are required for the apartment preparation business. You will also need lawn cutting and landscaping tools such as a heavy-duty weed trimmer, a pickup truck, padlocks, heavy brooms, a shop vacuum, a high-powered pressure washer, a small chain saw, a power paint sprayer, and a carpet steam cleaner.

If you don't have some of the more expensive tools listed here, remember you can rent heavy-duty tools from equipment rental stores.

Business Merger Idea. Since this business is very similar to the apartment preparation business, you should consider providing both services. Banks acquire foreclosed apartment buildings that need the vacant units prepared for rental. If you help them get their buildings rented, they will sell faster. Can you see how apartment rental preparation may be needed by the REO department of various lenders?

Your Best Source of Clients. The toughest part of any business is the initial year when you are seeking out new clients. After this period, you should be getting plenty of jobs from referrals. Investors and business people talk to each other a lot. If you provide a timely and good work product you should have plenty of business after your first year or two.

Tenant Investigation and Eviction Services.

When a property owner rents a house or apartment, the owner is giving the tenant custody to a very expensive asset. This asset can be physically damaged or be held hostage by a nonpaying tenant. Either way, property owners have much to lose.

In many cases landlords do take applications from tenants before they rent property; the problem is many landlords do a poor job of screening out high-risk tenants. Problems usually appear within the first few months when the landlord realizes he has selected a bad tenant. At this point, the only solution is to evict the non-compliant tenant from the building.

The Business Model. The tenant investigation and eviction service business is one that can be worked almost exclusively from a small home-based office. The service involves pulling detailed credit, background, and eviction searches on potential tenants for landlords. The second part of the service is to help landlords remove their bad tenants with various legal remedies or evictions.

This type of work doesn't have to be limited to residential tenants since commercial tenants require screening and credit verification just as much as residential renters. This means office complexes, strip centers, and even industrial landlords could use your screening services.

The landlord's job is to get a signed credit application and then allow you to do your work of researching the tenant applicant. This research or "investigation" is done primarily through credit bureau databases and on-line data resources. Along with gathering the raw data, you could possibly create a scoring system to rate the stability and credit worthiness of the prospective tenant.

There are several searches that could be conducted to determine the credit rating or risk rating for the applicant. 1) Multi-bureau credit check: Trans/Equifax/etc. 2) Criminal background search 3) Judgment index/database 4) Research truthfulness of stated info on application (job history, past length of residency, etc.) 5) Past eviction history.

Tenant Investigation Pricing. There are several ways that you can price your tenant investigation services. You can charge strictly on a per-use fee basis or you can charge a flat-fee on a membership basis. Another option would be a combination basis of a small membership fee and a small per-use fee. You could also charge different prices for different levels of investigation. You probably would want to push the premium service where you bundle all of the research/background checks into one nicely priced package. Most of the firms I have researched charge anywhere from $12 for a basic credit check up to $60 for a complete credit/background/eviction investigation using multiple databases.

Another pricing and marketing option is to charge a higher fee, but to offer some form of limited tenant guarantee on once your service rates as an acceptable risk. This could be a bit tricky, but I think it is worth considering as a sales proposition. One tenant investigation service that I am familiar with offers a six-month tenant guarantee. I'm sure there are some big loopholes in the guarantee to limit the legal exposure of the tenant investigation service.

Eviction Services. This part of the business would be considered a paralegal service. You will be assisting owners in filling out and filing of various court documents in order to have a non-compliant (non-paying or breach of lease) tenant ejected from a property.

This service could be offered with several levels of service and prices. It could begin with the company preparing and mailing out various late notices and demands for payment. From here, you could actually handle serving the notice to move to the tenant, and filing the court documents for the owner. The main area you would want to avoid is going to the hearing representing the owner, because this requires an attorney. You cannot represent someone else in a courtroom unless you are the property manager or an attorney at law.

After the actual hearing, you could continue to assist the owner with additional paperwork filings, since the actual eviction in most areas requires a second step of additional filings. It may sound complicated, but in most areas it is a matter of just learning the rules and legal process. **Note:** Depending on the area of the country, independent paralegals like this service are sometimes frowned upon by lawyers, because they think this is only their territory, and non-lawyers are not welcome. The legal term for this is UPL (unauthorized practice of law), and there can be legal penalties if the county or state bar association decide to fight you on this matter. With the proliferation of self-help legal materials and independent paralegals opening up document services this is changing in many areas of the country, slowly, but surely.

If you ask a lawyer if it is legal for you to do this business they may automatically say no, because they generally feel like they went to three years of law school and you didn't, therefore, you aren't worthy to fill out forms. Your best bet is to research this out yourself and possibly get help from any of the various independent paralegal associations.

Resource. Nolo Press is a good source of self-help law books and information on paralegal work. Their web address is: **www.nolo.com** or 800.728.3555. Ask for their interesting catalog.

Another Option. If you do run into trouble or don't feel comfortable operating an eviction services company, consider finding an open-minded attorney who you could work in association with in order to bypass this whole unauthorized practice of law thing. Just make sure that you are protected from the lawyer firing you and keeping your clients—maintain control.

How to Learn the Eviction Process. Eviction law varies from state to state. In most cases though, the process is similar. First, notice to move or as it sometimes is called—Notice to Quit is served on the tenant, because of some type of nonpayment or breach of lease has occurred. Next, papers are filed with the local District court or justice of the peace. Whatever it's called, it is usually a small claims type court, that is more user friendly than a large county courthouse which is more of a lawyer's court. Then a hearing is scheduled. At the hearing the judge will rule in favor of the landlord in most cases. Next, there is usually some sort of timetable that must be waited to expire, and then you can file for the actual eviction to be scheduled. Once filed, the court will have another notice served on the tenant giving them just a few more days to get out. Then Eviction Day comes and in most cases the people must be out or the constable or sheriff will have the non-payers bodily removed! Finally the owner or manager has the locks changed. That is a rough outline of how the process usually works.

You will have to do careful research to see precisely how the process works in your state. Call your local state representative and ask their office to send you copies of all the state's landlord tenant laws.

Tip: Go to the local law library and ask to speak to the head librarian. Ask this person who has written the definitive work on your state's landlord tenant laws. In every state there's some attorney who has written a landlord/tenant legal manual explaining in the process in detail. These manuals are typically written by attorneys and for attorneys, although many real estate practitioners use them as well. Also, ask the librarian if they have what are called practice manuals for attorneys on the subject of landlord and tenants. Again, every state has manuals for attorneys called practice manuals. They provide a large amount of step-by-step details on the process.

Additional Profit Centers. Anytime you have a business, you should be on the look out for additional services or products you could offer to your clients (as long as the additional service is not too far outside the normal services you provide).

There are several excellent add-on services you might consider, especially if you decide on a credit/tenant investigation business. The first is called Judgment Recovery or collections. We will have an entire section on this business opportunity later in the book. The thing to know is that it requires many of the same tools as does the credit check and investigation services, therefore it may be very complimentary to your credit and evictions service business. Also, keep in mind, many landlords are holding judgments from past tenants who never paid them. With your connections to the rental business you may have a captive market for this additional service.

The second opportunity could be collection services where you collect past due or bad debt for landlords, businesses, or anyone with a documented unpaid bill. Again, this could work hand-in-hand with your other credit investigation services.

Marketing Strategy. Many of the same strategies that are used in the other investor service businesses can be used in this business. Your main target audience would be real estate investors, realtors, property managers, CPAs, attorneys, and real estate investment clubs/associations.

Probably your best bet would be to use the small ads and direct mail to the target audience. I would advise you to collect as many names of landlords as possible and record them in your computer database mailing list. These names and addresses could be acquired through a variety of methods. In most areas there are mailing list marketing firms that have hundreds of thousands of names and full demographic profiles that could produce lists of local real estate investors. Beyond that, a daily tracking and logging of classified for rent ads could produce phone numbers that could be reversed searched to find the owner's address (see Appendix).

Your main message would be that you offer comprehensive credit checks and investigation in order to take the risk out of the rental industry. You would want to emphasize your proficient use of various computer databases in order to achieve reliable results. Another main thrust of your business could be the ease of using your service along with speed of your responses (in today's computerized society two days is too long—try thirty minute responses or faster).

Many large property owners may have their own on-line credit account with various bureaus, therefore, you may need to modify the pricing or service package you offer them in order to be competitive. Perhaps you could hook them to your own on-line databases for a monthly fee or per use fee.

Stress to the client that your service is not a cost, but a small investment to help protect their valuable assets.

Tools and Technology. This opportunity will require you to have updated high tech tools, including multiple phone lines, fax, internet service, computer gear, and possible subscriptions to various on-line data banks.

Here are a few resources:

Equifax Credit Bureau, PO Box 740241, Atlanta, GA, 30374-0241, 800.685.1111 or **www.equifax.com.**

Experian, PO Box 949, Allen, TX 75013-0949, 800.397.3742 or **www.experian.com.**

Trans Union Corporation, 800.916.8800 **www.tuc.com.**

Public Records research: Try **www.knowx.com.** Another public record resource is Pacer Service Center, 800.676.6856 or **www.pacer.psc.uscourts.gov.**

The Internet is teaming with on-line databases and information providers in the credit and public record industry. Before you sign-up for any service thoroughly research your options.

Closing Caution and Summary. This entire field of credit investigation and research is governed by federal laws. You will need to thoroughly research the regulations that govern pulling other people's credit before beginning operations.

There are two primary laws you will need to study and probably get legal counsel on before setting up operations. The first governs credit reporting and screening. It is the Fair Credit Reporting Act (FCRA). The other law is the Consumer Credit Reporting Reform Act.

If you get involved in debt collection activities you will need to know and understand the Fair Debt Collection Practices Act.

This whole area of credit and collections is heavily regulated, therefore, you will need to navigate your business through the various laws and possible licenses. If you are serious, get an attorney who specializes in credit and debt collection laws, and not a general practice lawyer. Also, before you visit the lawyer, thoroughly do your own research and reading on the matter so you can talk intelligently on this subject.

Property Management Business. A good portion of real estate investors love real estate but don't like managing it. This is usually because they don't have the time or expertise to manage tenants and buildings. After all, real estate ownership is not like having a mutual fund or bank CD. All sorts of tasks and jobs that need to be handled in the course of managing a property: tenant screening and selection, repairs and maintenance, rent collection, accounting and payment disbursement, code inspections, eviction laws, conflict resolution, security deposit issues, etc.

If you take the time to learn how to professionally manage property you can build a prosperous business helping people manage their real estate. By specializing in management you enable people to spend more of their time doing what they do best in their particular field while you handle their rental property.

Property management is not the hassle people think it is when you make it your specialty. Like anything else, when you are "geared up" to handle the business, everything flow a lot smoother than if you do it on a limited scale. Property management is a craft, not unlike carpentry, dentistry, sales, or any other business. The problem most folks have is they don't devote enough time to learn the business, and therefore have problems in the rental business. As a professional manager, you can help them.

Although starting a property management business does not require large amounts of capital, it does require some experience. As I stated, it is a craft that you won't learn at a weekend seminar, but if you have the desire, it can be learned and mastered in a few years.

Real estate management offers unique opportunity for investors who already own some real estate and need additional income. These people already have some experience. In addition they probably already have a small team consisting of a handyman, electrician, cleaning person, etc. that helps them with their buildings. They are already in this business, and many of the systems are in place, so why not expand?

Earning fees managing other people's property is a good form of leverage. You don't need to own the property to build an income; you just need to control it through some sort of management relationship.

Property management is lucrative because it builds a monthly cash flow based on other people's rental income. If you manage 100 units for a few investors who pay you 8 percent of the gross, that would be about $4,800 per month in fees based on a monthly rental of $600.

One cash-poor real estate investor I know managed a small portfolio of about 40 low-income houses that rented for about $400 each per month. Working straight from his own apartment he managed them earning about $1,600 per month. In addition he made significant other income from handling the maintenance and unit preparation—plus he had his own portfolio of rental units that he owned! The combination of his rental properties with his small management business made him a nice income. Best of all he had the freedom of being his own boss.

A Word About Licenses. There are real estate licensing laws in every state in the union. They are similar from state to state. As a rule, you do need a real estate license to manage property for other people. There are some exceptions and possible "loopholes" in these laws, which we will review further in this section.

Without going into a long dissertation on real estate licensing requirements, let me state that generally speaking, you need a broker's license to be the person directly in charge of managing other people's property. Generally, you can assist a broker by just having a salesperson's license. If you decide to get into management in a big way, you probably will want to acquire a real estate license and work under a broker who will give you a lot of freedom. We will cover more on this topic later.

Supplemental Income. You may already be a full-time real estate entrepreneur who owns buildings. If you are, you may find offering management services a dependable way to boost your income to cover the ups and downs in your cash flow that all business people face. For example, you might be making $60,000 from your portfolio, but would like to earn another $20,000 for a cash flow that would make things a bit more comfortable. Since you're already tooled up with management systems in place, you might consider offering your professional management services to other investors as a way to supplement your income.

Bridge To Ownership. Management is an excellent bridge into owning a piece of real estate with no money down. I have seen this concept at work, and can personally attest to its effectiveness. Here is how I have seen it work.

A savvy landlord in my town owns quite a few lower income houses and apartment buildings that she personally manages. Over the years she took on the management of other people's houses and apartment buildings. She explained to me that many of her owners were so pleased with her management that they sold her the very buildings she was managing with no money down and complete owner financing. They trusted her because she proved herself reliable during the years she managed their buildings. Because of her trustworthy management these owners converted their rental properties into mortgage notes with her as the buyer.

This worked for several reasons. First, they knew she knew how to handle the buildings and that their collateral would be in good hands. Second, they knew she was reliable and trustworthy with making payments since during the management term, she was forwarding those payments to them. Lastly, this created a stable cash flow to the owners with even fewer problems than ownership, because they would just be holding the note. This clever manager used her management as a bridge into ownership with very little of her own cash invested.

My second example is about a couple of young fellows who operated a landscaping and yard maintenance business. In addition to their landscaping business they had a maintenance service handling all the repair needs for an apartment building investor in a nearby small city. After a few years these guys took on more and more responsibility from the investor. They started doing repairs and ended up collecting rents and handling the bad tenants (a lot of low-income apartments). Eventually the finances of the property owner went sour and he defaulted on his payments to the bank for reasons unrelated to the property itself.

The bank ended up with the foreclosed properties. Banks are in the business of loaning money, not managing low-income apartments with all of the day-to-day operations—the bank was essentially losing their shirt trying to manage the 150 units they repossessed. Out of sheer desperation, the bank called the two young maintenance managers to help them run the buildings until they were sold. The amazing thing is that the bank, seeing that these guys were competent managers, offered to sell them the entire portfolio of 150 units. The problem was these guys didn't have a lot of cash or credit, and they were self-employed. No problem. The bank sold them the whole package with no money down and held the financing to boot!

Do you see how management gets you close to the real players in real estate and can offer unexpected opportunities?

A reliable, hardworking, competent property manager will attract plenty of opportunities for joint ventures and hidden deals in the marketplace! If you develop skills as a manager, are a trustworthy individual, and have a management team, you will get tons of referrals and offers to become a player in other people's deals!

The Business Model. In this business you will be handling the renting, collection, maintenance, and supervision of rental real estate. You will be managing both buildings and income streams for investors.

Your fees are earned from the services you perform. If you do not perform, you don't get paid. Perform well—get paid well.

Your customers—oops, clients—will be real estate owners who either do not have the skills or don't have the time to manage their properties. You will make owning real estate a lot easier, since you will be on the front line with the tenants and the building supervision. Your job will be to make the sometimes complex and burdensome world of real estate seem as easy to own as a mutual fund. These owners just want to get their check every month, pay their mortgages, and not be bothered with managing people or building maintenance.

Fees and Pricing. There are several ways people make money in the management business. Typically when a unit gets rented, the first month's rent goes to the property manager for screening and acquiring the tenant. Everything is negotiable though—perhaps, you would charge less on the up front fee and a little more per month.

Next, you typically charge anywhere from 7 to 10 percent of the gross rent each month for collecting the rent and handling the various management duties. This fee of course is nowhere set in stone and would depend on the number units per building that you manage. You might charge 10 percent of the rent to manage a house, but probably would charge less than 10 percent if it was a 38-unit apartment building. You would offer a volume discount.

In the property management business you build your income with a lot of small checks every month. Your average profit per unit will range from $35 to $70 per month. This may not sound like a lot, but start building a volume of business and the numbers can be impressive. Also keep in mind that this is an on-going income stream. Do look only at the $35 per month—look at the $35 per month multiplied over two or three years.

Another source of revenue could be earned by providing the owner with affordable repair services. In this case, you could use someone on your team to handle the service call, and you could charge a modest fee on top for arranging the service. The fee that you charge on top of the service work must be affordable or else you risk losing the clients for the more profitable monthly management services. Another option could be that the contractor would bill the owner directly and then pay you a finders/referral fee, although this system gives you less control over the client bypassing you. **Note:** depending on how you structure your business and whether or not you are licensed as a real estate agent/broker, referral fees may not be legal, although in most cases you can restructure or re-characterize the fees to be in compliance.

Your fees for arranging repairs should be in the range of 15 to 25 percent of the total, depending upon the dollar amounts being charged. Do not get greedy.

Hot Profit Tip. Consider setting up an advisory service for those landlords who don't want your management services, but who would want your expertise on an on-call basis. Consider a low annual fee of $100-200 for the client to call you and get management advice. Another possibility is to help vacationing landlords who need someone to field their tenant's calls while they go away on vacation. Consider charging $100 per month depending on portfolio size.

Marketing and Finding Clients.
You will find clients the same way as you do in the other investor services businesses. Real estate clubs, classified ads, direct mail, referrals, data base marketing, banks, networking with investors, flyers—and calling distressed owners who clearly are in over their head.

Many of the people that I know in the property management business have a lot of accounts in the lower-income sections of the city. This probably is due to the fact that these properties require more time and attention than more upscale housing. Even though it may take more time and labor, do not overlook low-income management as a way to break into the management business. Everyone must start somewhere.

There are a lot more distressed landlords in the lower-income areas, therefore this can be a very fruitful area to find owners who may need your services. Just make sure to avoid the real war-zone areas.

One way to locate owners might be to send letters to the owners who are listed in the eviction rolls down at the district justice court where most eviction suits are filed. These records are usually open to public inspection and you could periodically contact the various owners by phone or letter. These owners may be highly motivated to enlist your services in handling their building!

Additional Profit Centers. Really any one the investor services discussed in this book could be an additional profit center you can weave into your business mix. Here are some ideas: Eviction services, apartment preparation, maintenance contracts, master leasing, REO cleanup and management, tenant screening, tax reduction consulting/reduction, investment consulting, trustee services, and many more!

Managers, realize you have a captive audience of potential homeowners. Consider helping your tenant clients to find a home if they decide to become property owners instead of renters. I know one management company that makes some nice commissions helping tenants become owners.

Licensing Issues and Management Options.

As stated earlier, every state has some sort of real estate licensing laws that regulate the real estate business. Generally speaking, these laws are meant to be a barrier to keep amateurs out of the real estate business and to protect the general public.

I obviously do not know the laws of every state in the union, and even if I did, I would be a fool to try to explain them all here. But the general concepts or regulations seem to be consistent through the states. Let's now review the general thrust of real estate licensing and see what options there are.

The state real estate commission govern and enforce real estate laws enacted by the state's legislature. As a rule, they want to control as much of the real estate business as they can get away with; it is typical of governmental bureaucracy.

The Key Principle of Licensing. The general principle that seems to run through most state real estate licensing laws is: You do not need a real estate license to handle real estate that you own or real estate that you have a financial ownership interest in. But you do need a license to sell or manage real estate real estate for other people when you do not have an ownership interest in the property.

Because the organized real estate industry is composed mainly of licensees or brokers, they have a vested interest in keeping non-licensees out of the business. It's a form of a trade union, just like the State Bar Association for lawyers. These folks want you to jump through their hoops and pay their fees to let you in the game.

These laws are written very broadly, so they can exclude as many people from the game as possible to protect the union. If you want to be in the management business in a big way, you probably are well advised to jump through the licensing hoops, become licensed, and fall under their governance.

There are some exceptions and clever ways to possibly avoid licensing and still earn money doing management services. We will review several ideas shortly. **Note:** With any of these licensing and state regulation issues you must carefully read your own state law and even get a lawyer's advice. I am not advocating you break any state laws. This information is only meant to provide preliminary information that you should research yourself, seek professional legal advice, and then make an informed decision.

In most cases if you want to set up you own management "shop" you must have a broker's license. The much easier sales person's license will not be enough. But in many cases, a licensed salesperson, can assist a broker with management. In other words, you must work under a broker's license and supervision.

This can make it a little tough because many brokers are sticks in the mud, not wanting to try new things or be aggressive about acquiring new clients. After all, many brokers don't want the management business—they want sales. The other problem—what happens if you as the new aggressive agent—build this management business for the broker, and he or she terminates your employment? Then all of your hard fought for management clients (and buildings) may remain as the broker's clients.

Broker of Record.
One viable option would be to find a retired or semi-retired person who holds a broker's license and see if they would become your Broker of Record. This would possibly enable you to call most of the shots, while at the same time having this figurehead as the broker of record.

Having someone be your broker of record won't come free since they have spent several years working to get their broker license. In addition, there is some liability involved, since the person holds a professional license, subject to fines and penalties for misconduct or malpractice.

In most cases, the broker of record will want a piece of the monthly profits and some sort of errors and omissions insurance policy for yourself and his name. The actual percentage to pay the broker will have to be researched in your local area. Many big city newspapers will have ads run by brokers seeking to offer their license as the broker of record. Shop these names first to see what they have to offer. Probably your best bet would be to run some small ads saying, "broker of record wanted." Along with the regular classified sections consider running small ads in various real estate publications. Then research the character and past history of the broker with the local real estate board and their colleagues.

If you work under a broker of record you in most cases will still need a real estate license, although these are a lot easier to acquire than the broker's license.

Other Possible Options. Over the years I have seen a lot of people provide management services for others without a license. There are a variety of ways these people handle the licensing issue. What we will now explore are just my observations, and not recommendations, although I believe some of these ideas to be basically legally sound, while others are marginal at best.

The Employee Concept. I know several attorneys who own large amounts of real estate. These attorneys all have employees who handle most of the day-to-day management of their properties. If you checked into it, you would probably find that this is a technical violation of the licensing statutes in most states. But since they are doing this in a very low-profile way, they don't have any problems.

I know another investor who handled the management side of a small group of investors who owned about a million dollars worth of property. This individual also has never had a problem managing these properties for a fee. Again it is low profile.

I know several other entrepreneurs who started out handling a lot of the maintenance duties for other investors and gradually moved into more management work. They show units, screen tenants, evict, handle repairs, etc. all with no problems from the real estate commission. They probably have steered clear of the state commission because their front-line business is building maintenance, with management being a secondary service. Again, they are below the radar screen since their main service is maintenance.

I am aware of several companies who have been managing huge portfolios of low-income housing for other investors and have told me they never have had a problem with the real estate commission. It seems that many of the local brokers don't feel threatened because they simply don't want to manage the type of properties these folks manage.

There seem to be two factors that the above examples share. One is that the management is done in a low profile way. Second, several of these entrepreneurs have their own properties they manage at the same time as they manage their investors' properties.

Master Leasing. Another concept to bypass the whole licensing issue is called master leasing. This is the method where you go out and acquire a master lease on a building at a wholesale rental price and then re-lease (sublease) the units out to tenants at the retail price of the units. In this scenario, you are a principal to the deal, holding a master lease as a lessee (which is an estate in land), which in most cases effectively circumvents the real estate licensing regs.

Become a Tiny Owner. I have seen the ownership method of managing other people's property as an extremely effective way to bypass licensing. Remember what we said earlier that you can manage your own properties without a real estate license? State laws generally say that if you are an owner (called a principal) in the deal, you do not need a license to handle the buying, selling, or renting your own property. Being an owner makes you a principal party (someone with authority to direct the property or an agent).

With larger properties I have seen the manager acquiring a tiny half or one percent ownership in the real estate which effectively makes the manager an owner. As an owner, even a small fractional owner, you probably get by most of the licensing issues (always research your own laws). Who's to say how much you pay for your tiny ownership? In real estate, even a token amount is usually binding.

Also, in real estate, ownership is typically evidenced by a deed, but the deed does NOT have to be recorded to make you a valid owner. To protect the main body of owners you might choose not to record the deed and have the deed held by them in escrow to ensure your performance. You might even have a quit-claim deed held in escrow to deed your interest back in the event you don't perform.

Your best bet is to get copies of all the pertinent real estate regulations for your state. Read and study them. Look for what clearly is and is not defined and covered. There are many creative ways to work around this management issue. Be advised that if you brazenly and aggressively advertise and market yourself as a real estate management company, you eventually *will* be visited by the state real estate commission.

Investors and entrepreneurs have used other ways to deal with the management/licensing issue. Some have used a limited power of attorney to control property and gain sort of a proxy ownership. For a power of attorney the owner signs over control of the building and allows you to control it in their stead. This may be difficult to obtain since POA contracts are extremely powerful and run the risk of the proxy person selling the property and running with the money. Consult with an attorney to see what protection could be offered to the owner.

Become the Trustee Owner. Another angle might be to become the trustee of the property for the owner, thereby providing some privacy and asset protection services, since the real owner's name is not on the public record. You as trustee, would become the straw party owner and therefore a principal in the deal, possibly avoiding the management license issue. This trustee method typically involves creating a land trust or some other form of a revocable trust. To make the owner more comfortable, the trust might not even be recorded and thus him or her even more control and assurances. Furthermore, the trust agreement could be written to give the beneficiary maximum control and powers to dismiss and replace the trustee at anytime.

Another possible method is to acquire an interest in the property via a leasehold. If you acquire a lease on a property, you become the owner of a leasehold estate, which is an interest in real estate. Then if you re-lease the property/units you become a sandwich lessor to effectively make you a manager in the deal. In this arrangement the original lease must state that you have the right to sub-lease the property to tenants.

What if you drafted a performance lease or a percentage lease like is used in commercial deals, whereby your lease payments to the owner are based upon your success in the venture? Wouldn't this help control your losses during vacancy and at the same time allow you to partner with the owner in the management? Hmmm.

What if you acquired an option-to-buy agreement on all the properties you managed? Would this make you a principal in the deal? A holder of an interest in real estate? I'm not sure it would make you a principal in the land, but I believe most real estate lawyers would agree that you would have an interest in the real estate. It is worth exploring with a good creative real estate lawyer who is open minded.

The Maintenance Company Approach.

This approach may work well with those of you who are good at the more physical aspects of property repairs and maintenance. As mentioned above, many management services companies start out handling just repairs and maintenance of income properties, and from here the owners gradually put them in charge of more and more responsibilities.

A few individuals I have interviewed who use this approach say they effectively bypass licensing requirements because they are not actually managing real estate. They prepare properties for rental and show units but don't actually get into lease signings or actual final selection of tenants. The main strategy is to provide a lot of services but still let the owners select the tenants and pay the mortgage payments. They handle most of the day-to-day problems like roof repairs, collecting late payments and posting notices to move, but anything involving lease contracts and tenant selection is left to the owner.

Tools and Skills.

The tools you need depend on the types of services you will be providing. If you are involved in the property maintenance end of services you or your contract help will need the full gamut of tools used in the apartment preparation business. A basic set of plumbing tools will also be in order, especially a drain cleaning snake. If you are involved in more of the people and administrative end of the business you will need all of the home office tools suggested in Chapter 2—copier, fax, two phone lines, a computer, and so forth.

A good management software package is also be a must. There are two basic types of rental software out there—software for owner-users, and software for management companies. For starters you should check out Tenant-Pro software or Tenant File. Whatever you do, make sure the software has the capability to produce full reports based on all the management variables and expenses by owner, vacancy, utilities, repairs, advertising, permits, etc.

Skills and Habits. Managing other people's property means you are being entrusted with hundreds of thousands of dollars in assets. You must take this responsibility seriously and handle yourself in a professional, business like manner. This means keeping promises and always doing what's best for your clients and their money.

There is a lot of paperwork that flows from the ownership and management of real estate. This will require you to be a reasonably organized person. If you're not, you better hire someone who will make you be organized. Owners will require an accounting of income and expenses; therefore, your computer and filing system must be maintained every week.

People and Building Knowledge. Being an effective property manager requires you to know and understand basic property repairs and maintenance. This doesn't mean you have to actually do this work, but a good base of knowledge will be valuable in handling many of the repair problems that you will encounter. I recommend studying the basics of how the mechanical systems in a building work. There are literally hundreds of books and how-to videos available on this subject.

Many problems associated with owning rental property originate from mechanical or maintenance issues. In fact, many of the people problems landlords encounter have their roots in leaky roofs and other malfunctioning structures. Even if you consider yourself totally inept at fixing things you need to learn the fundamentals of property repairs and maintenance. If you aren't knowledgeable yet, then it will be mandatory that you have an experienced handyman to troubleshoot problems.

This area of property maintenance, repairs, and mechanical systems is a totally learnable subject. Even if you consider yourself not mechanically inclined you can easily learn and even master the basics in a year or two of experience and study. The more you learn in this department, the better property manager you will become.

People are the next thing you will need to manage. They range from your tenants to the support personnel that will help you. Make the effort to learn people skills. Much of this type of expertise comes from just being out in the business world and learning from experience, but there also are plenty of books that will teach you how to handle people.

Tenants can be your greatest asset or your greatest nightmare. Be sure to study tenant screening and management. Read as much as you can on this subject. My book, *Perpetual Income,* has a lot of information on both property repairs and tenant management. Although it is mainly about lower-income property ownership, most of the information applies to any rental property investment.

Rental real estate is governed by state landlord tenant laws. It is an absolute must that you know the basic rental laws in your state. Get a hold of the entire body of landlording laws for your state. The local law library should be able to direct you to a comprehensive manual explaining the duties and rights of landlords and tenants.

Land Trust Trustee Business. This is another investor service that could serve as a profit center for other asset management services, or it could possibly stand on its own as a full business opportunity. It is a business idea whose time has come.

One of the problems in the ownership of real estate is the fact that real estate ownership is a public record. Go into any courthouse, and you can see what someone owns and how much they paid for it. It is a very open system. This openness creates privacy and asset protection concerns for investors.

As we all know our society is very litigious. You can be sued at the drop of a hat. Real estate holders are especially vulnerable since real estate can be attached by a lawsuit judgment easier than almost any other asset.

Challenges involved in real estate ownership like governmental regulations and city codes sometimes makes large property owners vulnerable. Although it may be unfair, overzealous codes inspectors have been known to target property owners that they deem as unfit to own property. The result can be having your properties be the target of harsh and unreasonable code demands and liability.

Consider a land trust to help reduce this problem. In the past few years, investors across America have been using the land trust device to gain privacy and protect assets. A land trust is basically a legal contract with one party holding title to property in their name for the benefit of someone else. The benefiting party, or beneficiary, as this entity is legally known, gets all of the benefits of owning the property, but not in the personal name of the individual. All of the income and tax benefits flow to the beneficiary even though their name does not appear on the deed. The trustee serves as the legal title-holder, but in most respects is just a straw party.

The controlling contract is called the trust agreement. This contract is kept unrecorded and in the confidential possession of the trustee and beneficiary. Basically this document spells out the rights and duties of the parties involved in the trust. Most trust agreements call for the trustee never to reveal the actual (beneficiary) owner unless by a formal court order. This creates extreme privacy for the investor-beneficiary.

In most every state of the union trusts are used to hold property. Trust law is a fundamental part of American jurisprudence. Although laws vary from state to state, generally speaking, well-established common law controls trusts.

The Business Model. This business would be a title holding service with you or your company serving as a gatekeeper or legal straw party for the property owner, thereby concealing the investor's identity and helping preserve their privacy. In addition, the investor would gain a smoke-screen type shield to legally and ethically keep assets below the radar screen of money hungry plaintiffs and lawyers seeking an unjust enrichment.

Another big advantage to a trustee service is its potential estate planning benefits. Real estate held in one's personal name is typically subject to probate proceedings upon the passing of the owner. In contrast, when a person dies having their real estate held in a land trust, the real estate flows directly to the designated contingent beneficiary named in the trust agreement, thereby avoiding probate and costly legal fees.

So you can see, a land trust can serve many functions in that it keeps the ownership as private as a Swiss bank account and helps bypass costly probate proceedings. I know this sounds like a complicated tool of the "rich," but land trusts are not complicated after you have spent some time studying them.

The Trust Problem. One of the challenges in using land trusts is finding someone you trust to be your trustee. In many cases you won't want a relative or friend doing it because you don't want them knowing the intimate and personal details of your finances. The problem then becomes choosing someone you know and trust

who is willing to serve as trustee. You may find that the one or two persons you might approve of being your trustee may be afraid to do it because they don't know the legal ramifications for their liability in doing this.

By offering a professional title holding service you can solve the problem many investors have in finding a trustee to hold their legal title. For a fee, your company can hold the investor's title, thus preserving the investor's privacy and offering some ancillary estate planning benefits.

While a basic land trust or living trust type arrangement is somewhat simple to arrange, there are a number of details that need to be considered.

As trustee, for instance, will all of the tax, water, trash, and city notices be coming to you or to the beneficiary/owner? Will you be dispersing payments out of a trust bank account for mortgages and taxes? Or will you just be a mail receiver and forward all bills and correspondence back to your beneficial owners for them to handle? For the service to be most effective, especially from a privacy standpoint, you probably will need all or most of the correspondence to come to the trustee company's mailing address.

Services and Pricing.
As mentioned, there are numerous services that could be offered. You will need to think through the type of services you want to offer and the pricing. A menu approach probably works best.

For example, Service Package A—Basic Title Holding Trustee Service Annually $100. Service package B—Trustee services with mail receiving and forwarding $100 plus $6 per month. Service Package C—All of the above plus bill paying service and accounting $125 and $15 per month. These are just examples, of course.

You will also have to decide how to price services for investors owing multiple properties and who may want individual land trusts for each property. This service might have an initial startup fee in the $195 range that could include the first year's service fee. After the first year the price could drop. The key is to price the service so that each additional property gets significantly cheaper. After all, your actual costs in doing business per customer won't change significantly whether the investor has one property or ten placed with you. For instance, if you are forwarding monthly mail to the beneficiary, the actual cost in doing this will only rise a few dollars for postage if they own more than one property.

The area of pricing must not be taken lightly since the only way to make real money doing this is by handling a decent volume of business. The only way to generate volume is by making the price affordable. As a group, real estate investors are a cheap lot! If the service costs more that about $200 per year, chances are many investors will find alternative options.

Liability and You. The question that will arise in your mind is, How much personal exposure will I face as the trustee to the property, especially doing this on a large scale? This is a valid question that should not be taken lightly. The answer, of course, depends on the state you live in and what type statutes govern trustees and their duties. I will not attempt to answer these questions, but I will review general legal principals regarding trusts.

Generally speaking, there is no personal liability for trustees who hold title for the benefit of another party as long as they have not committed fraud or some other criminal act. As an added precaution, it probably would be highly advisable to have the actual trustee be a corporation, therefore it would not be the John Doe Trustee, but something like, Maxton Inc., Trustee.

Whatever the case, do as much research on your state law and then hire a good creative lawyer to help advise you. Keep in mind, lawyers are conservative in their advice and often will say no when they don't know the answers rather than risking looking bad if something goes wrong.

Another issue bound to come up is how to make investors comfortable with the tremendous control you have as trustee. This possibly could be handled a couple of different ways. First, consider getting bonded with a third party covering you up to a certain dollar amount. Another option would be to have some sort of legal document recorded that prohibits additional borrowing against the real estate. Lastly, consider having a large debt or security instrument like a mortgage recorded against the property to ensure that there is no marketable title (salable or mortgageable) until it is released by the beneficial owner. There are a lot of options here so get legal counsel with a lawyer in trust and real estate law.

Marketing and Strategy. This service could be marketed using many of the same ideas and methods used for other investor services. The one possible difference is this service could possibly be used over a much larger geographical area since you are handling documents and paperwork, not actual tenants or maintenance issues.

Additional Profit Centers. Most of the investor services mentioned in this book could be additional profit centers in the land trust trustee business.

One additional service that could be offered is asset protection consulting, but unless you are an absolute authority in this area you probably should steer clear. Asset protection consulting would require you be somewhat of an authority in the area of real estate, litigation law, corporations, limited liability companies, limited partnerships, trusts, and privacy issues. The challenge here is you would almost have to be a lawyer to have a solid grasp of all these issues. Another challenge would be the charge of UPL (unauthorized practice of law), which can have some stiff legal penalties— lawyers don't take kindly to people they feel threaten their business. I have seen trustee services offering this kind of service, but proceed with caution in this more legally complex arena.

Resources and Additional Information. Nolo Press and Z-Law (see appendix) would be a good place to start to learn about trusts, corporations, and limited liability companies through their various self-help books and software programs. Your local law library would also be excellent, although most of these books are written for lawyers and by lawyers, therefore they may not be as digestible for the new student.

The 1031 Tax Deferred Exchange Facilitator. This is a business idea with your company acting as an exchange facilitator for 1031 tax deferred real estate exchanges.

A 1031 exchange is an IRS-sanctioned method of handling the sale and reinvestment of the sales (exchange) proceeds into another investment or business property without paying capital gains taxes. In most cases it is actually not an exchange or swap of real estate, but more like a rollover. The exchange allows an investor to dispose of one investment property and roll over essentially tax free the proceeds into another property, thereby creating no taxable event.

The Internal Revenue Service code section 1031 covers the rules for these exchanges. As stated, most of these so-called exchanges are delayed rollovers. The basic guideline is that upon the closing sale of the first property the investor cannot touch the money or have constructive receipt of cash. This money must be held in escrow or a trust account by what is called an IRS approved qualified intermediary exchange facilitator. Other names for this facilitator include "exchange accommodator" and "qualified exchange intermediary."

The qualified exchange facilitator holds the money until the seller/exchanger notifies him within 45 days of the date that the next property is to be purchased or "exchanged" into. Then that property must be closed within 180 days from the first sale. If all of this is handled in conformance with IRS guidelines then the sale and repurchase really becomes an exchange.

The Business Model.
In this business you act as an exchange facilitator that helps investors save capital gain taxes by using the rollover exchange. You are paid a fee for your service, and your fee will be considered small compared to the potential tens of thousands of dollars in saved taxes.

Depending on the type of exchange being done, the intermediary handles the various titles and monies from the parties of the exchange to prevent them from receiving the money. One of the advantages of this business is that investors cannot do an acceptable exchange without using a qualified intermediary. Therefore, investors need you and can't do it themselves.

Skills and Tools.
In this business you will definitely need to be a detailed paperwork type of person, preferably someone with an accounting or heavy real estate background to handle the sometimes complex nature of tax and real estate laws.

You probably will need to work this business out of an existing professional office, perhaps a title company, accounting firm, or law office. This is because of the need to meet clients for settlements and meetings in a suitable professional atmosphere. You probably could work out an arrangement with a business associate to use their office on a fee per use basis. Believe it or not, most of this work can be handled strictly over the phone and fax, along with using electronic wiring of money.

You will need the full range of high-tech office equipment and computers to operate this professional services company. You will need some exchange software in order to handle the various calculations and forms that will be needed.

You will also need to become insured or bonded to handle all of the money involved because CPAs, lawyers, and smart real estate brokers will not allow their clients to trust you with large sums of money without protection.

There are IRS guidelines you must follow to become a qualified intermediary for the exchange. For example, an intermediary cannot have worked with the exchange parties in the past two years as an employee, agent, CPA, attorney or financial planner. There are other rules as well, so you'll need to thoroughly research and conform to make sure your exchange is legitimate.

Marketing and Strategy. Your best bet for marketing is to network and market your services to lawyers, accountants, real estate brokers, real estate investors, real estate investment clubs, and financial planners. It's a no-brainer that your main message will be that you can save investors tens of thousands of dollars in unnecessary taxes.

Develop high-class brochures and marketing pieces to bolster your professional image. Because trust and personal character are important when handling other people's money and assets, consider including several bank and legal references for prospective clients to see. Make sure you explain to your prospects that this method is fully authorized and sanctioned by the Internal Revenue Service. Provide copies of the code for them to see for themselves.

If you're not shy, consider doing presentations for business or professional clubs. These groups are always looking for good speakers or presenters to share informative information to their group. You will find this to be your best advertising ever. Take along plenty of cards and brochures, and you will begin to see results within a few presentations.

You will also find that by giving these free mini-seminars you will be asked by more and more groups to speak. You don't need to be a good speaker. Just provide a brief (20-25 minutes) talk with some question and answer time, and the group will be happy. Virtually everyone hates paying unnecessary taxes, so you'll have an attentive audience.

Pricing and Fees. There is a wide range of fees for this service, but the average seems to be around $1,000 per exchange. Some companies charge a lower initial fee such as $495, but then add on a lot of smaller fees which typically makes the service price out at about $700 to $900 in total.

Research and Further Information. If you consider

this business opportunity you must strictly adhere to the IRS guidelines for what constitutes a qualified intermediary exchange facilitator. Furthermore, you must make sure any exchange you facilitate is in conformity with the Internal Revenue Code (IRC). See their publication number 544 (titled Sales and Other Dispositions of Assets) at **www.irs.gov** under the clickable publications option. You will also need to study IRC section 1031.

You of course will need to research any state regulations there might be to engage in this business. A national association represents exchange facilitators in this business. Contact the Federation of Exchange Accommodators at **www.1031.org.** Or call them at 916.388.1031

Because real estate licensing laws are written broadly to protect the interests of real estate brokers and agents, be careful not to market yourself as a real estate "consultant" unless you are actually licensed as a broker. Ditto for legal advice. No matter what anyone says, these various fields do overlap, and there will possibly be times when you tread on these grounds. Your best bet probably is to use the industry term of 1031-exchange intermediary.

The Real Estate Buy/Sell Business

In this fascinating chapter we explore over a dozen business ideas for buying and selling real estate as a business. Although this opportunity typically requires larger amounts of capital, I will explain several ways you can get involved even if you have very little cash of your own.

I need to say out the outset that all of the business models in this section involve the same product, namely houses; therefore, we will not repeat all of the how-to explanations since many of them would be the same. We will explain the concepts for the first model, and then only include new information for the next buy/sell business model. It will be to your benefit to read through all of the buy/sell models even if you have interest in only one particular model. You will learn ideas throughout this book which will be applicable in many business models.

What Type of Real Estate? The principles explained in this section apply to all types of residential real estate. But for simplicity sake, we will be focusing on the buying and reselling of single-family houses. Also, I define single-family houses as any type of one-family dwelling, whether it be a townhouse, detached single, semi-detached, old fashioned row house, or condominium.

Houses are the perfect type of property to buy and sell. They have the greatest consumer demand, they are the easiest type of real estate you can buy and sell fast, and houses are the easiest type of real estate to finance. Furthermore, houses are the safest all of the real estate vehicles since they are the most liquid in terms of ability to exit quickly (either by selling or refinancing).

Profit Potential. Buying and selling houses is an excellent way to build a high income without tenants, but it must be stated that long-term, net worth growth is not a by-product of the buy/sell game. If you want financial independence and a high net worth, this will be achieved more effectively in the long-term holding game involving rental property. We will cover those excellent opportunities further along in the book.

The buy/sell house business—or "flipping" as it is often called—can generate chunks of money that range anywhere from a low of $2,000 to about $25,000 per house. The average or benchmark profit goal is about $10,000 per house, although many new investors seek a per house profit goal of $15,000, especially on rehab deals needing a lot of work.

No License Required.
Buying and selling real estate for your own account does not require a real estate license. This is another great aspect to this business opportunity because for the most part you are working under your own rules. The key licensing factor is that you can buy, sell, manage, or rent properties for your own account without a license since you are an owner or principal in the property.

The Three Big Opportunities.
In this chapter we will break the buy/sell house business into three categories: the Rehab Business, the Buy Low-Sell Low Business, and the Installment Financing Business. All of these opportunities are exciting and by the time we are through you might have a tough decision deciding which game you like best. Some folks do a little of everything, but it's usually better to specialize in one strategy.

The Rehab Business.
Of all of the buy/sell business models, the rehab business offers the biggest potential for profit. But keep in mind it also involves the most time and expertise of the three models. This business is a tried-and-proven method for making money. Thousands of people actively buy and sell houses for a living. There is competition, but there is always room for a high-quality person to make their mark in the field. As the saying goes, "It's never crowded at top."

The Business Model.
The rehab business is the business of buying distressed houses that need repairing and cleaning at a deep discount, then reselling these houses to owner-occupied users at retail prices.

There are three main stages in making this program work, and each one involves a separate set of skills. They are Buying Right,

Fixing Right, and Selling Right. If you fail in any of these categories you can have a difficult time making money in this business.

While buy/sell house business can be an excellent business opportunity, keep in mind, it is harder than it looks or sounds. This is actually a good thing. If it were easy, everyone would be doing it, and it would be an overcrowded field.

Distressed Houses. The term "distressed house" means different things to different people. To me distressed real estate is any type of property that is either physically rundown and deteriorated, or financially distressed, as in a foreclosure or forced sale situation.

In many cases, distressed real estate deals are both physically and financially distressed. This combination drives the retail value of the property below market prices. If the real estate has neither physical or financial distress, the chances are slight that a profitable deal will be made.

Nasty Houses Are Where the Money Is. Sometimes when you watch late-night infomercials they show some slick guy driving a Rolls Royce claiming to have made a fortune buying and selling beautiful homes that he bought at foreclosure. They then show pictures of gorgeous waterfront mansions bought for 30 cents on the dollar. I would not say it's impossible, but 99 percent of the time this is not how it works.

The reality of the situation is that distressed houses are smelly, nasty, rundown wrecks that need a lot of work. This is what scares away regular amateur buyers and creates the desperate seller who is willing to unload the property for 50 to 70 cents on the dollar. It is rare to see great looking properties selling at major discount.

Over the years real estate investors have used a lot of terms to describe these rundown houses: junkers, handyman specials, fixer-uppers, yuks, wrecks, or shacks. Whatever the term used, the pros love these properties because this is where the serious money is being made.

Concept: Dirty rundown houses are where the big money is made.

Cleaning and Renovating Creates Value. In the rehab business you are creating your profit spread primarily by cleaning, repairing, and fixing the rundown house to a fresh, like-new standard. You are not building new houses; you are renewing old ones.

Regular Buyers Are Afraid. In the housing market, dirty, rundown houses scare away traditional buyers. You can work this to your advantage by being able to see through the filth and repairs and then correct the problems. It's called vision. Inexperienced buyers do not have vision to see through the filth, and they typically have no comprehension of how to repair a property.

Fixing Up Houses to Sell Fast. Besides giving the property a good detrashing and cleaning, learning how to repair and make improvements will make you a lot of money. The fix-up side of the business is not hard to learn, but there is a definite art to it. You do not have to be an expert at this, but you will need to hire out some of the work until you learn how it's done. As many other books have pointed out, the most value is created by about half a dozen improvements: cleaning, painting, carpeting, vinyl flooring, kitchen spruce-ups, bathroom spruce-ups, and basic repairs.

You Don't get Paid 'Till It Sells. The final stage in the process is marketing the home to sell. This can be accomplished in a variety of ways, but perhaps most important is to price the product correctly. You don't want to sell too cheaply, and you don't want to price too high. Fair market or just under market, usually makes the most sense in normal market conditions.

Cautionary Tip. Home buyers are typically choosier and demanding than home renters. So be a little more picky about which houses you buy to flip. It's harder to sell houses than it is rent them!

How to Buy at Least 30 to 50 percent Under Market Value.
In the buy/sell business the most critical part of the process is buying wholesale. If you buy right, you will have a lot more margin for mistakes. As the old saying says, "Buying right will cover a multitude of sins."

Hot Tip #1. In the rehab business, never pay more than about 70-75 percent of the true fair market value.

If you follow this rule you should stay out of trouble and have enough profit to make it worth your time. In fact, many experienced investors shoot for more like a 35 to 50 percent discount when buying, but keep in mind, the discount isn't fully realized until some of the repairs and cleanup are completed. In other words, you usually couldn't resell the property the next day for 35 to 50 percent more until you get it cleaned up and made less scary.

Hot Tip #2: If the house is for sale and VACANT, it is the single biggest indicator it can be bought at a discount. Vacant houses equal desperate owners.

Hot Tip #3: If the house is dirty, smelly, and needs repairs, you know the seller is highly motivated.

Hot Tip #4: Only, ONLY, deal with motivated sellers! If the seller doesn't really need to sell, you probably won't make a deal. Don't waste time trying to strike a deal with someone who is not highly anxious to sell.

Hot Tip #5: In order for the seller to be motivated, they probably will fit into one or more of the following situations: estate (owner died), divorce, foreclosure, back taxes, vandalism, bad tenants, fire damage, failing business, rundown building, deferred maintenance, condemned building, bankruptcy, or drug or alcohol problems.

Ninety-five out of every one hundred motivated sellers will fit into one or more of the above categories. The more combined problems they have, the more willing they will be to sell the house at a price and terms that will work for you.

Hot Tip #6: Always get the seller to tell you their price first, then test the price by knocking it down with a lower-counter offer (the exception would be those extreme situations where you know right off the bat it is a killer deal which you better snap up because it doesn't get much better).

> **Hot Tip #7. Knowing values is critical. If you aren't an expert on the type of houses and their values, consider finding a flexible appraiser and pay him or her a reduced fee for a simple walk-through inspection. You're not asking for an appraisal, but more like an opinion of value with no guarantees or liability. It's important to secure the deal with a contingent contract and then get your reduced fee opinion of value. If you pay more than about $75 you're probably paying too much (explain to the appraiser you will need this service many times).**

If you follow all of these guidelines you should be on your way to knowing a good value when you see the above circumstances. But remember, you still have to know what the property will be worth after the cleaning and repairs are done.

Finding Motivated Sellers. Some people describe real estate investors as vultures who swoop down upon ignorant people and take advantage of them. This really isn't the truth. In most cases, real estate investors are helping people convert their unwanted assets into cash. You see, the regular marketplace of conventional buyers does NOT want these rundown properties. In fact, the market has rejected these properties. The fact that these properties sell at deep discount is a matter of supply and demand—frankly, there's no demand for junky houses, so the price goes down.

If you are buying and selling houses as a business you will need to stoke up a marketing campaign that will generate leads. You will not find bargain properties every day, or even every week, but they are out there. Your job will be to fill your pipelines with prospects so you can sift through most of the dead leads to get the gold nuggets.

Estates make one of the richest sources for finding good real estate deals. In most cases the people who inherit real estate are looking to sell it as fast as possible and at a nice discount. If the property needs a lot of updating and repairs, then you have a good chance of buying a bargain.

Good old foreclosure property is the old standby source for making a good deal, but you need to know that many, if not most, foreclosures are not a good deal until after the bank gets the property back after the sale. In today's market many people have bought their house with very little money down; therefore, there's no equity. Once the lender has taken the property back into their possession (REO) through a foreclosure sale, it can then be negotiated at whatever price you want to offer.

The next category of real estate deals is the abandoned house. These fall under a variety of scenarios (back taxes, repair problems, vandalism). These typically have a combination of problems that make the owners highly flexible on the price and terms.

The last category of home would be the home up for auction. Like the above category, this type of property is not a single category. For example, homes being auctioned could be available through estates, REOs, bankruptcy, back taxes, etc. Whatever the case, remember, auctions are one of the best sources for buy/sell deals.

So there you have my recommendations for what type of property to hunt down. If you focus on property in these categories you will be on the right track.

Advertising and Marketing Ideas For Buying.

Let's first deal with auction property. Your best bet here is to get yourself a bulletin board or big piece of flat cardboard and start posting all of the auction notices, advertisements, and letters about upcoming auctions.

Local newspapers and freebie papers typically have advertisements for upcoming auctions. Get on various mailing lists and auctions house notification lists. Start attending auctions and sign in on the mailing list sheet. Get on every list you can so you can be notified of auctions: IRS, bankruptcy trustees, sheriff sales, foreclosures, auctioneers, lender lists, REO auction houses. Post all of the various ads you save and the notifications you receive on your board.

Next, attend as many auctions as possible, even if you're not ready to buy—just to get educated. Keep a log of the addresses and sales prices and try to calculate what level of discounts these auction properties are selling at.

Your strategy with vacant houses will be to track down the owners by doing a little detective work. Your best results will come from talking with the neighbors. My experience has been that the neighbors love to tell the story of the troubled property and its owners. In many cases, they can tell you where the owner is now living. Once you find the owner's name and address, consider calling, writing them a letter, or even paying them a personal visit. If they don't respond right away, put them in your database and mail them a letter every month or two. Also try to determine if the property is up for an upcoming forced sale auction like back taxes or bank payments—typically they are.

Estate Property. When someone dies, the property the person owned is controlled by the executor or administrator of the estate. In most cases, the estate will choose to liquidate the property in order to settle the estate and probate the will. (Estate property is sometimes called probate property.)

From my experience some of the best real estate deals are estate property. There are several reason for this. First, these houses frequently are debt free; therefore there is 100 percent equity. Second, because the houses are mechanically outdated and in disrepair, they sell at heavy discounts. Third, the heirs can't wait to spend the "found money" therefore; they will sell cheaply in order to get the money as soon as possible. Fourth, because there are estate taxes and attorney fees due, the lawyers are eager to get the house sold so they can clear the estate and get paid themselves.

Estate property can be purchased through a variety of channels such as through realtors, at auctions, sales by owners, and attorneys. Along with these conventional ways to buy estates, you can send out direct mail letters explaining that you buy estates. (In fact, I purchased a good rental house from this very method.) You can track estates down by the public notices in newspapers or legal journals sent out to lawyers in each county.

Foreclosures and REOs. The two best ways to buy foreclosure property is by the "knocking on doors" method and the REO method. For the "knocking on doors" method, you just stop by and ask the people if they have any interest in selling the house. You have to be discreet about doing this, but this direct approach can work well if they have some equity in the property. You might get twenty people telling you no, but the twenty-first person might be willing to make you a terrific deal. Many old-timer foreclosure pros buy with this method.

Probably the best time to buy the property is after the foreclosure sale, since in many cases no one bids at the sale because there are too many liens against the property. After the bank takes back the property because of no competing bidders it is classed as a repo or an REO.

Call the lender after the foreclosure auction and see what they are asking for the property. Even if their price is high, mail them a written offer at a number that will work for you. Do not be afraid to offer a lot less than what they have invested in the house. If they don't immediately accept your offer, periodically call them and see how they are doing with the property.

Classified Ads and Signs. One of the best ways to find motivated sellers is to run small classified ads telling people you buy houses. In most markets there are already people doing this, but that's okay because these ads come and go, and sellers seem to shop their house through several investors. Here are some ads that seems to work well.

We Buy Homes: any area, any condition. Will make offer today. Liens, repairs, financial difficulties—ok, call...

We Buy Houses. Fast cash—call...

We buy houses: we will make your next mortgage payment: Call...

Unwanted Real Estate Wanted: Cash for Houses, call...

We will Buy Your house in 5 days, call...

Can't Sell Your House? We'll Buy it, call...

These ads work well because motivated sellers call you, which greatly cuts down on the time you spend prospecting for deals. Also, having the sellers call you creates a more favorable negotiating position.

Free or Low-Cost Signs. Signs are an excellent way to generate sellers' calls. Look for places where you can legally post small signs or mini billboards that tell people you buy houses. Some folks use bright yellow banners that you can have made at the quick-sign shops. Usually, these banners can be bought for about $80 to $120 each.

Signs can be very cost effective because you pay for them once, and they keep working for many months or even years. Look for opportunities to place these on the sides of old buildings or anyplace where a lot of traffic drives by. I have used this fixed marketing approach myself and have found it to be some of the best money spent.

Don't forget about using plenty of signs on houses you have for sale. This includes having a For Sale Sign and a We Buy Houses Sign posted on all houses for sale. This double duty signage will help you both sell and buy houses from people living in the local area. This technique is used successfully by roofing contractors. When I had my roof replaced on my home the roofing contractor immediately stuck a small sign in my front lawn telling the neighbors who was doing the roofing work. He said he gets a lot of roofing work just from that simple yard sign.

Word of mouth and referrals. Over the years I have
bought several houses just by talking to people I meet. If you keep your radar turned on you'll come across lots of people who are selling houses or know of friends trying to sell houses. Most of these people won't be in a position to give you a deal, but every once in a while one will pop up.

A unique method a friend of mine uses is to offer people rewards for information about houses for sale. His flyers and business cards offer a $300 reward for anybody who brings him a real estate deal. He hasn't bought a lot of houses using this, but he has bought a couple. The whole idea is to get as many fishing lines in the water as possible. No one method will produce an overwhelming amount of leads, but having several ads, letters, and flyers going at once will work.

Don't forget our lawyer friends. These guys can be great sources of leads. Get to know lawyers. We will cover a lot more on marketing in a separate marketing section so you'll have plenty of additional ideas to implement.

Placemat Ads. Advertising on diner and restaurant placemats
can be a cheap way to get your message in front of a lot of people. Although I don't think these ads are appropriate for every type of business they can be good for the house buying business. The important thing is to try different headlines and different positions on the placemat. The four corners are best because they are visible even after the food is served.

How to Finance the Deal. Of all of the actual business opportunities (not investments) reviewed in this book, the buy/sell business requires the most capital. The good thing is that this money does not need to be out of your pocket. Even though buying real estate is cash intensive, you can buy properties fairly easily with various forms of leverage.

Leverage is a business term that generally means borrowed money or debt, but it can also mean any financial instrument or arrangement that enables you to control an asset with very little money.

There are scores of ways to buy real estate using various forms of leverage. What I want to cover in this section are the best ways to buy houses where your single goal is to quickly resell the house. The methods used in this application will be different than those used when buying rentals or selling on installment contracts.

I will review in this section the four best ways to buy when doing a rehab and then reselling out of the deal for cash. One of the ways involves using some form of all cash. The remaining three ways involve creative leverage. Let's get started with the more creative ways for cash-poor investors to buy houses.

Option Contract. An option to buy contract is one way I have used to buy houses with very little money down. This technique won't always work, but it can work enough times to create some start-up cash.

Rather than give you a bunch of textbook explanations of option contracts, allow me to explain a very creative deal I did a few years ago. Several years ago while working at our family business I met a customer who in the course of conversation mentioned that she was trying to sell a house. At this point in time she did not know I bought houses. I began to ask her various questions and learned that she inherited the house and was the executrix of the estate. The reason she was in our store was to purchase some appliances for the house she was selling.

Within a few minutes into our discussion about the property I told her that I sometimes buy houses as investments. I asked her a lot of different questions to see just how anxious she was to sell the house. She told me that the house was currently listed with a local real estate broker. At this point knowing the location of the house and the fact that it was only a two bedroom, I did not have much interest. I essentially brushed her off by telling her I didn't like buying through realtors (true), but to call me if it didn't sell and when the listing contract had expired. She agreed to do that.

To my surprise about a month or two later she called me telling me her contract was due to expire in about a week. We made the appointment for my inspection of the house.

The house was in a clean neighborhood on the border of an area that was somewhat run down. The house itself was in fair condition, although it had a basement full of junk. The upstairs needed a good painting and some general sprucing up. It wasn't run down, but it looked outdated and pretty blah. At this point I still didn't feel too excited about the deal since it wouldn't make a good rental and it was only a two-bedroom house. I was cool to the deal.

This seller seemed very anxious to make some kind of deal, but at the time I didn't have a lot of cash and wasn't eager to borrow the money to buy it. It looked like a marginal deal—not a great rental, and not a great resell deal.

The Offer I Hoped She Would Not Take. Not

feeling excited about buying this property, I made her an offer I felt sure she wouldn't take. I asked her for a three-month option to buy on the house with $1 (yes, one dollar). Now, I didn't phrase the offer quite like that. I did use some salesmanship. I told her I wanted to fix up the house a bit and then possibly buy it. I would invest my time and energy into cleaning it up and the worse thing that could happen to her is she would get back the house in much better condition if I didn't buy it at the end of the three months. I also explained that I didn't think the house would make a good rental and that I might try to sell it.

As a creative twist I also requested two additional conditions. One, if I decided there was a very good chance I was going to buy the house I wanted the right to extend or renew my option for four additional months giving me a total of a seven-month option to buy contract! Secondly, I asked her that in the event I did not purchase the house, she would reimburse me for materials (no labor) used to fix up the house based on my receipts not to exceed $2,000. I also explained the planned repairs and improvements such as new carpeting, paint, ceiling fan, and other items.

She seemed open to the idea, but wanted to review my offer with the attorney handling the estate. She was ready to accept my offer, but wanted his opinion. I was not surprised when about a week later she said her attorney advised her not to do the deal. This is understandable since my deal was totally off the wall in terms of the standard way real estate is bought.

What did surprise me was that she said in spite of her attorney's advice she was willing to do the deal, and that she really trusted me and liked me. I prepared the option contract and a simple repayment agreement for the materials in the event I didn't purchase it. With two pages of paperwork and one dollar down I controlled a $52,000 piece of real estate for seven months! If you want the translation, that equates to ZERO INTEREST, NO PAYMENTS, NO DEBT, NO TAX BILLS, NO WATER BILL, NO INSURANCE PAYMENTS!

In real estate we call this leverage. I optioned the property at a price of $52,000 for three months with a four-month renewal option for $1 down.

After signing the option with the seller I immediately began the cleanup and light rehab of the property. I did a lot of it myself, although my handyman did hang the ceiling fan and install three rooms of carpet. Altogether it took about a month until it was ready working at it part-time. I paid out about $2,000 in materials and labor.

I placed my classified ad in the paper with the headline: Estate Liquidation. After three weeks and several showings I had a buyer for the house. Within another 35 days we went to closing. My net profit after ALL expenses was a tidy sum of $5,200. Nobody's getting rich on this type of deal, but it certainly made me a nice profit using virtually no capital or credit.

The option contract is an incredibly powerful tool because it enables you to control a property, giving you the right to resell it. The price you pay for this contractual right is called the option consideration. The option fee or consideration can be whatever price you negotiate. Many times it can be a nominal amount such as with the deal I just showed you—if the seller is anxious enough to sell. Even though option contracts are power leverage tools, remember they are just that—tools. They do have limited application, and you will need more tools and techniques than just this one.

Owner Financing Techniques.
The biggest barrier to investors buying real estate is always where to get the funds. Without some capital or credit, buying real estate can be difficult. What most investors fail to realize is that some sellers, especially motivated ones, will hold all or part of the financing for them.

If you've been investing for any amount of time you soon realize that most highly distressed sellers want cash. This appears a roadblock for many investors. I want to show you a way to get sellers their "cash" and still give you owner financing. Here's how.

If you're like me you have asked a lot of sellers to provide owner financing or as we say in the industry, "hold the paper." Most sellers don't give it a second thought and say no. Although many sellers won't change their mind no matter how much arm twisting you do, probably about one-third will say yes if you present it right.

Most sellers won't hold the financing because they don't want the deal to drag on for the next ten or twenty years receiving small monthly payments. They just want to get on with their life and get a nice chunk of cash to spend or pay off debts with. But before we get into the actual technique, let me give you a few quick guidelines to help you see if the seller is a candidate for an owner financing offer.

The seller should own the property with a high equity or, even better, free and clear. Estate property works well because they typically are free and clear and have no pressing foreclosure problems. Next, the property should need a lot of fixing and cleanup, which will keep a regular buyer from even considering it. Lastly, the seller should be an exhausted seller, meaning they are tired of showing the property and see buyers reject it.

In this business opportunity you are interested in buying and reselling the house fast, so you do not need long-term financing. In most cases you want to be in and out of the deal in six or seven months. As investors we run into trouble with owner financing by asking for long-term notes. **Note:** Rental investors need long-term financing—buy/sell dealers do not.

The Preferred Owner Finance Term. If you are buying the property strictly to resell it you probably should start by asking the seller for a three-year owner financed term until the balloon payment. If that isn't acceptable, consider shortening the term, but be careful if you don't have a back up financing source in the event the property doesn't sell by the balloon date.

If the seller still resists financing, ask the seller to hold the note for 10 to 12 months. Explain that you need a few months to get the property so it's bankable (for the next guy) since regular long-term lenders don't like to lend on junker houses. Explain that in a short time they will get their money. Use some salesmanship. Many times it's not what we say, but how we ask for it.

Many sellers will hold the financing for a short time as long as they know the real money is coming in several months. If the seller seems exceptionally cautious or fearful, you can ask them if there is something wrong with the building that they aren't telling you. Is the collateral bad?

Most real estate experts will tell you that these short-term balloon type notes are bad. I agree that they can be very bad. But if you are in the buy/sell business where you plan to be in and out of the deal in less than a year it is not as risky. If worse comes to worse and the house doesn't sell, you can refinance the house, since it will be worth a whole lot more when you are finished the rehab.

Profit Tip: put a safety clause giving you the right to extend the note another 6 months if refinancing is not completed. It's probably best to negotiate this after you've come to a general agreement on the deal. Sometimes it's better to iron out the broad details before you get into the little extra kicker clauses that sweeten the deal.

The actual terms of the note are up to you. Many sellers like some down payment to pacify their fears of not knowing you. My general recommendation would be to tailor the down payment based on how bad the condition of the property happens to be. If it's a total wreck I might ask the seller to hold the whole note since I will need all my cash to rehab the building. You are in charge in this department—ask for what you need to make the deal work. Perhaps you might even ask the seller for a six-month grace period of no interest and no payments. It works—investors do these deals every day.

A word of caution: Real estate deals involve entrepreneurial risk. You can minimize your risk by conducting your business in a very precise and professional way. If you buy properties for quick resale you cannot fritter away your time. The clock is against you. You must get on the job and work day and night to get the house ready. Empty houses will eat your profits—fix them up now!

Leverage the Existing Financing. A certain number of deals will come your way in which you can take over the existing financing. This method is kind of like a mortgage assumption, but technically you aren't be assuming the loan. The main benefit with

this method is that you can leverage the property using the existing mortgage without having to come up with cash.

The vast majority of existing mortgages out in the marketplace have what is known as a due-on-sale clause. This clause is a contract provision in the mortgage which says that if the property is sold, the lender has the right to call the entire loan provision due and payable. In other words, they can, at their option, make the property owner pay the entire debt balance due if the property is sold without paying off the existing mortgage.

The due-on-sale clause is meant to stop mortgage assumptions, which were very popular up until the 1980s. Although very few truly assumable mortgages remain in the marketplace, professional investors have come up with a variety of ways to handle these loans. Following is the current thinking among many professional distress real estate buyers.

The due-on-sale clause can be a problem, especially if the deal is to be held long term. But if the deal is to be bought and quickly resold the clause often times is a non issue. This is especially true when dealing with sellers who are behind on their payments—lenders do not want to own the house; they want the money.

The professional buyer will often take title to the house subject to the existing loan and continue to make the payments to the lender using the seller's coupon book and loan number. In most cases these loans are processed in big payment departments where thousands of checks are processed each day. The clerk who clears these payments into the lender's computers typically just reads the account number and check amount and not the nitty-gritty details of the mortgage. The bottom line is that many investors will risk using existing financing during the six or ten months of the rehab and resale and then pay off the existing mortgage on the resale closing. This of course, does involve some risk in the event the lender calls the entire existing mortgage due via a loan acceleration demand.

Over the years many investors have developed creative ways to circumvent the due-on-sale clause. The old contract for deed, lease-option, trusts, delayed closings, purchase option, and the "just do it" method all have been used with varying degrees of success.

Caution Note: There always is the risk the lender could call the note due and payable. This could place whatever investment you have in the property in jeopardy. I would not advise this method unless you have significant experience in real estate or have the cash or credit line available to pay the mortgage balance due if called. If the lender calls the note, frequently they will just try to get you to qualify and write a new loan to you directly. If the property is a real junker, often times showing the lender a picture of the deplorable condition of the property will be enough to get them to reconsider allowing you a few more months to make the payments until you get them cashed out. Be aware that many new mortgages are known as "assumable" but in reality they still require you to submit an application and qualify to take over the mortgage. In essence it is just like getting a new loan and is not truly assumable like the old FHA and VA mortgages of past decades.

Using Existing Financing and Structuring Offers.

When you are dealing with a distressed house seller, one possibility for buying the house with very little cash is to use a combination of existing financing along with a note from the seller. With this technique you give the seller a few thousand dollars down and then take over the existing financing along with a note for the seller's remaining equity.

For example, let's assume that a distressed seller has a run-down house worth $70,000 with a mortgage balance of $42,000. The seller is willing to sell the house for $55,000. With about $5,000 in repairs and sprucing up the home will be worth about $85,000. The seller is very motivated but only needs about $2,500 in immediate cash for moving expenses and to get an apartment. You could offer something like this:

Take over the existing mortgage of $42,000.

Give the seller $2,500 cash down.

Give the seller a note payable for $10,500 payable in 12 months with $100 monthly payments.

Although this offer may not be as desirable for the seller as getting their entire $13,000 equity in cash, it does serve to get the problem property sold and provide them some initial cash relief. The investor in return leverages a $70,000 rundown house for a modest $2,500 cash investment. The bulk of the leverage is derived from taking over the $42,000 mortgage. The remaining leverage comes from the seller's holding a second mortgage. In many cases sellers will reject that offer, but since the buyer will pay the seller the balance of their equity within one year it becomes acceptable.

Normally these short-term note arrangements are not considered safe, but the risk is not a huge issue since the property is going to be resold in 6 to 10 months, which will provide the funds to pay-off the first and second mortgages. You should always have a back up plan on how to pay off the seller's note in the event the property does not sell quickly. If things do not go as planned, you may need to get a refinance loan or discount the property so it sells quicker. Another option would be to renegotiate the note with the seller. Often paying a partial installment ($1,000 or $2,000) of cash to the note holder will make them amiable to a note extension.

Power Buying with All Cash.

If you survey buy/sell rehab investors you will find the number one buying method will be all cash. This can appear to be a problem since many investors don't have fifty or sixty thousand dollars in the bank to make all cash offers. I will explain how to handle this problem, but let's first talk about why most of the pros use all cash offers to buy real estate.

Professional buy/sell investors have one main objective in buying. They are looking for big discounts. The easiest way to get big discounts when buying property is to buy with cash offers and fast closings. After all, many distress sales involve deadlines or absolute terms like auctions. These deadlines (pending foreclosures) and absolute terms (auctions) require you to have ready money waiting without contingencies. This fact alone chases away window shoppers and leaves only serious investors who demand great deals for their precious cash. At a typical absolute auction a distressed house sells for about 75 percent of its market value.

Over the years in real estate I know at least a dozen serious rehab investors whom I consider to be professional buyers. The most used method among this group for buying bargain properties is the all cash method. This is not to say they never use creative offers, because they do. What I am saying is they find all cash offers to be the most powerful way to buy distressed real estate. After all, everyone accepts cash. In fact, sellers often accept cash offers that are far less than competing higher offers involving creative financing.

The Credit Line Buying Method.

If you have decent credit, a stable life, and equity in some assets (your home, stocks, etc.) you should be able to find a lender to offer you a credit line. A credit line is a short-term loan service whereby the bank will provide capital to buy real estate. Typically, the loan is paid monthly with interest-only payments, and the balance is due in one or two years. This short-term financing is seldom a problem, since most investors will have the property resold within a year. In those cases where the property has not been resold, the same lender or others will usually refinance the property enabling you to pay back the credit line.

Banks will rarely give you a credit line unless you have some assets to collateralize the loan. In most cases business people have a piece of real estate or other valuable asset which is worth as much as the desired credit limit. If you do not have much net worth to back up the loan, the lender will require you have excellent credit and a reliable income. This is where many real estate investors find the snag in finding money from banks. They either have limited collateral, poor credit, or inadequate or unproven income.

If your credit is poor and you have very little in the form of collateral, the chances are slim that you will get a sizable credit line—banks will not loan on your good looks. In this case it will be critical that you document a proven winning track record in real estate in order to get the money.

Hot Profit Tip. Avoid using the term "flipping" properties when dealing with commercial lenders. Lenders don't like "flippers." I guess it sounds like something fishy is going on. Consider using the terms "property redeveloper," "renovator," or "housing investor."

Private Lenders.
Many investors don't like the hassle of dealing with commercial lenders and seek out private lenders who have cash or credit lines that they loan to investors. Many times these people are easier to deal with than banks. The drawback is you typically have to pay more for the money. The going rate is usually 12 to 15 percent interest to the private lender. This isn't as bad as it seems since this is short-term money that you use only until the property is sold.

The best bets for finding private money lenders are local investment clubs and small classified ads. Also, networking with accountants, lawyers, and business people can be effective at finding money investors. Shy away from investors who seem too fearful and only have a few thousand to invest. You want investors who have at least $10,000-15,000. Explain to your investor that this money will be safely secured by a mortgage against real estate.

Credit Line Tip: If you are new to real estate and have limited banking credibility, make getting a credit line your top priority. Start out doing your creative deal making and get some experience and cash flow. Document your deals along the way with before and after pictures and a written narration of each deal. Create a professional looking portfolio showing who you are and what experience you have. This should be a combination resume and company profile. Create a mission statement and business plan to be included. If you have some assets, consider drawing up a personal financial statement showing your net worth. In the event your credit is a little shaky start today to pay your bills on time and clean it up.

In closing this segment on financing I cannot overstate the importance of developing private or commercial credit lines to be an effective buy/sell rehabber. If you can do this you will be able to buy houses for 50 to 60 percent of their market value. As the worn out cliché goes, cash is king—it really is.

Learning How to Repair and Dress Up Houses.
If you are in the rehab business you will need to learn the process of repairing houses and making them show well. This does not necessarily mean you will be personally doing the work, but I can promise you that the more you learn about repairs and fix-up techniques, the more money you will make.

From my experience of knowing rehab investors who survive in this business over the long term, the vast majority take an active roll in the rehab process. I have rarely seen armchair investors make it in rehabbing.

This does not mean you have to become a plumber or an electrician, but you will need to learn as much as you can about the many creative ways to repair and renovate houses to maximize your profits.

Avoid the "Professional" Contractor.
You will have trouble making a profit in the rehab business if you use what I would call "professional" contractors. These are the companies that

spend a lot on advertising and have the big expensive lettered trucks. The price these companies charge will not leave you enough profit in the rehab.

The solution is to find hungry new contractors who are either just starting their own company or ones looking for some side work. These folks know their business but are willing to work at a price that leaves some profit in the job for you. You can find these enthusiastic contractors by running small classified ads with the headlines like this:

Handyman Wanted
Rehab Contractor Wanted
Retired Carpenter/Handyman Wanted

These ads will usually bring a lot of calls from people looking for some extra work. You may need to try several until you find the right person.

Doing It Yourself.

Fixing up houses is not brain surgery. Even if you are really clumsy in this area I highly advise you learn how to do this work if you are going to be a rehabber. There are plenty of ways to learn. I learned a lot just from watching and helping my various handymen over the years. There are tons of money-making tricks to learn.

Some folks will say you should waste your time doing any of this work yourself, but to be honest, there are serious profits made every day doing contractor and construction work. If you have the skills and apply it to rehab real estate you can do very well financially. One thing I have noticed over my eighteen years of investing is that the rehab investors who actively participate in the rehab rarely go belly up. This is because materials are relatively cheap. It's the labor that accounts for 70 percent of job costs. If you are cash poor, rehabbing the job yourself may be the most workable way to build your income and net worth.

I highly advise you learn the rehab and fixing business even if it means you will be mainly supervising your workers. If you already know how to repair houses you have a big jump on your competition. Here are a few tips on learning how to creatively and effectively repair and rehab houses:

Take the free how-to clinics at the big home supply centers.

Buy or rent the various how-to contractor videos.

Watch and question your contractors to pickup pointers.

Talk to other real estate investors to see how they do it.

Check out the public library—a huge source of free books.

Invest a couple days a month helping a trades person for free.

Just do the repair yourself—old trial and error.

The big key is to get some knowledge from studying and asking lots of questions combined with buying the right tools to use. Having the right tools is most of the battle. Next, just get out there and do it. The hardest part will be the first time—it's called the learning curve. Also: Check out the magazine, *The Family Handyman* (see resources). Great tips for rehabbers.

Estimating the Deal with a P&L Statement.
Your best bet is to build a small P&L (profit and loss) statement for the deal. From a pure accounting standpoint, I use this term loosely. On your P&L statement you list all of your costs, and this requires some guesswork, that will be incurred in the deal. Your costs would include your desired and actual purchase price, property taxes, insurance, interest, advertising, agent's commission, repairs and rehab costs, overruns, utilities, and your target profit. From these numbers you calculate the needed selling price. In many respects it's wise to work this backwards since the marketplace will determine the actual sales price. Take future market value and work costs and profits backwards to end up with what you should pay for the house.

Selling the Property Fast.
You won't make a dime until you sell the property. There are several things you can do at the outset to make selling easier. Number one, deal only in houses with three or four bedrooms, not just two. The demand in the house business today is for homes with a minimum of three bedrooms. Number two, buy houses only in clean middle to lower-middle class areas—avoid trashy areas that are rental neighborhoods. Number three, make sure you know all your numbers when you are buying.

Many investors are weak in this area and do not know the true fair market values of homes. This is critical because you must price the home correctly. If you buy the house right, clean and repair it nicely, you should be able to sell the house in two to three months. If the house does not sell within 90 days you probably are doing something wrong.

Hot Profit Tip. You need to know that buyers are typically a lot more picky and choosy about buying a property than renting. Buyers, especially buyers with good credit and cash, are exceptionally demanding. They usually won't accept houses with built-in obsolescence, major defects in location or floor plan. Be careful to buy only marketable houses with private bedrooms, adequate closet space, etc.).

Once you really get rolling in this business and are selling several houses per quarter, you may want to develop your own house buyers marketing program. With this marketing program you develop a list of first-time home buyers who want to buy houses from you. This will require running various ads and developing various creative buying programs for helping people buy houses with little money down. This will require you hooking up with creative mortgage brokers and knowing the newest first-time home buyers programs, but it can save you $4,000 or $5,000 per house if you can sell without a realtor.

Along with running lots of ads for your houses for sale you should use as many small signs and informational flyers as you can when selling a house. Go all out and draw as much attention to the house as economically as possible. Your study of marketing as I recommend in Chapter 8 will greatly aid you.

Resources: Following are some recommendations for further information on the buy/sell house business.

The web site, **www.dealmakerscafe.com** has a lot of how-to articles, discussion forums, and helpful resources for folks interested in buying and selling houses. A friend of mine, Matt Scott, runs the site and I'm sure you won't be disappointed by the information he provides.

One excellent book, especially if you'll be working on classic older homes is *Renovating Old Houses,* by George Nash. This book is loaded with detailed explanations and illustrations on handling old homes that need to be restored.

Creative Real Estate magazine, 858.756.1441 is the only monthly magazine on the market that broadly covers a range of topics in the area of creative finance and do-it-yourself investing in houses and income properties.

You can find out about government repossessed properties from the **www.hud.gov.** web site. Through this site you can get a hold of theVA, HUD, and IRS Repos.

The Buy-Low Sell-Low Business.

The second type of real estate buy/sell business is the buy-low sell-low business, also known as wholesaling. This is a perfect business opportunity for someone with very little capital because in most cases you will be acting as a middleman. If you structure your deals correctly you should not need more than about $1,500 to get this business started.

This business is in sharp contrast to the rehabber business, since in this business you aren't fixing houses or looking for big profit spreads. Instead, you will be looking to buy and sell houses quickly as-is, leaving the larger profits and work to other investors. Furthermore, you will not need near the capital or credit that a typical rehab house business needs.

This is a unique opportunity that will deliver smaller per-unit profits, but the secret is that you will be able to handle a high volume of deals. In the buy-low, sell-low wholesaling business your typical profit will be in the range of $2,000 to $5,000 per deal. This isn't bad considering you usually won't be taking title to these houses. Basically this is a paperwork and marketing business!

The Wholesaling Business Model.

In this business opportunity you will be buying distress real estate at wholesale prices and reselling these same properties to investors at a slighter higher wholesale price. This is why it is called the buy-low, sell-low business. To make wholesaling work, you must price your products so there is an adequate profit for the next investor.

Wholesale buying and selling is a business-to-business service. Your customers are other businesses (investors), and not the people who will live in the houses. In the business world there are two main types of distribution, wholesale and retail. In retailing, the business distributes products to end users, while in wholesaling the business sells its products to other businesses at a price that is low enough to leave a healthy profit for the next business, which will either resell the product or use it in some way to make a profit. One of the key ingredients in this business will be how you price your properties. We will discuss this a little later.

Your main product will be houses, although we will cover some additional profit centers that can be incorporated into your business. Your primary clients will be real estate rehabbers, landlords, and installment house sellers.

Hot Profit Tip: While most of your clients will be investor types, seriously consider offering some of the less distressed houses to regular home buyers.

As with any buy/sell business models you will be buying only distressed real estate in order to buy it wholesale. The basic mode of finding deals is the same as the rehab business. This is accomplished by a comprehensive marketing campaign of classified ads, signs, word of mouth referrals, direct mail, flyers, and attendance at various auctions.

Financing. In most cases your goal is to sell the property before you close on it. Instead of personally taking title to the property, you sell your position in the deal to another investor. This sell-before-you-buy strategy enables you to buy and sell without actually needing much cash or credit. However, as your business begins to get rolling, you will want to set up credit lines (via banks or private investors) for those deals that aren't sold before you buy them. We will explain a little further on how to handle those deals when you are not able to find a buyer.

Pricing Houses in the Buy-Low, Sell-Low Business. I cannot over emphasize the fact that you must price these wholesale deals correctly. This requires you do two things right. First, you must buy ONLY outstanding deals at wholesale or sub-wholesale prices. This means buying houses at prices anywhere from 40 to 65 cents on the dollar! Second, you must remarket the property at a solid wholesale price of anywhere from 60 to 75 percent of the fair market value! Unless you are dealing in a truly hot seller's market, pricing the resale above 80 percent of market value will not leave enough profit on the table for the buying investor.

If you buy the property at the right price you will have enough profit margin spread in the value for the investor. Never forget that investors can buy good deals without you. Therefore, it is critical that you DO NOT GET GREEDY when pricing the house. You want your investor to make lots of money because they will be buying more deals from you. Plus, they will refer other investors to your business!

How Much of a Fee? The general rule in the house wholesaling business is to make about 10 percent on a deal. If the house is bought for $40,000 then your fee to sell is about $4,000. If the house sells for $25,000 the fee is about $2,500. These rates are, of course, only rules of thumb. I have seen wholesaling fees range from $1,000 to $10,000 with average fees of about $2,500. The ultimate rule should be not what the percentage of the fee is but how good the deal is. If you truly are able to buy a $150,000 house for $100,000 there's no reason not to charge a fee of $20,000 and still leave plenty of profit for the next investor. Conversely, if you buy a marginal junker property for $15,000 and have a tough time finding a buyer because the location is rotten you may have to settle for a $500 profit.

Type of Houses and Location. The type of property you buy will depend on what type of houses your investors want to buy. If your primary customers are rehabbers who need to resell the house and get cashed out, then you must be selective and buy only starter family houses in cleaner neighborhoods. If your buyers are rental investor (landlords) then you probably will be dealing in a broader area which would include marginal areas also known as borderline locations. This could also hold true for installment selling investors.

You certainly don't want to buy in bombed out war zones, but don't be afraid of marginal areas, because these areas can yield a lot of good deals. The key is to buy only well-priced deals. The rule of thumb in marginal areas is never to pay more than about 50 cents on the dollar.

Additional Profit Centers. Although houses should be your primary product, you may eventually consider buying distressed apartment buildings to wholesale to income property investors. The strategy will be basically the same, except that these investors will be seeking cash flow rather than large discounts off price. Your goal will be to structure purchases that have a strong income potential which often is a result of the financing you obtain from the seller holding the mortgage financing.

Another profit center could be in the forming of a Real Estate Buying Group. You would sell your subscribing members a monthly service including a host of products and services such as a newsletter, consulting, product sales, discounts at various vendors, renovation or management supplies or whatever product or service you think investors would want. One real estate investor I know has a business of selling carpeting and cabinets to investors and along with it he gives out free investment tips and advice. He is a very successful investor himself and it seems a lot of his customers buy carpet and supplies just to get his brilliant advice! Another investor I know buys distressed building supplies for his own use at auctions and sells the overflow to other investors.

Marketing and Business Strategy.
In this business you will be doing two types of marketing: marketing to find distressed real estate and marketing to find investor-buyers.

Since we have basically covered how to find distress house deals in an earlier section we will focus our effort on finding investors and selling deals. There are several ways to find investors.

Run classified ads offering actual house deals.

Real estate investment clubs.

Run ads in investment club newsletters.

Networking in real estate circles to learn who the player are.

Collect names of landlords from classified ads using reverse directory.

Collect names of rehabbers from the ads they use to sell their houses.

Your advertisements will generate leads that you will need to record into your database mailing list. Your database should include a lot more than a name and address. It should be a confidential investor profile detailing their buying preferences, dollar limit, email, fax, phone, cell phone, physical address, investment guidelines, area preferences etc.

Your goal should be to accumulate at least a hundred names, preferably several hundred, of serious rehabbers and rental investors whom you can notify when you have a good deal.

Develop various ways to contact your investors so you can let them know immediately when a deal is secured. Set up your fax machine to do batch fax broadcasts to your investor list notifying them of your newest deals. Collect email addresses and send announcements this mode also. Lastly, send out a hard copy flyer to your list notifying your investors of the deal. Include pictures and specific details.

Funding the Deal.

I promised I would explain how to get into this business and buy houses with minimal amounts of cash, so here's the scoop.

There are two primary ways to buy and sell houses in this business using very little of your cash or credit. The first we touched on earlier in the rehab chapter which is to use an Option to Purchase contract. This is not the preferred way. The second is to use a Real Estate Purchase contract with a contingency clause. This is the method I recommend.

The Option to Purchase contract works because it enables you to control the property with minimal cash down and no legal obligation to buy the property. But many distressed sellers (banks, estates, etc.) will not be as comfortable with an option as they would with a bona fide purchase contract.

You can handle much of the risk of not knowing if you can sell the property by including a strong contingency clause in the contract. A contingency clause or subject-to clause is wording stating that the deal is valid only as it meets some preset established condition.

Contingency clauses are used every day in real estate. For instance, most purchase contracts are subject to the buyer's being approved for a mortgage within a set time period. This is a mortgage contingency. If the buyer is rejected for a mortgage, they are almost always released from the contract. You can do the same thing with your own custom contingency clause. Here are a couple of samples:

This contract is subject to approval by the buyer's partner within 14 business days. In the event the buyer does not elect to purchase said property, seller will return all earnest money within 7 days of notification.

118

This contract is subject to the inspection and approval of said property, title report, mechanical systems, and zoning ordinances, by the buyer any time before title transfer.

You want a purchase contract that provides some wiggle room in the event the deal does not pan out like you thought it would. In that case you can either exit the deal or renegotiate it with the seller.

Deposit/Ernest Money. In most cases sellers want some down payment or what we call earnest money. You will be wise to limit the amount down you give the seller as much as you possibly can since you don't know the condition of the title report or salability of the property. Most wholesalers give a token $10 to $100 deposit. Another option would be to give a larger amount like $250 or $500 but have it held by your title company to limit your risk of a fight over the deposit.

Assignability of Contract. According to common law contracts are assignable, meaning they are transferable to another party. There are legal exceptions to this principle, but generally contractual rights are salable and transferable. The biggest exception would be if the contract would have a provision forbidding assignments. Caution: Most real estate contracts used by brokers and licensed agents forbid assignment.

This is important to us since this is the primary way we will be making money. In wholesaling, you sell your contract to the investor who will close in your place. This is called contract assignment.

Your fee, as discussed earlier, will typically be an assignment fee, which will save you from having to do a double closing and pay extra closing costs. This is important since our profits on each deal will only be about $1,000 to $5,000.

One great way to secure this assignment right is to place the words. John Doe, and or Assigns, in the buyer's name spot.

The assignment is typically handled using a relatively simple document called an Assignment of Real Estate Contract, which you and your nominee buyer sign.

Preparing the Property for Resale. In most cases you will not personally close on the property. But you will want to get keys for further inspection and to show it to other investors. Make sure your agreement permits your access to the property.

Some wholesalers strictly sell everything as-is without lifting a finger to clean up or repair the property. This works, but keep in mind that some investors like to clean out the junk and trash to help boost the perceived value for their buyers. In most cases though, you will be selling to experienced investors who can see through the filth and trash.

There are advantages to cleaning up dirty and trashed houses because even experienced investors will pay more when the deal looks like it requires less work. I have even seen some wholesale house dealers do a quick three-hour paint job using a power-sprayer and ten or fifteen gallons of paint. Again, it makes the property sell quicker and doesn't cost but a few hundred dollars. Is it worth spending an extra day to make an extra $1,000? I think so!

The Plan and Resources. So there you have it—a great way to build a buy-low, sell-low business with very little cash or credit. You become the master deal maker and help investors find great deals. The fees are smaller, but the nature of the work allows you to handle twenty or thirty of these juicy little deals per year. Check out our friends at **www.dealmakerscafe.com.**

My book, *The Hidden Secrets of a Real Estate Technician,* has extensive information on understanding real estate contracts, assignments, title searching and more. Call 800.724.0724 or write to me at PO Box 13246, Reading Pennsylvania 19612.

The buy/sell Installment Contract Business.
This opportunity is the third buy/sell business opportunity that we will explain in this book. I consider it among the very best opportunities reviewed in this book.

Although much of the general business model strategy and tools for this opportunity are the same as in the other buy/sell businesses, there are major variations in how this business is deployed. For the most part, I will explain only the new facets of this opportunity without repeating information. Generally speaking, the methods of finding and buying distress property are the same no matter what method you use to ultimately sell it.

Of all the methods I have seen investors use to sell houses this one is the most consistent winner. The strategy works year in and year out. In fact, the majority of successful buy/sell investors use some form of installment selling (also known as land contracts/lease-options) to sell their houses.

In the following pages I will explain four top strategies that investors are using to buy and sell houses fast using the various installment techniques. This information is extremely valuable and is true "insider" information that the pros won't tell you. I know these methods work because I have used them and know many other investors who also use them.

The Business Model. In real estate circles you will hear the term, "Hold the Paper." Holding the paper is business jargon that means the investor will provide the financing for the sale. Quite simply it means owner financing.

The business of buying and selling real estate with your own in-house financing is a great business because providing financing for your buyers greatly speeds up the process of selling houses. In fact, any business that provides easy financing for its customers will find a lot of new buyers for their product.

In most cases you won't be earning such large chunks of cash as with some of the other opportunities, but you will be building a predictable monthly income. It can be a bit slower to get rolling, but the advantage is you can build a large monthly income that will work even when you're not. It's not uncommon for installment investors to build a cash flow of $5,000 to $10,000 per month that continues to work even when they are not.

In this business your goal will be to buy houses with the sole purpose of reselling or renting them with some sort of financing program. You might be lease-optioning the house or using some sort of rent-to-own contract to market the house. Whatever the case, you will be acting as the bank for your buyer or renter.

The Big Secret. The biggest problem typical house investors have is finding buyers who are bankable. To be "bankable" the buyer must meet certain credit requirements and have enough money for down payments and closing costs. In most cases the financing is the sticking point in selling the property. If you, the investor, can create your own financing for the property you will have an almost unlimited supply of buyers.

What Investors Can Learn from Sears. Anyone who doubts the power of easy financing only needs to look at the Sears and Roebuck Company. Without question it is safe to say that Sears is the most successful merchant in the history of merchandising. A major part of their success centers around the easy financing they provide their customers. Some business observers even question whether Sears is in the retailing industry or in the financing business because the merchandise they sell really is just a medium to create finance paper. Many analysts have also said Sears makes more money from their "paper" and insurance (service contracts) than they do from actual product sales. Nobody knows for sure, but there's no doubt that Sears knows the power of in-house financing to help sell products

Do you need a new lawn tractor but don't have the $1,900 to buy one? No problem. Sears will sell you the tractor with no money down and a low monthly payment of about $24 per month—you'll hardly even feel it. For another $2 per month they'll sell you a service contract to protect you from any surprise repair bills.

Sears has mastered this game like nobody else. They know that controlling the financing process greatly expands the pool of potential buyers for their product. In addition, they are able to develop large profit centers in the form of finance charges and service contracts. You can use the same strategy Sears uses by creating your own customized financing for your buyers.

The Many Advantages of Installment Selling.

There are a multitude of benefits gained by providing some sort of financing program in your buy/sell house business. The biggest advantage is you can sell your property easier and faster by becoming the "bank" in the deal because you can create your own terms and guidelines to suit the needs of the buyer. Doing this greatly enlarges the number of potential buyers who can buy your house.

When you offer owner financing for your buyers you can often sell these houses without doing a lot of fix up and property renovation. In other words, you can sell the property as a fixer-upper. Fixer uppers are hard to rent and hard to sell conventionally, but they are usually easy to sell when you offer owner financing.

Another key advantage of providing financing is you can sell the property for more money than you can without financing. A home can easily sell for 10 to 15 percent more when you offer your own financing. The buyer will gladly pay this added amount because you are providing a service few sellers are willing to provide. Besides, the buyer won't be paying a lot of the typical fees and closing costs they would pay if they bought through conventional lenders.

So you now can see how offering your own custom financing when selling can greatly increase the number of potential buyers, the speed of the sale, and the purchase price. Besides these benefits, in-house financing enables you to sell properties that may not be up to banking standards because of needed repairs. All of these things plus a few more things we'll discuss make the installment sales business a true home run for the real estate entrepreneur.

Buyer/Client Profiles and Guidelines. Let's look

at the typical buyer who buys using a lease-option or contract for deed. The buyers who make the best prospects are those who may have dinged or blemished credit but who generally pay their bills. Many times they are self-employed or perhaps a few years ago had some credit problems, but now have stability in their life. Also, people with excellent credit but no down payment are also good prospects since your custom credit program will help them accumulate equity in the deal that they can use when they refinance a few years later.

The Biggest Challenge. When you market most proper-

ties using the lease-option or contract for deed method, you will have plenty of buyers. The challenge is selecting the right buyer. You want to find buyers who have decent credit. Chances are their credit won't be crystal clean. But you don't want deadbeats!

In most cases you want people who not only will pay you the payments on the house, but also someone who will maintain the property and be able to afford repairs when they come along. From my experience many lease-option buyers will make the payments but neglect their duties of maintaining the property. In these cases, you can end up getting the property back in a few years in far worse condition than when they bought it!

My basic recommendation here is to find someone who is mature and reasonably responsible. Generally this means avoiding extremely young people who often haven't settled down yet. In these cases get them to find a co-signor.

The worse a prospective buyer's credit looks, the larger the down payment. Look for people who seem to be stable in their employment or past rental history. Avoid folks who constantly move around and change jobs.

Selling Tools and Contracts. One of the first tools you need in the installment business is a financial calculator. There are a number of different models on the market. The Texas Instruments or Real Estate Qualify II are good models. These machines are almost mandatory because they will precisely calculate principal and interest payments.

Once you get up and running you probably should have some software to track your monthly payments coming into your office. NoteSmith software is probably the software of choice here. It is powerful program that will do just about everything in the note business but collect the payment!

In the installment sales business investors sell property using a variety of contracts. In this section we will explain the various contracts and the pros and cons associated with their use.

Contract For Deed. One of the most frequently used contracts is the contract for deed. This contract goes by a number of different names, but generally speaking they are the same device. Some names for contract for deed include long-term sales agreement, land contract, bond for deed, articles of agreement, or lease purchase contract.

The typical contract for deed is a legal document specifying that the buyer will receive the deed after an agreed amount of payments or principal has been paid on the contract. In these contracts the seller-vendor keeps the legal title of the property in his or her name as security for the debt until a certain threshold of equity has been met by the buyer-vendee, at which point the seller must convey full legal title.

The buyer is somewhat protected in the contract for deed because ownership is based on the equitable title they receive from the contract for deed. From a legal standpoint (income tax, depreciations, etc.) the buyer-vendee garners all of the benefits of being an "owner" without actually having the deed in their name. At the same time the full legal title stays vested in the seller which affords them protection of keeping the buyer's name off the deed and shelters the deed from possible future judgments against the buyer.

Because of the protections and benefits that both buyer and seller receive in the contract for deed arrangement, these contracts are very popular among real estate investors. In addition, since the seller is not actually transferring the deed, there typically aren't many closing costs (transfer taxes), and this enables the buyer to become an owner (equitable) without needing as much cash at closing.

Caution and Explanation. The big caution here is that contract for deed laws change from state to state. In some states if the buyer does not pay under the contract you must foreclose the contract just like a mortgage. In other states the contract for deed law is very seller-friendly, enabling the seller-vendor to easily evict the non-payer with a relatively easy court procedure.

Be very cautious about selling with low down payments to people with shaky credit especially if your state requires full foreclosure of land contracts. If your state requires a foreclosure action you may want to choose another type of contract or require much larger down payments. Foreclosure actions, depending on the state, can be a long and arduous process to get people out of the property. Therefore, I can't stress too much the need to know what you are doing. I know this from experience. I ended up foreclosing one of these and it took about one year.

Lease Purchase, Lease Option, Rent To Own

Contracts. The next category of contracts are the rent-to-buy contracts. These are a tricky to pigeon hole into a single category because depending on the terms, they may or may not be the same contract. For instance, the typical lease purchase contract is often just a land contract with "lease purchase" as its title. The same thing goes for a rent-to-own contract.

The danger to the new investor using the lease purchase or rent-to-own contracts is that the investor may not really know or understand his or her state law on these contracts. Just because a contract has a title calling it this or that does not make it what it is called. The determining factor is not the title of the document, but what the content of the contract says.

Lease Option. You can avoid many of the legal pitfalls of conveying too much power to the buyer by using a simple lease option. A properly drafted lease option is just a lease contract with a separate option-to-buy contract. In most but not all cases, this avoids the debate over whether the buyer-renter needs to have the interest foreclosed to get them out of the property. When properly drafted, the defaulting buyer-renter just needs to be evicted using a local small claims court action because they were just renting the property with the option to buy and did not actually have an equitable interest (ownership) in the property.

Wrap-Around Mortgages or All-Inclusive Trust Deeds.

If you become involved in creative real estate it won't be long until you hear the term "wrap mortgage." A "wrap" is a type of owner financing. A true wrap mortgage is a second mortgage created by the seller whereby the seller continues to make payments on the first mortgage against the property. The seller, in essence, has created a master mortgage whereby he collects payments from the buyer and then pays out a smaller payment on the underlying first mortgage.

An all-inclusive trust deed is the same as a wrap mortgage except that it uses a different type of security device. Some states use trust deeds as the security document for the note, while other states use just mortgages. Don't be concerned about whether to use mortgages or trust deeds, just use the document that is accepted practice in your state.

In reality all of the various installment sale devices (lease-option, land contract, wrap-around mortgage, lease-purchase) are "wrap" financing devices. This is because in almost all cases, the seller will have some sort of underlying financing where payments must be made.

To clarify the wrap concept let me briefly illustrate the concept with numbers. Let's say that the investor buys a property for $45,000 with owner financing. The investor put $3,000 down and the seller holds the balance of $42,000 in the form of a first mortgage. The investor then cleans up the property and resells it for $59,000 with $4,000 down and the balance on an installment land contract of $55,000. This land contract (contract for deed) is a wrap-around contract because the investor still has payments that must be made on the underlying first mortgage.

Four Selling Strategies for Installment Sellers.

In this segment I will explain the four main strategies that I have seen investor use in the buy/sell paper game. In most cases, investors choose one or two strategies. Rarely will you find an investor who uses all four of these ideas. Your best bet is to tailor the resale plans to the parameters of the deal.

Strategy #1 Buy Low-Sell Low to Investors.

Most real estate investors overlook buy low-sell low options to sell properties. In many ways it is similar to the traditional wholesaling of properties, but it is different in the fact you are providing the financing for the investor.

In this strategy your primary clients are landlord investors, especially newer investors without a lot of capital or credit. With this strategy you buy lower-end houses or small apartment properties at extremely distressed prices, and resell these properties to investors at a higher price, but with plenty of profit still in the deal for the investor.

In most cases you will buy bottom feeder properties that require a lot of clean up and repairs. The nastier the better because you want deals that nobody else wants so you can buy them at rock bottom prices. The key to this strategy is you will not be doing any of the fix up or renovation work. This is left for the enthusiastic investor to handle.

Tax sales, bankruptcy, and various private sales are the type of deals you will be looking for since they offer lower income properties at extremely discounted prices. You will focus on lower to middle income properties because you will get the most bang for the buck in terms of purchase price and markup. Also, lower-income properties should still provide a good cash flow for the investor, which is important since this money will be used to pay you.

I have seen this strategy work well with women who wanted to buy and sell houses but didn't want to handle the repair and renovation work. This works great because in most cases they will not be doing any of the physical work—everything is sold as is. In this strategy the main thing you are selling is the easy financing and the future profit, which is created from the sweat equity of the investor buyer.

In my area there is an attorney who buys low-end fixer properties and then resells them to investors on easy terms. In most cases she sells with very little down payment, since the investor is going to need a fair amount of cash to handle the repairs and clean up of the property. The properties she buys are real steals which she uses a credit line to buy. She then sells these with no or low down payments to responsible investors who turn the property around and rent them out. She uses an installment contract as the sales conveyancing method.

This program will only work if you do two things right. First, you must buy fixer-upper properties at severe discounts. And, second, you must offer the property to the investor with plenty of profit still in the deal. If you get greedy by charging too much interest and too high a sales price you will have trouble selling the deals. Besides, if the deal isn't good for the investor they will get discouraged as soon as problems start occurring and give the house back to you. Also, you want it to be good enough that they come back and do additional deals with you. Caution: be cautious about selling too many deals to one investor because new investors often bite off more than they can chew—I probably would not do more than three deals per investor to spread my risk of default.

A Typical Deal. You buy a distressed house for $22,000 that needs a lot of clean up and repairs. You buy it by taking over the seller's existing mortgage of $20,000 and payments of $195 per month. In this case you will have about $2,000 invested in the deal. You do nothing to the house but run a classified ad in the local investment club newsletter. You offer the house for $31,000 with $1,000 down and payments of $270 per month. You end up investing only $1,000 in the deal with a wrap installment contract that yields $75 per month ($900 annually) in cash flow. This may not sound like a great deal, but remember you aren't doing any fix up work and have almost no money invested to create the cash flow.

Strategy #2 Buy-Low Sell-Low to Homeowners.
This strategy is similar to the one just explained except in this case your buyer will be a homeowner. The home buyer you will be targeting will be the type that doesn't mind doing some clean up and repairs as long as you will be providing the financing.

With this strategy you essentially duplicate the investor strategy previously mentioned with a few modifications. First of all, you will have to handle some repairs and improvements before you sell the property in order not to scare away typical home buyers. This means getting the major mechanical problems handled—things like roof leaks and major plumbing problems. Leave most of the cosmetic and minor repair work to the buyer to handle since you are selling the property at below the fully cleaned up and repaired retail price. A key benefit in leaving some clean up and fix up to the buyer is it gives them a time and energy investment in the deal which will make them think twice about walking away from the deal and the payments.

Because you will be doing some of the cleanup and repairs you will be able to charge more to the buyer than you could to the landlord investor mentioned in Strategy #1. But, again, it is important to make the deal attractive by leaving some equity in the deal for the buyer. Also, it is important to collect a good down payment from the buyer to help prevent them from defaulting and tying up your property in some sort of foreclosure situation. Try to get at least 10 percent down.

Strategy #3 Buy High Sell Higher. This is another interesting strategy that you won't see a lot of investors using. It is very different from the first two strategies because it works well only with nicer properties that don't need much work.

In this strategy your goal is to find nice middle class homes in move-in condition. Obviously you will want to buy these houses at as low a price as possible, but because these homes are in better condition they will not sell at a deep discount like a fixer upper house.

You will look for those houses in this category that need you to take over the existing financing. As with most of the distress buying strategies, your prime candidate will be the vacant home with a distressed seller.

Your basic goal is to buy the home for the mortgage balance. Why would someone allow you to do this? Because the seller probably doesn't have much equity and is strapped with double mortgage payments. For whatever reason (divorce, job transfer, relocation) the seller in such a situations typically has moved and is making double housing payments. This can be tough after a few months. These folks need to get out from their house payment or face foreclosure and bad credit. You can help them by taking over their payments.

After you buy the property, preferably with very little cash down using a lease-option or an installment contract, you immediately re-market the house (remember, the goal is to tie up the property with very little cash down.)

The money in this strategy is not made in the repairing and renovation of the house, but by selling the property with an attractive financing package.

Typical Buy High Sell Higher Deal. You buy a clean townhouse for $70,000 with an installment contract or a lease-option. Your basic agreement with the seller is to make their existing mortgage payment of $640 per month. The house is worth about $77,000 in true fair market value. You are buying at only about a 10

percent discount, but the terms are excellent. You have only about $640 invested, the amount needed to make the next payment coming due.

You re-market the property for $84,000 with $4,000 down. Why would someone pay 10 percent over regular market value? Because you are offering "owner financing." Owner financing can create a price premium of 10 to 20 percent because you are offering buyers the opportunity to buy a home without strict bank qualifying and without all of the costly closing costs associated with conventional financing. Does this mean you let any willing buyer buy the property? No. You will be inundated with eager buyers, but you must screen them. You want someone with reasonably clean credit and who leads a stable life. Self-employed people are often good prospects because they have a harder time qualifying for traditional financing. Caution: if their credit is trashed this is a warning sign.

Along with the 20 percent mark-up in the deal you should create a monthly cash flow from the difference in your payments and the payments offered to the new buyer. This usually can be achieved by the small spread in interest rates between what you are paying and what you are charging.

While this strategy is somewhat simple, don't underestimate its effectiveness. A large pool of buyers are looking for nicer homes that have creative financing packages. If you can go into the marketplace as a skilled buyer and purchase these houses you can build a nice business servicing this clientele. In most cases there will be plenty of buyers. Your job in this strategy is to select the best candidate who will make timely payments and take care of the property.

Strategy #4 Buy Low, Rehab, Sell High . Of all the
strategies this is the one professional investors seem to use the most, probably because it provides the greatest total profit potential and an effective way to sell houses fast.

The biggest hang-up in selling houses is usually finding buyers who have enough down payment and good credit. With the buy low, rehab and sell high strategy you create your own financing terms to sell the house. Then, after the buyer has developed a track record of paying, you take them to a skilled mortgage broker, get them permanent financing, and you get cashed out of the deal.

In this strategy you buy fixer-upper houses in clean, lower to moderate income neighborhoods. Next you clean and repair the houses by painting, carpeting, and refurbishing the kitchen and bath

areas. Make sure you also take care of repairing most of the maintenance areas. Your finished product should be clean, painted, and
fresh looking.

Once the cleaning and refurbishing are completed you need to
market the property. Advertise the house in the classifieds with any
of the following headlines: Buy Like Rent. Owner Financing. Lease
Purchase. No Bank Qualifying. Rent to Own. Describe the property
by stating the basic features of the house and terms of the deal.
Note: long classified ads don't seem to work as well as short
punchy ads. For example—

**Buy Like Rent: 3 bedroom single—Oak St., freshly
renovated. $625 per month, $2,500 down.
Call 777-7777.**

You will notice the sales price is not mentioned. This is
because most buyers are mainly concerned with down payment and
monthly payments and not the sales price. Ultimately your sales
price must be in line with fair market values, but a small price premium is typical because you are offering good financing terms.

The Best Sales/Rental Contracts. From my own
experience and the experience of countless contacts, lease-options
and installment land contracts are the two most commonly used
contracts. I personally favor a lease-option as my selling/renting
tool because it affords me the most protection against buyer default,
while installment contracts often need a foreclosure action to boot
out non-payers.

Whatever contract you decide to use, make sure to collect
enough down payment to protect yourself against buyer default. If
your state has tough rules on getting people out on installment contract it is probably smart to collect at least 10 percent down. Since
lease options are typically safer to use you probably can get away
with a 5 percent down payment (option payment). In any event,
consult with experienced investors and real estate attorneys from
your region.

Two Philosophies of Installment Selling. Inves-
tors generally have two lines of thinking when it comes to using
these various lease option and installment sales contracts. It comes
down to whether to do a short-term or a long-term deal.

Short Term Contracts. Investors who favor short term installment or lease option contracts view them as temporary or bridge financing. Their goal is to get the buyer or renter permanent financing through a mortgage broker or bank as soon as possible. These investors typically only provide financing for one to three years at which time the buyer-renter must obtain permanent financing.

In the opinion of these investors it is safer to get cashed out of the property so they can roll their capital into another deal and repeat the process. These investors look forward to the monthly spread in payments and the large chunk of cash they will earn when the permanent lender refinances their temporary installment contract. The investor doesn't have to be concerned with the buyer's defaulting since he or she will have been cashed out of the deal.

Most of the short-term installment sellers I know like to turn their new buyers over to their mortgage broker within a year so the mortgage broker can begin the process of getting their credit cleaned up. In most cases if the buyer makes timely payments that are verifiable, the mortgage broker can find a lender to handle their mortgage. Also, make sure your lease-option gives a suitable rent credit towards the purchase in order to create the needed equity or down payment required by the lender—consult an experienced mortgage broker for guidelines.

Long Term Contracts. The opinion of investors who choose long-term contracts is that they don't want to kill the goose that lays the golden egg. If the buyer is making timely payments, why not carry their financing as long as possible and earn the interest? After all, building a nice cash flow is what it is all about.

Many of the investors I know hope the buyers never refinance because that will end their income stream from the property. I know one investor who sells all of his houses with a 40-year mortgage. This provides low payments for the buyer and lots of interest for the investor. Interest can be a major profit center.

Profit Centers In the Installment Business. Besides the regular markup in sales price there are a number of profit centers in the installment house business.

Interest. Interest can be a major profit center in the "paper" business. To prove this, look at any long-term mortgage. About 95 percent of the average mortgage payment is interest.

Mortgage Interest Differential. The difference between the rate of interest you are paying on the underlying mortgage and the rate you are charging is called the interest rate spread or differential. The lower the rate you are able to buy at, the more profit you can earn in the spread. For example, if you buy with 7 percent owner financing and resell on a land contract at 10 percent you have created a 3 percent rate spread. This spread is a profit you make by leveraging the underlying note. This is common practice with various "wrap" contracts and is very lucrative.

Price Premium. I have already mentioned this, but it is worth reviewing. For the owner financing wrap deals you create you are able to charge a modest price premium for the terms you are offering. Typically 10 to 15 percent of the value can be added to the price if you offer attractive financing terms. Buyers usually won't blink an eye at this as long as you are offering them a good house with affordable payments.

Repossession Profits. I hesitate to mention this but there are times when buyers will default, and you will end up with the property back. Although most of the time the house will be in worse condition than when you sold it, there will be times when a buyer will actually improve the property before finally giving the house back. Although I would never count on this, it does happen. I've had a few houses come back with new kitchens and heaters. To be fair I must also tell you I've had some houses come back as total wrecks.

Option Money Benefits. On those deals where you rent the property with a purchase option, you need to realize that option payments fall under a unique tax treatment. Generally speaking, option money paid by a prospective buyer is not taxable until the option is exercised, abandoned, or lapsed. This means that the up front option payment is not reported on a tax return as income until the option is exercised or expired.

Buying Strategies for Contract Sales. I now want to briefly explain the ways most investors buy houses where the plan is to resell on a contract.

Owner Financing. This method can be tough because a lot of sellers don't want to hold the mortgage. The big exception is with lower income neighborhoods. Because these areas are already distressed you can often buy rundown houses with great owner financing terms like no money down, low or no interest. Just be careful to avoid heavily blighted areas.

Take over Existing Mortgages. This method can work well and many sophisticated investors use it, but you need to be careful of the due-on-sale clause that most mortgages contain. The due-on-sale clause could be triggered when you buy the property or when you resell again without paying it off. If you use this method it is probably wise to use a lease option when remarketing the property to avoid triggering the due-on-sale. Also, it is probably smart to keep the lease option or contract time limit fairly short to minimize your risk in the event the due-on-sale clause is called.

Credit Line then Refinance. Most of the real pros I know who buy and sell houses buy distressed houses with all cash from a short-term credit line. They clean and refurbish the property. Next, they refinance the house with a permanent mortgage (usually a 10-15 year term) that is a low closing cost mortgage (at a slighter higher rate). Finally they resell the house using either a lease-option or a contract for deed. The new mortgage they got on the property still has a due on sale clause, but according to the investors I know most of the lenders don't seem concerned that they have "sold" the property, since the investors don't record the installment contract and make their payments as agreed. In fact, with two of the investors I know, their lenders know exactly what they are doing and really don't care.

Just Get into Title. This a philosophy, not a method of buying, that says you want to buy houses any way you can as long as you can minimize the cash you are investing in the deal. The important thing is to gain control of the house so you can build the profit into the deal with the financing in your resale.

Lease Options and Installment Contracts. Since most mortgages have some sort of callable due-on-sale clause, the land contract or lease with option to buy makes a good way to garner control of the property and avoid alerting the lender of the transfer. The drawback with either of these methods is that the legal title stays in the seller's name, which can be hazardous if the seller gets a judgment against his or her name. Some sharp investors seem to have beaten this hazard by having the seller deed the property to a trust with another party as trustee, thereby getting the seller's name off the deed.

Pitfalls and Issues Installment Investors Must Watch

Usury Violations. The rate of interest you charge needs to be in compliance with state usury limits. Some investors charge whatever they feel the market will bear without concern for state usury limits. In many cases this is not an issue if you charge a fair rate. What happens is that investors get greedy and start charging loan company type rates. Then when the buyer goes into default and hires a lawyer, the seller gets nailed with a suit alleging usurious interest practices. Check with a sharp real estate lawyer to be sure your rates are legal.

Due-on-Sale Clauses. I have already addressed this pitfall, but it is worth mentioning again. If you sell a property that has an underlying mortgage with a due-on-sale clause, you run the risk of the lender calling the entire loan due and payable. In most cases selling or renting on a straight lease coupled with a pure option to buy contract will solve this hazard since a technical transfer has not occurred. Also, remember if your credit is good and you have lenders who work with you, they sometimes won't mind if you resell the property as long as you always make your payments and are responsible. This is often true with smaller local banks who are holding the mortgage in their own portfolio stock.

Do Not Give the Buyer the Deed. In most cases you should avoid transferring full legal title to your buyer until you have been completely paid you. What often happens when you give the buyer the deed is that they end up defaulting on various bills and are served with judgments. These judgments will attach to the real estate. This can be a problem if you take the property back, since it will come back with the additional liens unless you foreclosure and clear them off.

Avoid High Credit Risk People. The next pitfall is that of the major credit deadbeat. These people can make your life miserable. Not only will collecting your payments be a hassle, but if they get a lawyer they will try every trick in the book to stay in your house without paying. This could mean that you have to foreclose them out of the property or fight them in a bankruptcy.

Wrap Around Hazards. Wraps can be the greatest tool in the world, but keep in mind that you may have to make payments on your underlying mortgages, while there is no money coming in, if your buyers stop paying you. Landlords face the same problem, but landlord evictions are cut and dried take about 30 to 60 days at the most. Whereas these various installment sales devices can take anywhere from 2 to 10 months to get the people out depending on the state you live in and the contracts you use. This is why I like regular lease-options since they generally make it easier to evict and terminate. Whatever the case, all of these conditions are manageable with the right knowledge and experience.

Greed Pitfall. Because this business can be so good, some investors get greedy and think they can over charge people. This is a mistake because when you don't leave any sweetness in the deal, the buyer may get sick of paying your ridiculous prices and go into default or end up getting a lawyer to fight you. Avoid charging full price for everything. Over and over I see investors charge folks excessive interest and extreme sales prices. Don't be a vampire. Leave something in the deal for the buyer. In the end you'll have less defaults and less fights with angry buyers.

Installment Sale Tax Problems. There are many advantages to selling houses on installment contracts, but be aware that if you do a large volume of these as strict buy/sell deals you can run into a tax problem. Generally speaking you can use the installment sales tax reporting method when selling investment property with some sort of owner financing. The problem comes in when the IRS determines you to be a dealer and not an investor. In this case you may have to pay all of the taxes on the entire profit the year of the sale even though you only received a few payments. Consult with a sharp accountant who invests in real estate to help you structure your investments. One idea is to rent the properties first and establish them as rental investments before you flip them.

Hot Profit Tip. The Veterans' Administration sells many of its repossessed houses on installment contracts. Typically the down payments are extremely small and the installment contracts can usually be wrapped by investors or at the very least, offered to your buyer on a lease-option contract.

Summary and Resources. So there you have it—a good review of the opportunities awaiting you when you buy and resell houses on contracts. This can be a highly profitable business where many investors have made huge profits creating their own financing paper.

If you still have doubts, consider this: If you sell a $45,000 house on a 30-year note (contract) with 9 percent interest, you will receive a total of $130,000 in payments of which $85,000 is interest!

Not many books deal specifically with buying and selling houses on contracts, but there is one I can recommend. It was written many years ago, but the concepts are still valid. Its title is, *How to Build a Real Estate Money Machine,* by Wade Cook. Since it is an older book many libraries stock it or can order it for you via the inter library loan system.

6

The Home Inspection Business

The home inspection business is a relatively new business that has been created in the past twenty-five years. It is a service that educates and informs home buyers about the mechanical condition of their prospective home purchase. The business is primarily an educational and advisory service.

This business is relatively easy to enter, but many people underestimate the broad range of technical training and knowledge one needs to stay in business. If you have a lot of knowledge of the construction trades and are somewhat technically inclined, this business may be a good opportunity for you to consider.

Home inspection can be profitable and rewarding because you are providing a service that truly helps people. Few consumers have the knowledge that a home inspector has, so they will trust you like a valued counselor. Most importantly, a hardworking and proficient home inspector can earn upwards of a $100,000 with a mature practice and a large real estate market.

The Business Model. The home inspection survey is primarily a service to alert and educate buyers about the structural and mechanical soundness of a property. In addition to reporting potential problems to the home buyer, the inspector will give a general advisement on what is needed to correct the problem.

Consumers consider this a valuable service since they are making what amount to the largest purchase of their life. To pay $250 to learn the detailed condition of their future home is money well spent. In fact, it could easily be argued to be the best money they will spend, since a major mechanical problem or defect could cost thousands to remedy.

The demand for this service as increased in recent years due to a multitude of factors. First, many states now require seller disclosures which alerts buyers to the presence of past and present mechanical problems. Because of this, many buyers need a professional opinion of an unbiased third party. The typical contractor is not suited for this since they often just want to sell their services, rather than provide an opinion. Furthermore, many contractors are limited in their expertise to their own field of work. Second, the high cost of buying a home makes the purchase a huge investment, which makes consumers nervous, therefore they need something to help reduce the risk of buying a lemon. Third, more and more lenders require inspections and mechanical testing to reduce the risk on their end of the deal as the lender; lenders want to know beforehand about things like lead, asbestos, and polluted water.

In a typical home inspection the consumer will receive both a verbal report and a written report explaining the condition of the various mechanical systems in the property. In order to give a detailed report the inspector must methodically inspect and test every system in the property along with making general observations of the current level of maintenance.

The Inspection Survey Process. Once given the job the inspector makes an appointment with the seller to conduct a 2-3 hour survey of the property. In most cases the inspector wants the buyer present for the inspection so he can communicate the results of the inspection.

As the inspector you will develop a ritual to follow when inspecting the property. This ritual usually involves making multiple passes through the property to get a detailed feel of it. Some inspectors use the double pass method doing a pass in each area as a general overview and then a second, more detailed pass when the actual testing is done.

The average house has 6 or 7 mechanical systems that need to be inspected and tested. These systems are as follows: roofing, electrical, heating, plumbing, structural, air conditioning, basement/slab (foundation), and sub-systems including the cooking range, water heater, kitchen, bath, windows, and cosmetic coverings.

After a detailed inspection and testing, the inspector then gives a verbal report and explanation to the buyer about the property. This is important because buyers are notorious for not reading the written report. At this point the job of the inspector is not to alarm or scare the buyer in an effort to justify his or her fee, but to clearly explain the overall condition and possible problem areas of the house.

Smart inspectors should major on serious problems, which generally is any problem or hazard requiring more than about $500 to fix. In addition to pointing out the home's serious problems, the inspector should identify all of the minor maintenance or repair problems; but should realize that most homes are not perfect and are already priced to reflect the current level of maintenance and mechanical soundness.

After giving the verbal report the inspector takes his handwritten report and produces a professional computer generated report, which is then delivered to the various parties in the transaction. The written report is *critical* because it will help protect against future claims saying the inspector missed something. Disputes can often arise over a verbal report, but the written report should insulate the inspector from false charges.

Earning Potential and Fees. As with any business it is difficult to estimate earning potential due variables that are hard to measure. The general range of income for an established home inspection practice is in the $60,000 to $80,000 range per year, although some inspectors have been known to make even more.

In most cases a single inspector can perform no more than about 500 to 600 inspections per year. More than this becomes physically impossible for one person. The average inspection takes about 2.5 hours to complete (including the verbal report), plus an additional hour or two to process and package the report back at the office.

The inspection fee generally ranges in the $200-300 range, although most inspectors charge their fee on a sliding scale based on the size and or price of the house. Extremely large homes are often priced out at fees of $400-500 due to extensive work needed to thoroughly survey them.

Profit Tip: Be careful not to under price your service as a way to gain competitive advantage since some people will perceive it as a sign of an inferior inspection. Rather, find a way to create some other added value that sets you apart from the competition.

Additional Profit Centers. In addition to the standard inspection service, many businesses offer ancillary services and testing at an extra charge. Services like radon, lead, termite and water testing can all be offered as additional services.

Knowledge, Skills, and Training Needed. Success in the home inspection business requires a broad array of knowledge and skills. Although this can be a wonderfully rewarding business, most people underestimate the degree of skill and professionalism required to survive in this business.

As strange as it might sound, the home inspection business is above all a *people* business, not a mechanical business. You must have a great grasp on the various trades, but you will not survive if you are not a good communicator and people person. Many engineer types who are great at the mechanical end of the business run into trouble because they cannot reduce their observations into a comprehensible and digestible form. Furthermore, many engineers are not people persons and have difficulty dealing with the nervous buyers they encounter.

People with experience in the building trades who also have good people and communication skills make ideal candidates for the home inspection business. If you aren't a tradesperson don't despair because there are extensive training courses that you can take to learn the business. In any event, you must have some preexisting knowledge and talent in the mechanical end of the world.

Most people underestimate the large body of knowledge that is needed to be successful in the home inspection business. Even if you have an extensive background in the building trades you will still need to take various courses to be ready for all that you will encounter in this business. After all, your clients are putting all of their confidence and faith in you, and you can't disappoint them.

If you are not adequately prepared you *will* have problems in this business. It is too easy to miss something when inspecting a house. If you do, you are sure to hear about it after the property closing. Worse yet, you may hear from the buyer's lawyer. The liability is just too great to go into this business without the right knowledge and preparation.

Training Resources. One of the highest rated training companies is HomePro Services, Inc. at 800.966.4555. HomePro is operated by Michael Lennon, an expert's expert. His company offers both training courses and licensing programs which will set you up in business without the need for a franchise fee. HomePro also offers a full range of marketing and business forms that will save you thousands of dollars in trial and error experience. If you are serious about this business, check these guys out.

Book Resources. One of the highest rated books for the home inspection business opportunity is *Real Estate Home Inspection: Mastering the Profession,* available from Professional Equipment at 800.334.9291. A smaller, less comprehensive book, *The Complete Book of Home Inspections*, is available from the same source.

Barriers to Entry. Because this business is relatively easy to start many people mistakenly believe it is a fast track to financial success. Exactly because the barrier to entry is low, the business has become competitive with more people attempting to get a good start with home inspecting. The hard part isn't starting the business, but staying in business since mistakes and overlooking problems can happen easily. This isn't to say it is a bad business, just be prepared to know what you're doing. As one inspector told me, "Don't quit your day job." Figure at least one year to build up an acceptable flow of inspections.

Marketing Strategy. The home inspection business can be marketed using many of the same techniques used in other real estate service businesses. However, there are a few modifications. Home inspection businesses obtain a large portion of their jobs from licensed sales agents. This is due to the fact that home buyers rarely spend much time considering details about a home inspection until the house is under contract. Therefore, a lot of the advertising for home inspection service is not absorbed because it is the last thing in the buyer's mind. Because of this tendency, home inspectors need to focus a good part of their time in building a network of contacts within the real estate field.

A major share of your clients will come as a result of referrals from realtors, lenders, appraisers, and other real estate professionals. Build a database mailing and fax list for mailing and faxing your ads and informative marketing reports. The key is to be consistent and disciplined about doing your direct marketing. Try to keep in touch with your database prospects every month. Keep in mind that many of these real estate people already have a service they use, but keep marketing anyway. There will come a time when the service they're using lets them down or is too busy to respond fast enough. Then they will call you!

Real estate agents have teams that help them process deals. A typical team consists of mortgage brokers, appraisers, repair people, title companies, and home inspectors.

Profit Tip: Your number one goal is to become a team member for as many real estate agents as possible.

Ads in real estate home books are another source of advertising, but watch your expenses since these ads are often expensive and don't always bring the result you will expect.

Coupons can work well. Create a coupon that offers either a nice discount or a special offer on your service. You might think about a joint advertising venture with other real estate businesses offering the client a special package deal on a group of services such as title insurance, mortgages, etc.

Tools, Equipment and Software. This business does require a rather large collection of tools and equipment if you are going to do a professional inspection. One often overlooked "tool" is a nice uniform with your company name to create the professional image you want to portray. Next, you will need all of the basic inspection tools such as flashlights, an ice pick probe, an outlet tester, ladders, a tape measure, an angled probing mirror, camera, general hand tools, an oven thermometer, a clip board, and a compact tape recorder.

In addition to basic inspection tools you will need more sophisticated tools such as a carbon monoxide sniffer, a volt meter, gas leak detectors, a circuit locator, a termite sniffer, a water pressure tester, lead testers, and a host of other testers to ensure a quality inspection.

A terrific company for buying inspection tools and books is Professional Equipment. Ask for their catalog of books and tools 800.334.9291 or see them at **www.professionalequipment.com.**

Software is a mandatory purchase because you will need a program that will take your written notes and create an inspection report that looks professional. Important: you will need a pre-inspection contract signed that discloses what exactly your service does and does not cover. Again, these can be ordered from the above company.

Pitfalls and Liability Concerns.

Clearly the biggest problem associated with this business opportunity is the inherent risk involved in conducting an inspection and reporting in writing what a customer is buying. Because homes are a complicated combination of systems it is fairly easy to miss a concealed problem. It also can be easy to report a problem in your verbal report and then leave it out of the written report, thereby creating a problem later.

The challenge is that consumers treat the inspection like a promise or a guarantee that the home will not need repairs. Well, anybody associated with any of the repair or mechanical trades will tell you that something can be working fine today, but mysteriously break down next week. In the consumers mind, you missed the problem and they expect you to pay for it!

Pre-Inspection Contract.

All smart inspectors have the buyer sign a pre-inspection contract that explains what is and is not covered. This should solve most of your liability problems. But keep in mind, if your inspection does not meet general industry standards, you could be held liable for major problems that you missed, even if your contract disclaims liability.

The Balance Between Deal Killer and Responsible Inspector.

You'll want to maintain a delicate balance between being a responsible home inspector and being a deal-killing inspector. If you scare too many buyers into thinking their prospective home is a disaster waiting to happen you will cause real estate sales people to lose deals. If the sales agent loses too many deals because you frighten and alarm their buyers, you won't get any more referrals. On the other hand, if you don't honestly inspect properties you could exposure yourself to bad word of mouth advertising and legal threats. As usual, honesty is the best policy, but be diplomatic and don't scare people into thinking the house they are buying is a lemon. After all, virtually every used house has some repair and maintenance problems.

Additional Resources and Contacts.

If you want more information, contact the American Society of Home Inspectors (ASHI) at **www.ashi.com.**

7

Real Estate Sales Brokerage

Becoming a licensed real estate sales person is among the most promising opportunities that is reviewed in this book. There are many misconceptions and challenges that you need to understand before you jump into real estate sales. I will give you two seemingly conflicting statements with total confidence. First, real estate sales is a unique opportunity because a highly ambitious person without a lot of capital and formal education can make the same level of income as a lawyer or even a medical doctor. Second, in real estate sales if you're not suited to the industry and do not have a tenacious personality, you won't make a lot of money, and you probably won't be happy.

The Business Model. Real estate sales is a rare businesses that requires you to work for somebody else because licensing laws do not allow salespeople to own an office until they qualify and pass the broker's exam. To qualify and pass a broker's license you must first earn your wings working in an office owned by a broker. The subject I will be reviewing here is working as a licensed real estate salesperson, not a broker. It should be the goal of most agents to work towards a broker's license, not because you should open your own brokerage firm, but because the broker's designation increases your marketability and prestige in the eyes of clients.

The Business Within a Business. You may be having a hard time understanding how I can call real estate sales a business. The reality of the matter is that no matter what brokerage house you are working for, you are really working for yourself. Becoming a real estate salesperson is in effect building a business within a business. As an agent, you are basically on your own. In most cases, the brokerage firm doesn't care how you market your services as long as it's legal and not in conflict with their rules.

Cutting Your Teeth as a Licensed Agent. Many specialties and sub-specialties work within the licensed real estate brokerage field, but I will focus on the area that generally is the most profitable for new agents who are cutting their teeth.

This area is acting as an agent for buyers and sellers of residential and small commercial real estate properties: Houses, apartments, land, warehouses, offices, etc.

The "business" of helping people buy and sell real estate starts with becoming a licensed sales person. As a rule you cannot help people buy and sell real estate for a fee unless you are licensed to do so within the state you are conducting business. As I have mentioned in earlier sections, there are some exceptions to this rule as in the cases where you are a principal or owner in the transaction.

The business of being a real estate agent is really one of being a deal making facilitator. In other words, your job is to bring parties together and assist them in putting deals together. Don't underestimate the value of being a facilitator since most transactions involve problems and unforeseen complications which buyers and sellers are unprepared to handle by themselves. In real estate it is rare for a deal to go down without a glitch.

In addition to being a facilitator, you advise sellers in the pricing of properties. This is a key part of the value you bring to clients. Without good information for correct valuation, sellers run the risk of either over pricing or under pricing their property.

The next part of the service is marketing the property. The agent's job is to get maximum exposure for the property, so the property can be sold in the shortest time possible. This is critical because in most cases the agent only controls the listing for six months.

After properly pricing the property, marketing it, and bringing the parties together, your final job is to facilitate the financing. At this stage of the transaction you will be advising the parties as to the best options in financing and lender selection. This of course will be done with the aid of your many contacts with mortgage brokers and loan officers.

Your Best Days as an Agent. No doubt the favorite day for all sales people is closing day. You won't be paid a penny until all of the problems are handled and everyone sits down at the closing table. Here is where you pick up the check to take back to the office and hand over to the broker.

The Big Money is in Listing Property. It may sound like a contradiction, but any experienced agent will tell you the big money is not in "selling" real estate but in listing it. Here's what they mean. The easiest and fastest money is not from driving buyers around to buy houses, but it in listing property for sale. You see, when you list a property, you are controlling it. It is almost like becoming a tiny owner in the property because all of the parties must work through you. Although you will have little say as to what price the sellers sell for, you do hold a contract that states if the property sells, they MUST pay you.

The secret many beginners don't know is that most of the property you list will be sold by *other* salespeople and not you. You will be credited with "selling" the house, but the agent helping the buyer usually does all the work.

Profit Tip: It is in your interest to control as many listings as possible and let the other agents do most of the work! This is the fun part.

The Advantages of this Business. There are many advantages to this business and at least one career opportunity. First, as mentioned, the money can be extremely rewarding. Agents who treat this like a business rather than a job and who work long enough to break through the learning curve earn anywhere from $80,000 to $250,000 per year. This won't happen your first year, but agents who create a strong referral base really do make this amount of money. In fact there are top agents who earn much higher amounts, but most of them work with builders and control a serious new construction inventory.

Another advantage to this business is the fact that the listing contract enables you to control real estate with none of your own money. Think about this. You can control millions of dollars in listings with no capital of your own. This is super leverage without any corresponding liability except your reputation. In many respects it is like being in the house "flipping" business without having to buy the real estate yourself. In essence you are partnering with the property owner.

Along with the inherent leverage in this business is the fact that you don't have any house payments to make while the property waits to be sold. If you personally bought real estate to resell you would have to make mortgage payments every month until it sells.

Lastly, it is a relatively simple business in the general way it is conducted. As a one highly successful agent told me, "This is not brain surgery—it is a simple business." Although the business is not nearly as basic as it was twenty years ago, it still is a very learnable and manageable way to make money. Caution: don't confuse "simplicity" with "easy" because it is not easy, especially the first year or two.

The Old Approach to Getting Started. The old approach to getting started in real estate sales was to take a few hundred dollars and take the required courses and tests. Upon passing the exam, the agent would select a company and begin working. Buy a few business cards and you're in business. This will work, and if you really are strapped for cash you may have to start this way, but there is a new, more business-like approach that I would like to offer you.

The New Business Mentality Approach. In this approach you begin with the understanding that this is not a job but a business. To start a business you need some capital. If you don't have the capital consider borrowing it or consider dedicating a certain amount of your income into this business until you are fully geared and tooled up.

This business needs a decent amount of capital (about $5,000) to be effectively deployed. You will want to spend some quality time seriously researching and exploring this business to make sure it is something you will truly enjoy. If you don't have a lasting passion, you won't make it in this competitive field!

Try to meet and talk with successful agents to get a taste for what it's all about before you invest several years only to discover it bores you or doesn't fit your temperament. If possible, spend a couple of days shadowing a good agent. If need be, go outside your market area and talk with a pro agent to get unbiased information. In many cases the brokerage house broker will let you spend a few days with them to get a feel for the business.

Assuming you've done your homework and are committed to the business, you should be prepared to invest in your sales career just like you would any other business. You will need a good chunk of capital to fund your business and living expenses while you get rolling. You probably won't see a check for at least three months!

The cash needed to invest in your business will be used for a variety of things: business attire, computer hardware and software, advertising and marketing expenses, courses and training, license fees, living expenses, office supplies, errors and omissions insurance, etc.

Although it may be initially hard to scratch together the cash to run this business, you will be better off because like any business it is hard to run it effectively if you are broke. If you don't have any capital, running advertisements, marketing campaigns, and buying the proper business tools becomes very tough. It's like being in a financial straightjacket.

Skills, Tools, and Technology You Will Need.

First let's talk about the traits and skills needed to be an effective real estate agent. Perhaps the number one trait is that of persistence. The best agents I know are not quitters. They will work with a buyer or seller for as long as it takes to make the deal happen. I have seen good agents go to extra-ordinary lengths to get a buyer approved for a mortgage. In fact, I've been a party to several deals where I would have given the buyer almost zero chances of getting approved for a mortgage, but their dogged agent never gave up on them and finally found a lender to give them financing. If you plan to succeed in this business you must resolve to be a pit bull in terms of determination!

Number two, you need to have thick skin in this business. Don't let my enthusiasm for this business fool you into thinking it is a walk in the park. It is not! Real estate sales is a highly competitive business where only the fighters survive. If you get easy frustrated and tend to quit quickly then you need to either change your attitude or do not get in this business.

You will need thick skin in order to keep going through rejection and to stand up to the many ruthless people who work in this field. I don't want to scare you, but inherent in this field are a sizable number of agents who lie and cheat to make deals. Of course, these nasty people only comprise about ten percent of the total field, but these people will run right over you and you're clients if you're not careful.

Third, you need to be a problem solver. In almost every transaction there are unexpected quirks and bugs that pop up that need to be dealt with. You cannot become frustrated over these normal occurrences, rather, expect them. If you expect each deal to have a certain amount of last minute complications you won't be stressed when they happen. To be a successful agent you will need to develop a good attitude towards unexpected problems. Consider them a challenge and take them head on.

Fourth, you need to be well organized to be a successful agent. The typical real estate deal involves at least fifteen to twenty documents (letters, contracts, forms, disclosures, checks, etc.), therefore, you need some semblance of order and structure. When you multiply the number of documents per deal times ten or twenty open cases per month and you have one giant pile of papers that needs to be controlled.

Lastly, you need to be able to handle a fair amount of uncertainty. You see, in a real estate deal the agent doesn't earn one penny until the property goes to the closing table. The agent can spend forty hours working on a deal, but if the buyer's credit does not pass or the home fails some inspection the agent gets nothing for their effort. Only sold properties pay. It is sort of like a contingency arrangement where the lawyer doesn't get paid unless they win the case.

This succeed or don't get paid condition creates a subsurface level of stress and anxiety for agents. If you think about it, the agent is the guy in the middle who has very little control. Their life is greatly dependent on many outside parties who can make the outcome of the deal uncertain; mortgage brokers, appraisers, inspectors, buyers, sellers, all have a say in the deal, therefore the agent needs to navigate the deal through these outside parties in order to get paid. This delicate process requires a persistent personality who learns how to work with people and problems.

The Team. One of the ways a good agent learns to cope with the many challenges involved in this business is to build a good team of players. These "players" will greatly help the agent get the deal to the closing table. The team consists of mortgage lenders, title companies, home inspectors, repair people, other agents, and in-house staff.

Tools. You will need all of the standard business tools mentioned in earlier chapters (fax, computer, copier, cell phone, voice mail, etc.) so I won't spend much time replaying this topic, but I do want to make a few new points.

A digital camera will be a much needed tool you will be able to use to email clients digital pictures and to post pictures on your web site. Along with a digital camera you should also get on board with using video equipment to record guided tours of properties on your web site. All of these power tools will definitely give you a high-tech leg up on the competition.

Most real estate offices provide small cubicles for agents to work out of. At the same time the office provides MLS computers, copiers, faxes, and other tools. Although it is fine to spend time at the office and use their supplies and tools, I believe a chief goal of yours should be to build you own well-equipped office at home. This includes getting directly connected to the MLS computers system. By building a fully operational office at home you should be much more prepared to succeed in this business. Frankly, you won't be missing much not hanging around at the company office since there's almost no walk-in business in most offices.

By having your own high-tech office connected to various real estate databases you will be much more efficient than the typical sales agent. Furthermore, you won't need to travel to work in the morning to learn about expired listings, new hot listings, or sold properties. This will all be at your finger tips in your home office.

Communication Tools. In this line of work you really are in the communications business. The easier you are to contact and the faster you respond to various information requests the more business I believe you will do. To prove this point let me give you the example of one top real estate sales person that I know. This top producing sales person checks his voice mail messages from his cell phone once an hour throughout the day. He believes it is absolutely critical to be this close to his customers that he checks voice mail about ten times a day! That's responsiveness!

The three most important communications tools you have are: cellular phones, voice mail, and email. All of these tools along with the regular telephone will be your most critical profit making devices that you can use. Do whatever you can to reduce the normal barrier and friction in communicating with your customers.

Why You MUST Use the Internet.
If you plan to become a successful agent you must plan to use and exploit the Internet in your real estate practice. This is not a suggestion—this is a command. You must learn to use the dozens of on-line databases, links, sites, listing services, referral services, and email programs if you plan to succeed in real estate in the twenty-first century. If you fail to know the Internet as a marketing and informational tool you will quickly find yourself falling further and further behind.

The net is critical to your success for two main reasons. The first reason is that if you don't have a personal site your competitors, other agents, will use this information against you when competing for listings. In many instances sellers interview several agents before choosing one. The agents will sell against you by talking down the fact that you don't use web marketing.

The second reason is that an increasing number of buyers are using the Internet to shop for properties by searching popular real estate web sites. If you don't have one (or are linked to one) you will be missing out on a valuable channel for selling properties. New statistics show that about thirty percent of all buyers check the net to research properties in their area.

Building the Site.
You can pay a programmer and designer to build and maintain a site, but this becomes costly and cumbersome to handle since all changes and updates must be worked through the designer. I believe a smarter way is to use a user-friendly program and build and maintain your own site. It is faster and cheaper.

I believe that the best software by far for the amateur is Microsoft's FrontPage. Get the most updated version and I think you'll be amazed at how easy building a site can be. You can constantly update the site by adding links and content to keep your clients and their friends coming back for more. A good resource is the book, *Internet Marketing in Real Estate* by Barbara Cox and William Koelzer. This book explains why you need a site in your real estate practice. Along with answering the how's and why's, it provides a lot of information about what type of content and links to build in your site to draw the most traffic. Another good book on using the net to buy, sell, and rent real estate is *Sam's Teach Yourself E-Real Estate* by Jack Segner. This is more of a consumer's resource book of real estate web sites, but it gives dozens of helpful net sites for both consumers and real estate professionals.

Profit Tip: In today's time-crunched world people want facts about a property immediately. By you having your web address on your signs you can give buyers immediate information about the properties you are selling.

Increasing Your Competency. One of biggest challenges of real estate sales is to gain competency. For example, you need to learn property values. The best way to learn about property values is to get out in the field and tour as many listings as possible. Many offices conduct weekly tours with agents, taking several hours to view all the new listings for the week. My advice, whether you're a new agent or veteran, is to see as many listings as possible. Learn the values in the county you sell in and the inventory other agents have. If you work in an office where tours are not conducted, I organize six or ten agents and begin previewing about ten houses per week.

My next bit of advice is to take as many of skill and education enhancement courses as possible. Seminars and training courses can greatly increase your real estate knowledge. Take courses in appraisal, income property, and all the advanced residential specialist courses that you can find time to take. Many of these courses award certification designations, which you can use to enhance your credibility and knowledge.

Don't wait to take these courses. One expert agent I spoke with recommends taking a new course every six months. Enroll in a class as soon as you pass your salesperson's exam.

Strategies for Finding Listings. Your key to success in finding listings is to create a steady flow of sellers who list property with you. This will happen if you take responsibility for yourself and create an aggressive marketing campaign that never shuts down. Eventually, you will make a good living off referrals, but you've have to pay your dues first.

Selling real estate is not like getting a job at the local automobile dealership where almost all business comes from walk in-traffic. The big surprise to many first timers is to learn that the typical real estate office provides you with almost *no leads.* You will have to generate almost all of your own business. If you believe you will secure a lot of leads from phone duty or from walk-in traffic you will have a rude awakening. Phone duty and walks-ins may account for one or two deals a year—at the most!

The World's Most Powerful Prospecting Tool.

Most don't like it and most don't use it, but what I'm about to share is the very best way to find and create listings that I know. The secret is cold calling. Not cold calling just anyone, but cold calling for-sale-by owners, expired listings, and people in the market area you are cultivating.

Cold calling is highly effective because so few people use it. In addition, cold calling puts you belly-to-belly with prospective clients, whereas a letter is distant and impersonal. Furthermore, cold calling truly shows the seller that you are an aggressive agent who is not afraid to work hard to earn their business.

There isn't any magic way to perform a cold call other than just being friendly and making a brief introduction (always wear your company name badge so people aren't afraid to open the door). Do your best to ask some basic questions without appearing nosy, and you will be way ahead of the crowd when it comes to meeting sellers.

You should cold call people in the following three main groups: FSBOs (For Sale by Owner), expired listings, and neighborhoods of interest.

First, and easiest, are the FSBOs. You can find their property from ads in the paper or just from driving around the marketplace. Don't call first—just visit them. Most of these people will be highly resistive to considering listing the home. This is okay. Just be nice and explain that you understand they want to sell the house themselves, but that you will be happy to give them some free assistance if and when the home sells. Tell them to call you. Then just keep in contact with them by making brief phone calls and perhaps periodically drop by and offer them some forms or other helpful information. Chances are about 80 percent that they won't sell the house themselves and by this time they will be practically begging you to help them!

Hot Profit Tip: Some savvy agents have learned they can still make a few dollars even if the FSBO sells the home themselves. They provide the seller a paperwork service whereby they assist the seller with putting the documents together for a fee. This fee usually is around $750-1500 (or 1 percent). Of course, this has to be cleared with the managing broker.

Second, cold call expired listings. You cannot solicit listings from sellers who are currently under contract with other agents. You must wait until the listing contract expires. These expired listings are published every day in the MLS computer system. Be sure to print the updated list just as soon as the information is released in the morning.

Most agents call these expired listings on the telephone. But the pros do a cold call in person. Screen the list and pay the people a visit around 5 or 6 o'clock in the early evening. As dumb as the old cliché sounds, the early bird really does get the worm in expired listings.

Third, after a few months in the business, pick out an area and begin to work it for listings. This is the old farming method. Make daily cold callings to your zoned area. Take cards and some brochures and get out into the market and meet people. Most folks won't want to sell their home, but you will learn about their friend at work or relative across town who does want to sell. After periodic visits to your zone send postcards and flyers by mail to keep reminding these folks about you. You will begin to harvest some great transactions in about three or four months, almost guaranteed. The tough part is having the gut determination to keep the practice up until the deals start flowing. It will work.

Take Some Crumbs Until You Get the Steak.

This strategy involves finding and taking some weaker, lower quality listings in order to get exposed to the marketplace. You use this strategy by working less desirable neighborhoods or by taking some over-priced listings that are normally considered "junk." These will clearly involve more work since the properties may not be choice listings, but you will find that the more sparks and heat you create, the more leads you will begin to uncover. For example, many licensees don't like working inner city properties since they are slower movers. But remember, many of these properties are being sold by people who want to move to the suburbs just as soon as their city house sells. Guess who they will buy their next home from if you sell their existing house?

Advertising to Find Sellers. Paid advertising definitely finds sellers, but it will cost several hundred dollars per month. Create a general target zone and begin to advertise your services. This can be tough since there are often several other agents all doing the same thing and the consumer has a tough time of sorting out whom to call. Use smart marketing methods that will differentiate yourself from the others. For starters, be bold in your claim. I saw one veteran agent say in an ad—"I guarantee to sell your home or I'll Buy It!" Now that's bold. I'm not saying you should use that technique, but the key is to create some excitement. Frankly, most ads run by real estate agents are stupendously boring.

The Seminar Strategy. This strategy works by creating a valuable free seminar offering irresistible information to sellers on how to sell their home. Make a bold claim to attract attention:

10 Rules for Selling Your Home for Top Dollar in 30 Days or Less!

Plan weekly or monthly mini-seminars at a local hotel or restaurant where you honestly give good information that will help people to sell their property. Do not turn the meeting into a 45-minute sales pitch! Make it an educational meeting that gives some true insider tips along with a low profile or "soft" sell of your services.

There will always be a few who learn lots of information for free without engaging your service, but there will be a solid percentage of folks who will be so impressed they will hire you! The more informative reports and advice you offer the more people will be impressed by your professionalism!

Strategies for Finding Buyers. In my opinion the most underutilized tool for finding buyers is the classified ad. Many agents spend thousands of dollars running expensive color display ads and forget about the good old classified ad.

The Trick about Classified Ads. Most brokerage houses make the agent pay for their own ads except for a token ad or two that come with the listing service for each listing. These

156

token ads almost never sell houses. You need to run your own ads where the calls ring directly to you and not the brokerage house. The strange thing is many of these ads don't sell houses either! The trick is to create a catchy headline with some short copy. Again, this ad probably won't sell the house be advertised. But, it serves two key purposes. First, it shows the seller (send them all copies of ads you run) you are taking action in the marketing of the home (even though 80 percent of all listings sell through the MLS computer listing service) and, second, it will provide you with dozens of leads on buyers who are looking to buy houses.

How it Works. Chances are that most of the callers responding to your smartly written copy won't be interested in the home once they learn the details about location, price, etc. But, these will be hot leads of buyers who are in the early stages of looking for a home! When they call, do your best to know inventory and search the MLS to match them to a house that meets their requirements.

The Buyer's Seminar. You can use an informational buyer's seminar to find sellers through informational mini-seminars. Create your irresistible headline or twist and begin to advertise your self-help workshop or mini-seminar. Try something like:

How to Buy a Home That Your Friends Will Never Believe You Could Afford

Make sure you can deliver what your headline states, but don't be afraid to use a little theatrics or mild puffing—people enjoy having their imagination stimulated!

At the meeting have all of the standard seminar things like name badges, coffee, pop, cookies, handouts, and a registration notebook. Then deliver a 45-minute workshop presentation giving time for questions and answers. After you've delivered a few of these meetings you'll get the routine down great and will be ready start to find some good buyer and seller clients!

Master First-Time Home Buyer Programs. One of the best ways to build a buyer clients is to become an expert in the various first time home buying finance programs. Mortgage brokers and the aggressive banks in your area will be happy to educate and work with you on these programs. The more creative, low-money down programs you know about, the more buyers you will

REAL ESTATE BUSINESS AND INVESTMENT OPPORTUNITIES

find. Once you do a handful of these deals with buyers you will get tons of referrals from their friends and relatives wanting you to find them a house.

In addition to lending programs make sure you learn about all of the local and federal governmental programs and grants that help first time home buyers. Some of these programs will pay a first time buyer's closing costs and assist in funding their down payment. The more you know, the more deals you will do!

The Free Market Valuation Certificate. With as many agents as there are in the business, it surprises me how few actually use the free market valuation certificate in their marketing documents. Here's how it works. Try to include in your ads, flyers, web site page, signs, and other marketing mediums a coupon or certificate offering a free market valuation to homeowners. The certificate enables homeowners to get your professional opinion (not an appraisal) of what their property is worth. While some folks may ask for a free valuation with no intention of selling, over time you will generate good prospects. Some folks who request your valuation may not use your services this year, but you will generate some goodwill referrals out of it. The more sparks you create in the marketplace by meeting folks and getting your message out the more business you will generate. Make sure you give your program at least twelve months to judge its effectiveness.

Creating Audio Brochures. Few agents use this method. Create a marketing message for your target audience on audio tape. After you have polished and edited the tape have it mass produced and labeled. Then hand these short messages out to prospective clients. This gives added credibility and lets the client meet you without you actually being there. Consider putting the tape in a clear plastic bag and placing it on the doorknobs of FSBOs, expired listings, and other potential clients. Label it with an alluring and curious headline.

Trends in Real Estate Brokerage. Take time to understand forces that are reshaping real estate brokerage and the way real estate is bought and sold.

The 100 percent Concept. The old way of running a brokerage house was to give a sales person an office and split the commissions. Although there still is commission sharing being

done, the new way is to become a 100 percent agent. A 100 percent agent is where the office charges the agent a set monthly "office" fee and the agent gets to keep all of the commission. In this new arrangement there still are commission co-ops where the selling office splits the fee with the listing office, but the 100 percent agent does not have to make a split within their respective office.

This relatively new concept truly makes real estate sales a business, not a job. Basically, the 100 percent concept enables the agent to create a fixed expense, which will greatly benefit the top producers because the fixed office fee is small in relation to the total commissions being earned. For instance, a typical commission on a $150,000 home is $9,000. If the agent is both the listing and selling agent he or she would earn $9,000 and not have to split this with anyone. This is not a small amount of money!

Office fees vary, but generally range from $700 to $2,000 per month, depending on the type of services that are rendered and the location of the office. **Note:** This concept is not good for brand new agents, but it should be the goal of all serious agents. This concept also benefits the office since it gives them a predictable cash flow and lets them focus on delivering services to the agents.

Office Consolidation.

Another trend is the merger and consolidation of small offices into large mega-offices. These mega offices often have one or two hundred agents working from one office. Many small offices within a city have either closed their doors or merged with the large offices.

The main reasons for this trend are economies of scale and sheer marketing power. These large offices specialize in delivering a lot of training, advertising, and high-tech services for agents, which makes it hard for smaller offices to compete. In addition, many of the large builders/developers that are so valuable to brokerage houses have given their business to the large mega offices.

My general advice is to make a serious comparison of about five different offices before you select one. I would probably avoid the smallest offices unless you just want to be an investor specializing in property management or, possibly, creative financing. I also would advise avoiding the largest mega-offices where you become a minnow surrounded by sharks. My advice would be to hook up with a flexible and aggressive, medium-sized company that is a serious player in the market. These mid-sized firms usually are more flexible and often make agents a better deal in terms of fees and services rendered. Also, when shopping for a company to work for, carefully scrutinize their fee structure. Many offices charge high service fees for using their phones and copiers.

Competition Trends.

Real estate brokerages can be highly profitable businesses for those who can work through and survive the learning curve. But it also has become highly competitive. Many of the newest agents are entering the field and making significant investments in technology tools and marketing. You, too, must approach this as a business requiring the use of computers and some capital investment to build this business. While you don't need a "formal education" to set up your brokerage business, you must be willing to spend time developing technology skills to prosper in this field.

MLS Is No Longer King.

For years licensed agents had a powerful tool known as MLS (multi-listing system). MLS is basically a cooperative of companies that share their listings in one central computer system. This network of listing is the agent's most powerful marketing tool. When an agent lists a property, it immediately gets put in the MLS system which opens the listing up to the hundreds of other agents in the county.

The system is still strong but there is a new force which is minimizing MLS. This force is the Internet. The Internet allows people to create their own on-line listing service bypassing the MLS. The web now has hundreds of real estate listing and advertising sites that is opening up real estate markets to folks outside the standard brokerage MLS system.

Many realtors are upset and feel threatened by these sites. But this won't change reality. The Internet is here to stay, and licensees need to stop complaining and face the future. The best thing you as a licensee can do is not fight it but learn how to use the web. For example, you can build referral alliances with many real estate listing sites and use their on-line listings as a source for leads and marketing.

Specialization Trend.

After your first year goes by and you have a handle on what this business is all about, you would be smart to begin choosing a specialty within real estate sales. In the chapter on real estate marketing consulting I have a large list of possible specialties (upscale homes, new construction, buyer's brokerage, etc.). When you focus on one or two main areas your level of competency and expertise will rise. You will also be able to create a focused marketing message that will make you stand out from all of the other me-too agents.

Miscellaneous real estate tips and ideas. In this brief section I want to give you several tips and ideas that will be worth their weight in gold in the event you decide to get into this business.

Forms and Documents. You will be using literally dozens of forms and contracts that you will be using in your real estate practice. In most cases, the home office will provide a forms closet where the forms you need are stocked. Although this may work for you the first year, make it a priority to put these forms into your own word processor computer program so you can print your own forms out on a laser printer. This does two things. One, it allows you to fill in the blanks with the computer without needing a typewriter. Two, it enables you to save the filled-out form in case it needs to be reprinted later. Also, these laser printer forms are much cleaner and professional looking than the old photocopied forms at the office.

An easier method is to contact the local and state real estate board and see if they sell their various contracts and documents as a software package so you can print them yourself.

How To Handle Over-Priced Listings. A problem you're sure to face as an agent is the unrealistic seller. These are sellers who believe their property is worth gold plated prices. These sellers will list with you only if you use their price and not your estimate of value. The problem is these listings do not sell.

The beautiful solution to this problem is one I learned from a top agent who earned several hundred thousand per year!

Hot profit Tip: The answer to the many unrealistic sellers you will meet is the listing contract addendum. What you do is kindly express your doubt over the seller's value and present your best case for a lower asking price based on comparables. If the seller still won't budge lower, you accept the listing at their price, but get an agreement from the seller for planned reductions in the asking price if the house does not sell.

For example, you might say, "Mr. Seller, We can start with your price of $139,000 and give it a try for 45 days. If the home does not sell, and I hope it does, we then will reduce the list price to $129,000. If after another 30 days we don't have any offers we will bring it down to my estimate of value at $124,900." Of course, you will leave a little padding for negotiation with the buyer).

This lets the seller prove that the property is overpriced without your having to lose the listing to another agent who will take the overpriced listing. It also gives you your listing price which is probably more realistic. All of this is put in writing in the form of a listing contract addendum with the specified timed periods and price reductions spelled out. It works!

Dare To Be Different.
In real estate sales it seems that everyone is a me-too. Look at the various real estate ads in the freebie books. Everyone's ad looks the same. They all say some version of—"Hi, I'm John Doe Realtor and I can sell your home. Please list with me. By the way, I'm great." Booooring.

After you've spent several months getting a feel for the business, begin creating a different approach with your ads and message. Be creative and dare to be different. Yes, others will feel threatened and jealous, but you have to get out of the same old me-too-ism mold (see the marketing consulting business opportunity chapter for additional ideas).

The Tom Hopkins Thank-You Card Tip. About twenty years ago Tom Hopkins wrote a book about listing and selling real estate. One of the better tips in his book, How To Master The Art Of Listing And Selling Real Estate, was his thank-you card tip. Tom says when he was an agent he used short little thank-you notes to send to all of the various contacts he would meet throughout the day. He was really radical about using these because he believes people really appreciate that you took the time to notice and thank them for the chance to earn their business.

Thank you notes work great at getting people to recognize you as a caring and thoughtful person. It also is a subtle way to show that you are a detail-oriented person who will most likely handle their account with follow through.

Building The Data Base. This business demands that you build a database of current and past clients which you will use for future lead generation. You will market to this database to keep your name and message in front of clients.

Referrals are the lifeblood of the real estate brokerage business. In most cases, when you give someone good service and sell them a property, they will refer their friends, coworkers, and relatives your way. This is why it is critical that you keep in contact with them. If you don't, it will be out of sight, out of mind.

On the other hand, you don't want to blitz these people with flyers and crass advertisements. Look for ways to periodically send (better yet, email) them handy tips about home ownership, maintenance, energy saving tips, or anything that will help them during their ownership. Wrapped around these various homeowner ideas and tips will be your soft message reminding people of your excellent, life improving services!

Open House Parties. If you become an agent you will conduct open houses. Open houses really aren't that effective at selling houses, but agents do them to help convince sellers they are trying to sell the property. In fact, most agents will tell you they like open houses as a way to prospect for buyers in general—not the specific house being sold. It usually goes like this, "Oh, you don't like the way this property is laid out? I have the perfect house for you at 423 Oakdale Court...."

Like many of the marketing methods agents use, open houses are as dull as watching house paint dry. Dare to be bold and different. For example, why not have your open houses on Saturday rather than Sunday? Now that would be different, wouldn't it?

Another idea is the party concept. Advertise and market the open house as a "party." Consider having soft drinks, coffee, cookies, cake, balloons, and music at the showing. Invite some of your friends over to help liven the party up. Be creative and continue to enliven your parties with innovations. They may cost twenty or thirty dollars more than the standard open house, but creative house parties should produce dividends in your efforts to differentiate yourself from the competition. Your sales presentation will have more sizzle when you explain to prospective sellers that you have open house parties rather than open house showings.

The Hardest Year. The hardest time in your real estate career will be the first year. This first year will be a major learning process and time to establish your team. It also will be difficult since you won't have a track record upon to show sellers you are qualified to handle their business. Furthermore, you won't have a base of past clients to give you those wonderful leads and referrals that most agents live off of. All of these conditions make the first year in real estate the toughest.

Successful people push through this hard part until they reach a point called the "positive break point," where everything begins to get easier. This threshold point occurs when you have established yourself and have actually started selling properties. It also marks the time when you begin to feel a decent level of competency. At this point, the real estate business becomes profitable and fun! My advice is to research and think through the business thoroughly before you formally get into it, but once you get involved, don't give up during your startup months because it will become easier in time after you push through the tough first year!

There will be times when many of your efforts seem like a waste of time and you may feel like quitting. These times will come. Again, push through these times knowing that a positive momentum will swing back your way soon!

Real estate sales is one a profession in which people from limited backgrounds without college degrees can learn a craft that can end up generating a substantial income. If you feel after serious investigation that this business is for you, by all means get involved.

Additional Resources. If you want to see a brokerage company that has dared to be different check out **www.housepad.com.** These guys are using many innovative tools and marketing ideas that are worth paying attention to. They realize that by offering some services for less they are gaining more clients, which ultimately means more profits.

Sanzo Specialties, Inc. publishes a nice catalog of real estate advertising and marketing tools as well as numerous books on the nuts and bolts of real estate brokerage. Their site is **www.sanzospecialties.com,** or you can call them at 800.222.4041. These folks have been around a long time and will help you out with many of the marketing tools you'll need.

Another resource that will help you learn the newest trends in real estate sales and brokerage is an excellent book titled *The Hottest E-Careers in Real Estate,* by Blanche Evans. This book explains why agents need to be using the Internet and on-line databases to make more money and gives practical information for using the Internet.

A giant on-line real estate news site, **www.inman.com,** is a site you'll definitely connect with to keep current with the industry.

8

Real Estate Publishing Opportunities

In this chapter we explore several opportunities in publishing and information marketing. Most people don't think of these fields as real estate businesses, but there are many opportunities to merge the two fields.

Just a few short years ago when you mentioned "publishing," people would think of some big Madison Avenue company. This has all changed with the advent of inexpensive publishing technology and the Internet.

Although real estate publishing is highly competitive (like most businesses), many good opportunities exist to create a business with very little cash investment. We will review half a dozen business opportunity ideas, whereby savvy entrepreneurs can create and sell valuable and profitable information products and services.

The Business Model. We often think about people selling all sorts of products, but we rarely think of people selling information. That's probably because we think of people selling newspapers, magazines, books, newsletters, documentaries, seminars, college courses, and so forth, which really is housing for the information, not the information itself.

People love buying information in many forms because they know information returns a high yield to the investor. We've all heard the wise words of past thinkers, that education is cheap compared to ignorance. Smart people know that a few dollars from their pocket to purchase a book, newsletter, or course can provide them solutions to problems, ideas to change their life, and wisdom to protect them.

In the information publishing business you are doing just that—providing ideas and solutions. Just as the McDonalds stores sell food to feed hungry people, publishers and information providers are providing solutions and ideas to people who are hungry for progress and an enhanced life. If you feel like you have some special ideas, skills of communicating, or life-changing information, then, you may be the right person to serve the info-consumer marketplace.

I appreciate content-rich books, reports, tapes, and newsletters as much as anyone because I know how much books and other information products have improved my life. These wonderful products have enabled me to live a hundred lives in one lifetime. I can read a book that may have taken the author six months to write and tap his or her brain for the cost of a good dinner at a fine restaurant. There is a difference though—five hours after dinner that food is gone; a good book will still be with me five years later. Good books, reports, manuals, and directories are wonderful investments that frequently make their readers twenty, thirty, or a hundred times their money in the form of time saved and trial and error frustrations avoided!

The goal of a small real estate publisher or information provider is to deliver high-quality, usable information that helps people save time and better their life! I will explain several ideas that could make a business, or they could be a spark to help you develop your own ideas. Whatever the case, these ideas are just that, ideas. Feel free to accept, reject or modify them as you choose.

The Tools and Skills. Twenty years ago becoming a small publisher or information provider was tough because much of the technology and tools were limited and costly. Today, for about $2,000 you can own a great computer and a complete publishing software package.

Without going into detail on all of the products on the market let me say your best bets are probably the Microsoft lineup of tools. These tools are user friendly and affordable. For word processing I recommend their most popular product, Word. For desktop publishing they have a product called Publisher. For internet publishing you can combine the above two products with their web site development program called FrontPage probably is the most user friendly web page program on the market.

These tools are not enough to put you into the real estate publishing business. You must also have the most critical ingredient: Ideas. Not just any ideas. You need to have a new outlook, explanation, breakthrough, twist, innovation, and organizing capability. If you don't have some of these skills or traits then you may not be suited to produce quality products.

Information Publishing Ideas

FSBO Books and Products. Whenever you develop a product you must ask yourself who is my target audience. Well, there's one target audience in real estate that is fairly large and hungry for useful information. This market is the For Sale By Owner (FSBO) market.

FSBOs are people who want to sell their home themselves and not pay a sales commission. The problem they lack knowledge about selling their home. This is because selling a home today is far more complicated than it was ten or twenty years ago. What if you took your expertise in real estate and did additional research and developed a comprehensive how-to manual for FSBOs in your state?

There seems to be plenty of FSBO how-to books that cover the general process, but there are few state-specific books which really are what is needed since many states have unique laws or twists in their home selling laws and disclosure requirements. By creating a detailed and state-specific manual you will provide an extremely advantageous product that will save sellers countless hours in tracking down forms, contracts, and guidelines.

Perhaps this FSBO manual or "kit" could contain a video that will show sellers how to prepare their home for maximum resale price. This video could offer dozens of low-cost fix up and value-added enhancements to help sellers sell their property faster and for more money.

In addition this state-specific kit could contain a directory of internet FSBO sites and advertising sources where the seller could "list" the property at little or no charge. This directory alone would save the seller a day's work in tracking down advertising sources!

Now we're really going to kick up our value in the FSBO Kit by offering an enclosed computer disc with professionally drafted real estate sales agreements, disclosure forms, and other needed documents. This alone could be worth hundreds dollars in legal fees (of course you will explain the seller should still take the documents to their lawyer for legal review).

Now you don't just have a manual to sell your FSBO, but a complete help-them-sell kit. The video, manual, forms disc, and

FSBO web site directory will all educate and aid the seller in getting their property sold without paying a commission.

This FSBO marketing kit could be sold via small ads or direct mail to FSBOs who are advertising in the newspaper. Another marketing avenue could be bookstores or office supply stores. Whatever the case, get as many people selling the product as possible. (The standard discount offered to resellers on this type of product is 40 to 50 percent.)

Real Estate Newsletter Opportunities. Newsletters bring you a wide range of publishing prospects. Depending on your expertise, you can target any segment of the real estate industry: Realtors, mortgage brokers, investors, buy/sell investors, or paper investors.

People pay good money for newsletters because a well-written newsletter provides very timely and specific information that the typical magazine or newspaper does not. In fact, most newspapers and magazine products only offer general information that is suited for the mass-market reader.

People $95 to $249 a year for a profitable newsletter because they are serious about their field and know that just a few ideas will return their investment many times. The upside for the publisher is this information is relatively cheap to produce; the cost to print and mail an 8-page newsletter is about $2 a copy. Better yet, if you follow my forthcoming tips you can write, print, and deliver the newsletter practically for free.

You can choose from two or three basic formats for a newsletter. Some newsletters contain strictly editorial and information content. Others are a combination of advertising and informative articles. The third is mainly a marketing device (catalog) with a sprinkling of informative articles and tips mixed into the "newsletter."

The newsletter that will bring the highest subscription dollar is the one filled with editorial content. You have to charge more for these letters because there won't be advertising revenues. Also, since the customer is paying more, they will be more demanding of the content.

The second format is a combination of articles and how-to information combined with space for advertising. These ads can range from small classifieds to display space. Some newsletters offer free classified ads to paid subscribers. Customers often like newsletters with a mixed format because the advertisements are centered around properties and real estate. Subscribers can learn about other helpful products and services offered by the advertisers. This format has two profit centers: advertising and subscriptions.

The final format isn't a true newsletter, although it is made to look like one. In this case the "newsletter" is mainly a marketing device that has helpful information salted throughout the pages. These newsletters command the lowest price and often sell for a token amount just to filter out non-serious readers. For instance, you might produce a monthly newsletter-catalog for only $19.95 per year, but the main profit center is in selling the additional products or services you offer. The $19.95 is used mainly to defray the printing and distribution costs, and not to be the main profit source. Frequently, people will pay the nominal subscription price because the publication offers enough informative articles and resources to keep them hooked. The main profits from this format are from product and service sales from the "subscribers." In addition, there can be serious money made from advertisers paying you marketing fees (joint ventures, drop shipping offers, ad revenue, insert flyer offers, etc.) to make offerings to your large subscriber list.

Hot Profit Tip. No matter what format you follow, remember, you can always produce separate offerings (flyers, letters) and insert them into your newsletter package. You're already paying for the envelope, stamp, and stuffing labor, so why not send other offers inside? The added cost is minimal. Subscribers don't mind additional offers as long as the newsletter remains mostly content filled. Just keep the ads on a different flyer or inserted letter.

The Problems with Newsletters. There seem to be
two main problems associated with the newsletter business. The first is the cost and time involved in finding and recruiting subscribers. This isn't always easy, especially when selling a $149 newsletter. The answer may seem easy—just lower the cost of the publication. This too, creates a challenge because you won't make any appreciable money unless you charge enough to cover your time and talent. Think about it. With 500 subscribers paying you $49 per year that only amounts to $24,500 in gross revenue. From this number you still have to subtract at least another $7,000 for operating and productions costs. Your net profit would be only

around $17,500, which isn't enough to make a living. My point is you have to charge enough to make a newsletter venture work.

The next challenge with newsletters is renewal management. What most people fail to realize is that even the top newsletters in the country only get about 70 percent of their clients to renew for the next year. In fact, a 70 percent renewal rate is outstanding and rare. This means that even the best newsletters in the country lose a major chunk of their subscriber base each year! Since newsletters live and die on renewal rates, it is critical that your newsletter readers become addicted to your writing style and content. Don't hesitate to be opinionated in this media format. People love reading an opinionated style because it conveys confidence and expertise. Your letter must make the reader want to come back each year for more or it will wither on the vine from subscriber erosion.

This second renewal management problem means that you as publisher need to spend a lot of time and money finding new subscribers or you will suffer from declining readership. In addition, there are many costs involved in persuading your current readers to re-up their subscription. Most of the experts say you should send five to renewal notices before you stop asking for their renewal! This process can be costly and time consuming.

The 21st Century Newsletter Process. If I were serious about starting a newsletter I would consider a 100 percent electronic format. The electronic newsletter delivered via the Internet from a web site or email report solves many of the traditional challenges newsletter publishers have. With a web site report and or an e-mail newsletter you save on every cost area. You have zero delivery costs; zero printing costs (the client can print it); zero delivery time; zero costs in sending renewal notices; zero envelopes to stuff. As marketing expert Jay Abraham says, "the Internet is the world's cheapest printing press!" It's a darn cheap marketing platform, too!

With a website newsletter there's another option in the delivery and production process. Traditional newsletters are offered monthly, but this letter could be an on-going weekly or even daily report where the subscriber can read it on the site or in an email. If it is a site read letter, you could create a password system where the reader enters the password to get the updates. Another option could be to create an archive category where readers with activated passwords could read past issues or buy them on a single copy basis.

The key to a newsletter, especially an on-line one is to provide valuable content. There is so much free information on the net that people won't keep paying to get general info that is available elsewhere. Another key is to discount the electronic version of your newsletter. Most people still prefer a hard copy over reading on-line, but if the price is right, they will print their own copy. This shouldn't be too much of a problem since you won't have the costs associated with printing and mailing a paper edition! Many letters offer both a paper edition and an electronic e-mail edition. If you have the time, this may be your best bet.

The Newsletter Advantages. In addition to all of these advantages, the newsletter is a great way to build an on-going income stream of paying subscribers while at the same time piggy-backing the letter with other products and marketing messages. In fact, most newsletter pros will tell you not to start a newsletter unless you have other products to sell, or the letter won't make a sustainable income. If you don't have other offerings you will need to work on joint ventures and strategic alliances of people who have products or services that will benefit your clients.

Real Estate Book Review Club. In this publishing gambit you can provide readers or listeners with the valuable service of reviewing and summarizing various real estate and business books. We all know there are far more good books out on the market than we'll ever have time to read. You can review and summarize real estate and business books on a monthly basis. The summary review service should be offered on a subscription basis just like any other periodical. The going rate for this type of service is around $100 per year. In addition, you can sell prior month's reviews based on the book titles or topics covered. These packages of reviews will sell for a slightly higher price if sold to an individual or they can be discounted for a multiple purchase.

Several companies offer summaries and critiques on regular business books, but few if any, offer such a service for real estate and investment books. If you're a bookworm, this might be a good way to profit from something you enjoy. In fact, I'd probably be your first customer, since I love good real estate and investment books but don't have enough hours in the day to read them all!

This service could be offered in both a written and audiotape format. The audiotape format is important since the people who buy these services often do a lot of commuting and this enables them to use travel time that would otherwise be wasted.

The essence of the service is to provide a book report review and rating of the book while explaining in depth a few of the major points of the book. You have to be careful to avoid being involved in a copyright infringement or like many business book review services, work in cooperation with the authors and publishers. After all, this is free advertising and publicity since a percentage of the readers or listeners will go out and buy the book after learning about it.

If you're seriously considering this type of review service your best bet would be to subscribe to a business book review service to get a feel for how it works. Also, you probably should invest a few hours reviewing your plans with a copyright lawyer to ensure that you are not overstepping any copyright restrictions. Generally speaking, copyright laws allow brief quotations and fair use applications when used in an educational context with full disclosure of the author and publisher. In any event—do your homework.

State Specific Landlording Manuals. Here's
another publishing opportunity that will help the landlording community. Consider writing and publishing a specialized, state-specific landlording manual. I say state-specific, because there are already plenty of regular landlording books on the market, but few if any state-specific manuals that give exact details on the landlord and tenant laws and guidelines for a state.

This manual could provide a general review of solid investment advice coupled with a detailed explanation of your state's specific landlord-tenant laws. In addition, you could consider providing a copy of the actual state statutes, a good rental application, along with a few state specific lease forms on computer discs. From my experience, most landlords are very fuzzy on their state's specific landlording laws. This could be a great product if marketed effectively.

E-Books and Web Publishing. One angle worth considering is creating a very specialized information product (report, book) that is distributed in electronic form. You create the product, advertise it on the web, and offer it instantaneously to your client by them ordering on-line, getting the report in their hot little hands within minutes.

Typically e-books customers are allowed to read one or two chapters free to give them a free taste, and then they can order the balance of the book with a credit card. The going price for these e-books is anywhere from $9.95 to $49.95, depending on the quality and value of the information. There are big pluses to this method of product sales and distribution: you have zero printing, packaging, distribution, and mailing costs.

Several software programs are available that will create and deliver these e-books for you. Research the web for software choices. Look for software that will not allow the download receiver to email to others. A lock in the downloaded book prevents this from happening.

Speaking and Seminar Opportunities. Providing real estate investors useful information by conducting workshops and seminars is a profitable opportunity if you are a good communicator and have something worthwhile to share with people. The key is to have some type of new information or a new twist on old information. If you are going to prosper at this you should have some personal hands-on experience in the field you will be discussing.

I cannot stress enough the need to have something unique or special about the topic you plan to speak about. There are legions of speakers and books on the market teaching real estate. Make sure you have a unique style or insight into your field.

Fees for these seminars and workshops range anywhere from $49 to $495. Your best bet is to be sure to charge enough to cover all of your hidden expenses and costs associated with marketing and traveling to deliver the seminar.

A good place to start is with the many investment clubs that exist across the country. These clubs are desperate for speakers and in most cases will book you to speak even if you don't have a track record in speaking. The general arrangement is to provide a free 30 to 45-minute talk that offers a few solid tips and ideas with the idea that if they like your talk they will sign-up for a half-day or all day workshop at a fee. Keep in mind that these investment clubs will typically allow book and audiotape packages to be sold after your talk. If you work the seminar in partnership with the investment club, the going rate is to split everything after the first $1,000, which usually goes to the speaker. You can contact local investment clubs by first contacting the national organization called REIA at **www.NaREIA.com.**

Teaching College Courses. One unique avenue I have seen a few investors take to make some extra money is to teach a class on real estate investing at a nearby college or university. In many cases you don't even need a prior teaching degree or college background if you have real world experience and are able to communicate well. These courses are typically offered as general self-help type classes and not as formal credit earning classes. Whatever the case, consider talking with the local colleges and universities to see if they'd be interested in your services to teach real estate investing! Even though this type of work won't be highly paid, it could be a good training ground for developing your speaking skills to get into the lucrative real estate seminar business.

First-Time Home Buyer's Monthly Guide. For this publishing opportunity you create a self-help guide targeted at helping first-time home buyers. This magazine/report could offer the new buyer a host of information and resources to help them buy their first property.

This guide would probably do best covering a limited market place (several counties) because you want to provide local information and contacts; a statewide publication might be too general. The list of helpful contacts, articles, and advertisements might include FSBO ads, mortgage interest rates and local lender programs, vendor coupons, articles by hot local buyer's brokers, mortgage rate factor guide for calculating payments, articles on negotiating with sellers, Q and A about applying for a loan, advertisements for real estate services, lease purchase how-to ideas, creative finance tips, and more.

In this publication you probably will generate revenue from both report sales and advertising fees. Keep in mind, the more ads you have generally the less you can charge and vice versa. In my area one company that sells a weekly mortgage guide charges $14.95 per copy, but they are strictly content driven with no advertisements.

Weekly Mortgage Guide. This idea is very similar to the first-time home buyers guide except it focuses entirely upon mortgage rates and loan programs. This gives you an advantage and enable you open the market up to all real estate buyers. In fact, because it is also offered as a subscription service many of your buyers will be banks and mortgage brokers keeping tabs on the market. People purchase these weekly reports because they provide a one-stop resource for all lender rates and because they also provide valuable self-help information on how to get the best mortgage for the buyer's needs.

The possible information services could include interest rate reports, complete explanations of lender offerings and fees, how-to articles of getting the best rates and terms, payment factor charts, formulas to determine your maximum loan, credit repair ideas, application secrets, etc.

Since the average home buyer may be unaware of the processes that occur from start to finish in the buying process, you will want to offer a core structure that doesn't change (like the weekly interest rate reporting), but change the weekly topics to keep the readers learning so they buy the next week' or month's issue!

Publishing and selling valuable real estate information can be a winner if you are able to develop educational and helpful products that people can profit from. The problem with most products in this area is they don't deliver what they promise. If you can be different by offering truly beneficial and time saving information, this business opportunity might be yours.

Without a doubt the best resource I can offer you about the information and publishing field is Dan Poynter's books and web site. You can reach Dan at Para Publishing at 800.727.2782 or at **www.parapublishing.com.**

9

Opportunities in Real Estate Paper

In this chapter I will review and explain the top three opportunities in the real estate mortgage and paper industry. In addition, I will explain a other related ideas and the pros and the cons of offering these services as part of your business.

The three main "paper" or mortgage business ideas that we will explain are mortgage brokering, judgment recovery and delinquent paper, and discounted note investing/brokering. These three businesses each have great potential for financial success when deployed properly with a good plan.

In many cases the mortgage business is one of the most profitable businesses you can enter with very little capital since in most cases you will be using good old OPM (other people's money). We will begin our discussion with mortgage brokering and end with some of the more esoteric opportunities in judgments and private notes.

Mortgage Brokering. There are two ways to find mortgages or business loans in this world: banks and brokers. Banks are often difficult and not user-friendly, so mortgage brokers have stepped in to fill the need in helping people go through the complex process of acquiring a mortgage loan. Mortgage brokers have not just entered the marketplace; they are now responsible for placing about half of all mortgages being originated.

Mortgage brokers generally do not loan their own funds when placing a mortgage. This is one reason mortgage brokering can be such an excellent opportunity for the cash-poor entrepreneur. Mortgage brokers are service providers who use the capital of large wholesale lenders with almost unlimited pools of money. The broker acts as a mediator bringing the borrower and institution together, and gets paid an origination fee for his or her work.

The mortgage industry can be an excellent line of work for almost any type of individual since it basically is a people and paperwork business—there's no heavy lifting, no built-in gender bias, and no physical requirements other than being able to read documents and communicate on the phone!

Your earnings will vary depending on whether you are a full mortgage broker or a mortgage consultant working under a broker. It is common for aggressive and expert mortgage brokers to earn deep into the six-figure range.

If you are a detail-oriented person who likes working with numbers and paperwork, this opportunity could change your life and career.

The Business Model. Banks, saving and loans, and other institutional lenders are often difficult for people to work with. This is especially true if the consumer has special needs or any kind of non-conforming circumstances. Because of the tendency of lenders to be difficult to deal with and their complex underwriting requirements, many smart consumers use the services of a mortgage broker.

The mortgage broker's job is to act as a facilitator for both the borrower and the lender. The mortgage broker in many cases really has two clients—the lender and the borrower.

Acting as a facilitator the broker's job is to guide borrowers through the complex world of qualifying and applying for the mortgage. It also is about finding the right lender for the needs of the client. In this business one size does not fit all. There are some lenders who only specialize in residential mortgages under $300,000 with A+ credit, while other lenders specialize only in commercial deals starting at $1,000,000. Believe it or not, some lenders even specialize in poor credit borrowers called C and D lenders.

In a nutshell, the business of brokering mortgages is about qualifying borrowers to the type and terms of a mortgage they can afford, guiding them through the application, processing the application (credit investigation), overcoming approval problems, shuttling papers via fax and mail to the lender, and ultimately closing the loan. So you can clearly see that mortgage brokering is a multi-tasked process of acting as a consultant to the borrower and a document collecting processor for the lender.

Why Consumers Use Professional Mortgage Brokers. Consumers enjoy five main advantages in using a mortgage broker over a traditional bank or saving and loan: 1) Convenience; 2) Brokers fight for a client's loan more than salaried bankers will; 3) Better Selection. Brokers represent dozens of lender loan products; 4) Competency. A good broker knows far more about financing and tricks of the trade in placing loans than do bankers; 5) All-round better service.

Mortgage brokers earn fees. The main fee is the loan origination fee which is paid out of the loan proceeds at closing. In residential deals the typical fee charged is between 2 to 3 percent, of which 2 percent is usually paid to the broker. There are additional profit centers that brokers earn such as: application fees, documentation fees, mailing fees, and certification fees. In some cases the industry has earned a bad reputation for piling on what are called "junk fees" since they are pesky little fees that borrowers don't understand but end up paying because they want to get the loan closed.

Broker fees are limited by state and federal lending laws, with some states having almost no limits on fees, while other states are regulated to the hilt. The department of banking within the state you do business is the agency responsible for mortgage lending licenses and laws.

The Nature of Broker Fees. Generally speaking, the broker's fee expressed as a percentage goes down as the amount of the loan goes up. For instance, a $60,000 mortgage for a person with bad credit may command a 5 percent broker fee amounting to $3,000, whereas a $2 million mortgage may pay only a 1 percent fee amounting to $20,000.

Also, fees tend to rise, as do mortgage rates, when the borrower has shaky credit or other sub-prime lending conditions. In fact, some mortgage brokers specialize on these marginal borrowers since they command higher fees and interest rates. Many borrowers don't realize that brokers earn a higher fee from the lender when they obtain a higher rate on the mortgage. It's sort of a premium kickback (the mortgage industry does not like or use the term kick-back, so they use the term, premium).

Additional Profit Centers. In addition to regular mortgage origination fees, you as a broker can earn fees co-brokering loans. In this arrangement you split fees with other brokers who help you get a deal funded. Or, you could be the one helping another broker get their deal funded. These co-brokerage deals occur when a transaction needs either special expertise or special loan programs that you don't have or offer.

Referral fees are another source of income. These are similar to co-brokering, but generally you only provide a referral client and and do not actually do the loan packaging or processing. In this arrangement the fees are smaller since there is less work involved for the referring agent.

Whatever type of co-brokering you become involved with, make sure you get a written co-brokerage agreement signed by the other broker and yourself. This will ensure you get paid in the deal.

In order to take advantage of additional co-brokers and referral profit centers, it is important to network and meet a lot of different brokers within the industry. Caution: some folks are not ethical in terms of making sure you get paid or may steal your clients, but these people usually have a reputation that precedes them. Create a network and keep in touch with people who know.

Types of Brokerage. There are basically three types of borrowers in the marketplace: residential real estate buyers, homeowners seeking to refinance, and commercial real estate buyers. Besides these there are business owners seeking money to aid their business. All of these categories can be lucrative, but your best bet is to break into the business serving the residential and small commercial deals first. After you have logged experience and have built your lending sources you can expand into bigger commercial deals if that makes sense for you.

Business and commercial lending can often be a good source of clients since these loans typically are short-term requiring frequent refinancing by the business or property owner. In most cases, commercial loans and mortgages are 3- to 7-year notes with balloon payments due at the end of the term.

Processing the Deal. The first job a mortgage broker performs is to qualify the borrower to see how much money he or she can afford to borrow. This is based on preset lending ratios. The general ratios for residential mortgages are 28 and 36 percent. The 28 percent ratio means the borrower's mortgage payment should not exceed 28 percent of their gross income. The other ratio means that the borrower's total debt obligations should not exceed about 36 percent of their gross income. Keep in mind that some lenders are changing these ratios based on new loan programs. It will pay you to have contacts with a multitude of lenders to see which loan product best meets your client's needs.

Next, you need to get the borrower to fill out a loan application and then study it to see if any red flags or problem areas need to be handled before formally submitting the application. Along the way, you'll also be pulling the borrower's credit to get an initial reading on their credit worthiness to see which lender would be the most suitable to handle their mortgage needs.

After passing these landmarks you order a property appraisal. This is part of your job because the lender will require a real appraisal to verify the quality and value of the real estate.

Along the way there will be scores of documents that will need to be signed, faxed, and mailed to the various parties involved. Many of these documents will be employment verifications and credit inquiries. The bulk of the work is done by special people called loan processors. These folks make the mortgage business flow smoothly. In effect, they are the workhorses of the industry since much of the organizing and document management is handled by them. The broker, on the other hand, is more of the front-line contact and sales person for the mortgage transaction. The broker or loan counselor also plays the critical role of being the problem solver. In the mortgage business, loan underwriting problems are a daily occurrence!

After all of the initial paperwork and appraisal are concluded the loan package is submitted to the lender. The lender then goes about verifying and double checking your work. Once this work is completed the lender gives a final mortgage commitment or rejection. Finally, the property goes to closing and the mortgage broker concludes the process by getting the appropriate papers signed, notarized, and overnight mailed to the lender. At closing, the broker gets his check and can close the file.

License Requirements and Laws. In most states you will need to be licensed in order to operate a mortgage brokerage business. As mentioned earlier, this is regulated by the Department of Banking within a given state.

Some states may require you to be bonded and have a certain level of net worth or assets before you are issued a license. This requirement is meant to keep charlatans and unethical people out of the business or at least make them put their assets up in a bond arrangement to increase the likelihood of proper performance. If your state requires a high net worth you may want to consult with an attorney who regularly represents mortgage brokers to see what possible legal loopholes or creative ways to get around this problems. Often the best advice comes from asking other brokers outside your trading area. Check with local or state mortgage broker associations for the name of an attorney who knows the industry.

You will want to ask department of banking to send you their mortgage broker's application and applicable legal regulations to be a mortgage consultant.

There are a host of other laws that need to be complied with also. For example, you will need to become familiar with The RESPA Act, Fair Credit Reporting Act, Truth-in-Lending, and Equal Credit Opportunity Act. Your best course of action is to join a mortgage brokers association to help you navigate through the legal requirements and red tape. The National Association of Mortgage Brokers would make a good start **www.namb.com,** or 703.610.9009.

Licensing Tip. Since this business requires a license in most states, you may want to first begin working under a licensed broker before you jump into this game without knowledge or capital. In many cases, you can work as an agent or mortgage consultant under the supervision of a broker, without needing a license yourself. In any event, research your state guidelines before doing anything.

If you decide to work as a "business within a business" as an agent for a mortgage company, you will obtain a great deal of training and business ideas before you venture out on your own. Another advantage of working under another mortgage company is the you will gain the experience some choosy lenders require. Some lenders require two years of brokering experience before allowing you to place loans on your own. (Whatever you do, be careful in signing restrictive covenants that will keep you from starting your own business or competing in the same market.)

Also, if you decide to broker loans make sure you do not sign any franchise deals or territorial restrictions by companies offering you expensive training or a "system." You don't need a franchise to do this business because mortgage lenders are dying to have you help them place loans.

Tools, Skills and Education. One of the great things about this opportunity is you only need a few general business tools that don't require a lot of capital to buy. The basic starter tools are: cell phone, fax, computer, a dba ("doing business as") company name, mortgage lending software program, marketing brochures, cards, lender relationships, and a financial calculator.

One tool you should acquire as soon as possible is a laptop computer. A laptop system will enable you to meet clients and take their mortgage applications in their home and at their jobs. Experienced brokers say this is their most important tool.

The Financial Calculator. As a mortgage broker you will need to own a good financial calculator and know the basics of operating it. There are several models on the market. Texas Instruments is my preference since it is powerful and easy to operate. Hewlett-Packard models are also popular, but in my opinion are a bit more complicated to operate. Whatever model you choose, don't worry about knowing all of the esoteric calculations that these machines will perform since in most cases you will just be figuring monthly payment calculations. Good financial calculators can be purchased from office supply stores.

You will need many forms and documents in your mortgage business, and to provide them you'll benefit from having a mortgage lending software program. I recommend The Loan Officers Store by Hark and Associates in Claremore, Oklahoma. You can call them at 800.456.1001.

You need a basic foundation of talents and abilities if you want to prosper in this business. If you are detail oriented, organized, a problem solver, a people person, and can work under deadline pressure, you meet the five basic requirements.

In your mortgage business you will spend a lot of time paying attention to detail, organizing documents and files, handling frustrating roadblocks and problems, and dealing with all types of people. If you have a major shortcomings in one or more of these areas, this opportunity may not be suitable for you.

This is a simple business. You don't need any special degrees or college training. But if you want to make a lot of money you will need to constantly add to your knowledge and understanding of the business. The best mortgage brokers know all of the tricks of the trade. They accomplish this by attending as many conventions, seminars, and courses as they can afford. In addition, network with other brokers in the field since these contacts will provide a lot of insider knowledge and advice. You can pick up some good training manuals and books from The Loan Officers Store.

Dress Tools. Since you will be meeting one-on-one with a wide range of people, you will want quality business attire to create the image you want. You want to look like a professional. This doesn't mean you'll always be wearing a three-piece suit, but you should own some classy clothing. Khaki pants with a button-down dress shirt and tie, outfitted with a sport jacket and dress shoes should fill the bill. Woman should wear appropriate business attire.

Building Relationships With Lenders. To develop

a profitable mortgage brokerage business you need to sign up with lenders so you can offer their loan products to your clients. Each lender has specialty loan products. If you only represent one or two lenders you will have problems placing many of the loan applications that come across your desk.

Think of the mortgage lenders you represent the same way that a retail merchant looks at brand name products. The more products retailers carry or have access to, the more business they can do.

Setting up your business relationship with lenders begins by contacting the wholesale loan division of the lender and getting a broker's packet. This packet will contain an application and other details about the types of loans they make and the states where they are licensed to loan money. Once you are approved, you will be an independent contractor (broker) for the lender and able to sell mortgages to them.

To find lenders for your business, start by doing research on the Internet. Another option is to purchase a lenders' directory that will give a complete rundown of various lenders across the nation. These directories list lenders by state, region, loan product, and loan amounts. You can find a company that sells a lenders directory at **www.wholesaleaccess.com** or 410.772.1161. Financial newspapers and magazines such as *Investor's Business Daily* and *The Wall Street Journal* may also prove useful in locating lenders. Many of the big lenders may not look like banks. Commercial lenders are often insurance companies, pension funds, trusts, venture capital lenders, commercial lenders such as G.E. Capital and mega banks like CitiBank.

Marketing Strategy. I recommend learning the residential and small commercial lending business first. Try to represent some sub-prime lenders along with some A+ credit lenders such as FNMA (Federal National Mortgage Association, or "Fanny May"). If you choose to represent only squeaky-clean borrowers you may have trouble, since these borrowers can go to any bank or mortgage company for a loan. Everyone wants these easy deals. You may need to cut your teeth by helping marginal borrowers first.

Like any of the businesses described in this book I would make a multi-front marketing attack. This would include high-quality cards, brochures, and stationery. Next, I would run strategically placed ads with clear, client-driven ad copy. Along with these tactics I would get out of the office and meet as many people as I could. A lot of this is like the old story about throwing mud on the wall—throw enough mud and some will stick on the wall. Get out and network.

Real estate agents and brokers are another source of deals, but you need to know that many brokers have added in-house mortgage companies as a profit center and a way of gaining more control over the transaction. Try to carry loan products that fill a niche that isn't being filled by in-house mortgage companies. Additionally, try to out perform in-house mortgage companies with your knowledge and speed of service.

Hot Profit Tip: Real Estate agents all have a support teams that help them close transactions. These team players are mortgage brokers, appraisers, home inspectors, repair people, and title companies. One of your critical jobs will be to become a team player for as many realtors as possible. This type of referral business is a gold mine because once it is established you will have a steady flow of clients. The key is to give excellent service and not take their referrals for granted.

Build your database with all of the contacts you meet. Fax and mail as many compelling, client-centered marketing messages as you can. Build a voice mail database as well. Send your database prospects a voicemail message on a monthly basis and remind them to call you if they have need the specific mortgage services you offer. You can also remind these same folks that you will help them with any problems or questions they might have. In business, if you are out of sight, you are out of mind. Make frequent contacts with your database contacts. Rather than making your ads and direct mail pieces strict sales copy, consider wrapping the ad around informative tips or strategies for obtaining financing. This will help make your ads stand out from among the many useless ads that bombard people on a daily basis.

Shotgun as many newspaper classified ads as you can comfortably afford. In other words, avoid the largest papers since their classifieds are often expensive and not read. Instead, try running in the smaller newspapers where people make a regular habit of reading the classifieds.

After you have some experience, create your unique marketing message. Once formulated, hammer the same message home in all of your ads. Avoid being another me-too.

Renter Prospects. Another source of loan prospects are tenants, people who rent rather than own their living space. You could create a direct mail letter and have a professional database mailing company do a mass mailing to a specific demographic profile of renters in your marketplace. Your letter could be an information piece showing tenants how easy it is to buy a home with the many first-time home buyer programs you offer. It could also explain the many tax advantages of buying over renting.

The Internet Challenge. Many mortgage brokers have begun to feel the effect of the Internet on their business. Although the net has been mostly an information tool for sellers of durable goods items (appliances, furniture, etc.), it has been very effective in selling intangible products and services like stock trading and financial services. You must recognize this fact and get on board whether you want to or like the idea or not.

The solution to beating the net brokers is superior service. No one likes talking to someone over email when it comes to a giant purchase or commitment (The typical mortgage deal involves well over $300,000 when you factor in the interest). You are a real person who can be reached by picking up the phone. You also can offer personal advice to the borrower's problems which they will never get from some "internet" broker.

Advertising Research. I hesitate to offer this tip since so many advertisements are boring with company-centered rather than client-centered messages that proclaim the benefits of doing business with the advertiser. But I will anyway. Pick up newspapers, real estate freebie books, phone books, flyers, business cards, and sales letters from mortgage brokers and banks from your state and local area. Also collect advertisements and publications whenever you travel. These ads will serve as a resource for your own marketing and idea generation.

Cut out the mortgage broker ads and save them for your marketing research. Next, study these ads to see which ones are the most attention getting and client centered. What headlines are being used? What benefit-laden copy is being used? Are there special promotions, coupons, or discounts being used? What are the strengths and weakness of the different ads? Do you see any gaping holes in products or services not being offered that you could fulfill?

The bottom line is to gather as much information as possible from as many different lenders and brokers in your region of the country. Clearly, you are not doing this because you want to steal somebody's advertisements, but to get as many ideas and marketing models from which to develop your own client-centered sales and marketing materials!

Additional Resource and Contacts. I am a big believer in joining state and national associations for whatever trade or business you are in. These groups provide workshops and conventions that will help you keep your skills and trade intelligence sharp and updated. You will also meet a lot of good contacts who will share insider knowledge and ideas they are using in their business. One such organization you might consider joining is The National Association of Mortgage Brokers, **www.namb.com,** or 703.610.9009. For great reporting on the mortgage industry try **www.inman.com.**

The Judgment Recovery Business. The judgment recovery business is a unique opportunity you can start and operate using very little of their own capital. In fact, about $1,000 is all that one would really need to get involved. This opportunity can easily be worked as a part-time venture while you conduct another business or retain your current job.

The judgment recovery business was virtually unheard of ten or fifteen years ago. Back then only a few "underground" judgment buyers existed. Today, the business is still in its infancy with plenty of potential to grow. This business is not for everyone, but it presents a huge, untapped potential for those individuals willing to work it.

What exactly is a judgment recovery business? First, a judgment, or more precisely, a judicial judgment, is a court order or declaration that a party to a civil lawsuit owes a specific amount of money to another party. In most cases, the party being awarded the money is the plaintiff, and the party owing the money is the defendant. The judgment is the legal document from the court that tells the parties who won and who lost and how much money is owed as a result.

People are awarded judicial money judgments every day in America, but few of them end up getting their money. This is where the judgment recovery business comes into play. In this opportunity you help judgment holders recover at least some of their hard won money while the rest goes to you.

Judgment recovery may not sound like a real estate business, but I have included it in this book for two reasons. First, many of the best judgment deals you will find will be those where the judgment lien is secured by real estate. In these situations a good understanding of real estate law will help tremendously. My second reason for including this opportunity in this real estate book is because most of the folks that I know in the judgment business are also real estate investors. This is because judgments are essentially a "paper" (debt instrument) business, and a lot of real estate investors also wheel and deal in paper. Furthermore, the judgment business is an ideal part-time business which many investors like doing to supplement their investing income. After all, investors collect rents and note payments, so why not collect judgment payments?

The Business Model. Before we get into the actual judgment recovery business, let me explain how and why there is a need for this business. But first we need to look a little more closely at judgments.

In the typical case one party files a lawsuit against another. This could be for a multitude of reasons: landlord/tenant issues, nonpayment of money owed from a personal loan, unpaid services rendered, breach of contract, etc. The important thing to know is one party sued another party for money.

In these cases the judge will hear the matter and make a decision as to the merits of the claims and who owes who what. This decision is the judgment. In those cases where money is involved, the judgment is a money judgment. There are situations where the decision or judgment happens automatically. These judgments are default judgments, where the defendant does not respond to the suit and loses out of default.

The judgment is not a "done deal" until the statutory appeals period expires. In most cases, the losing party has about 30 days to appeal the court's decision. If the losing party does not appeal the decision in the required time period, the judgment becomes a lock-tight set of financial handcuffs around the debtor's wrists. This is where things become interesting. Most amateur creditors believe that the debtor (the one who owes the money in the judgment) will automatically pay up. That is a joke. Probably 90 percent of these judgments never get paid. The problem for the judgment holder (creditor) is that additional court actions are required to force the debtor to pay. This is where the process often stops for most people who have won a judgment in a court of law.

Let me back up just for a moment and consider the state of mind and flow of events involved in the typical court judgment scenario. The process is an emotionally charged experience for the person who filed the lawsuit (the plaintiff). Usually the issue is that the plaintiff was owed money that was not paid. The plaintiff has tried talking and negotiating and has made several attempts to collect the money or resolve whatever the problem may have been. In exasperation, the plaintiff feels there is no other choice but to take the debtor to court.

The plaintiff has to pay cold cash (usually about $80) to file the suit. It is infuriating to spend more money in an attempt to resolve the problem. Then it's court day. The plaintiff wins! "Yes," the person thinks, "now I'll get paid what I'm due!" After a few months the realization sinks in that this guy isn't paying them anything. "Hey, hey, this isn't fair," the person says. "I won in court, but this guy still isn't paying me!"

The next step is a visit to the local small claims court to ask why the payment has not been made. The clerk informs the plaintiff that additional court costs and filing fees are required in order to collect. In addition, they may need an attorney since the court does not give legal advice as to how the process works.

There are no hard statistics, but nine out of ten amateur creditors quit at this point. They are emotionally upset and feel too agitated to keep throwing good money after bad. They don't want to pay a lawyer $150 per hour to pursue the claim and throw more good money after bad.

Judgment Recovery Specialist to the Rescue. About a year after the above situation the judgment holder gets a letter from a company that calls themselves "Judgment Recovery Specialists." In the letter the company offers to buy the judgment through an assignment of interest process that will result in payment to the person owed. This letter is a surprise out of left field for the winner of the judgment. By now he or she has considered the judgment to be a worthless piece of paper. Without hesitation, the judgment holder calls the Recovery Specialist, thinking "What have I got to lose?"

The JRS explains the arrangement, and the judgment holder becomes a judgment seller. Now the judgment recovery specialist controls the judgment, and things become interesting.

The JRS writes a firm and business-like letter to the debtor explaining they have purchased the judgment from the judgment holder and they are now the new holder of the lien. They also explain that they are judgment recovery specialists and that the entire process will be a lot easier if the debtor cooperates. In fact, as a good faith gesture, JRS offers to work out an affordable payment plan or consider waiving all back interest and court costs if they pay the amount owed now.

At this juncture the debtor must decide whether they want to tangle with these experts or just make some arrangements to finally pay what they owe. In many cases they will pay what they rightfully owe.

In cases where the debtor chooses not to pay, the judgment recovery specialist still has several methods to collect the judgment. The specialist can continue a letter campaign or begin the process of foreclosing against the debtor's real or personal property such as bank accounts, stocks, furniture, cars, antiques, wages etc.). At this point the debtor knows the game is over—they have to pay.

The Nature of Judgments.
In many ways a judgment is like a note. It yields an interest rate based on state law. It accrues interest until it is paid. It is assignable (transferable); therefore, it can be sold or traded. It is a general lien against most real or personal property. The current holder—the buyer—has all of the rights vested in the original holder. There is a time limit, although in most states these rights are good for 10 to 20 years. **Note:** even with time limits. judgments can usually be renewed for another term.

Two Big Profit Opportunities. The first opportunity is to buy judgments outright for cash. Why would anyone want to buy a judgment for cash when the last guy had such a terrible time trying to get paid? Valid question. The answer is you can buy these judgments at extremely low prices. The going cash price for judgments is from 10 to 30 cents on the dollar! Did you get that? You can buy these judgments for pennies on the dollar. The next question is why would people sell their rights to the money owed them for so little? That's an easy one: if they don't sell to you they won't get anything.

People will sell a $2,000 judgment for $200. That's only 10 cents on the dollar, but again, they most likely won't collect any money if they keep it. That is the secret. Do you see the profit potential here? That is a potential $1,800 profit! I like these kinds of yields, don't you? Do you see how you could buy $50,000 worth of judgment paper for about $5,000?

> **Hot Profit Tip:** There's another way of operating this judgment buying business. In many ways this is even better since this method requires almost no cash. This approach is to buy the judgment on a contingency type arrangement where you don't pay anything up front for the judgment. What you do is make a deal with the judgment holder that you will split the money with them as you collect it. This is truly win-win. They get a higher price, and you have less risk. If the note is uncollectable, you have no financial loss except your time. Your return on investment on this arrangement is infinite because you have no money in the deal!

The Dirty Little Secret About Judgments. The secret is you not only are buying a piece of paper worth 5 to 10 times what you are paying, but you also are entitled to all of the accrued interest that the judgment has earned. In most states this amounts to 6 to 9 percent, but compounding is usually not allowed. A $2,000 judgment over a handful of years could net an additional $200 to $300 in accumulated interest.

The Easy Part and The Hard Part. The easy part of this business is finding clients willing to sell to you. Most will take your offer, especially the offer to split. The challenging part is deciding which judgment cases to buy and then going about collecting your money.

The Recovery Process: Getting Paid. You are only limited by your creativity in coming up with ways to collect the money due. Following are four collection ideas, but if you can think of other ideas don't hesitate to try them—as long as they are within the bounds of your state's collection laws.

The Interest and Court Cost Discount Offer. Your first offer with the debtor will probably be a letter you send explaining that you now own the judgment and they must pay you. Your letter makes an initial "goodwill" offer of waiving all accumulated interest costs on the judgment. If the court costs weren't too high from the initial court hearings you might consider waiving these also. There's a good chance they won't bite at this offer unless their situation has changed dramatically since the original judgment. However, some judgment debtors who will be intimidated by the judgment recovery specialist and will pay off quickly.

The Payment Plan Offer. This is perhaps the most effective way of collecting judgments since you offer a payment plan for the judgment debtor. With this technique, you send a letter (probably your second or third in a series of attempts) stating that your company will work out an affordable payment plan to enable the debtor to pay. The monthly payment plan works nicely because getting some money is better than getting nothing. Even if the debtor defaults after six or eight months at least you got a partial payment. For example, let's say you collect $700 over eight months and then the debtor skips town. Isn't $700 better than nothing? It is especially good when you are the one who made the contingency arrangement with the judgment seller.

The Get Tough Approach. For some debtors nothing will work but a get-tough approach. After all, these people have used non-response and stall techniques to evade paying their bills in the past.

"Getting tough" means using the legal system to get your money. These methods will involve some additional costs but are sometimes needed to show the debtor you are serious about being paid and know how to enforce your lien.

There are several legal options available. (1) Seize bank accounts. (2) Garnish wages using wage attachment. (3) Levy (execute) on personal property. (4) Force the sale of real estate (sheriff sale).

Presenting these options in a letter will be very therapeutic in showing the judgment debtor that you are a recovery professional and mean business. After you begin these techniques you may want to offer a final repayment plan option. If no response is forthcoming, you will have to decide whether or not to follow through with the more serious legal actions of wage attachment or levying their property.

The Buy and Wait Approach. Some patient judgment buyers follow the buy and wait technique when real estate is involved. The basic strategy is to buy the judgment (on a contingency or severe discount cash basis) and hold the judgment as a lien against the real estate until it either gets paid off in a future sale or is refinanced. You can use this method only if the debtor owns real estate. You must make sure that your lien is "clouding" the title. A knowledge of state lien laws will help you understand when a judgment does and does not lien the property.

This method may not sound so good, but it can work. Let's say you buy a $2,500 judgment for $300, which is secured by real estate, the debtor's home. Let's also say that the judgment is three years old. It has probably accrued about $300 in interest by now. The lien is worth $2,800. Let's assume it four more years until the debtor sells the home. At that time your lien will be paid in order for the title to clear and the sale to be finalized. By now the amount needed to pay you off will probably be around $3100. Now in my book, buying a note for $300 cash, which yields over $3,000 in four years, isn't too shabby.

Hot Profit Tip: Being a creditor, you can take a few steps and get the judgment listed on the debtor's credit report, thereby making it virtually impossible to borrow money from mortgage lenders. If the debtor attempts to buy a house in the future, they will have to pay off the judgment to get their mortgage approved. Virtually no mortgage company will lend money to someone with an unpaid judgment against their name.

Stay In the Payment Loop. Once you start applying pressure to these folks to pay, there is a chance the person will attempt to cut a deal with the original judgment holder. When you buy the judgment be sure to make it clear that payments must not be made to the creditor and if payments are made they must be turned over to you—unless, of course, you have agreed to split the proceeds.

Tools, Knowledge, and Skills. The tools required to operate this venture are the typical tools used in any small business: a computer, telephone, business name, post office box (for privacy and personal protection), filing cabinets (lots of files in this business), on-line credit bureau access, and word-processing software for drafting the letters you will be writing. A financial calculator is another tool you will need to calculate interest and yields. (The fact that this business requires minimal tools or cash is one of its the best aspects.)

The knowledge needed to become a judgment recovery specialist may sound intimidating, but everything you need to know is available by hitting the books and using a little trial-and-error learning. In fact, a good way to learn fast is by reading case files at the courthouse and modeling the paperwork to use for your cases.

Buy a good legal dictionary to help you understand the legalese. Next, you will need a copy of your state's rules of civil procedure. This rulebook is updated annually and gives the rules and regulation for various court procedures. Another suggestion is to acquire legal practice manuals written by attorneys for other attorneys. Seek a judgment manual and a general collections manual. Most law libraries have these. Important: make sure it is a state-specific manual that provides the detailed answers you need! Lastly, acquire a few books on federal collection laws and regulations.

This business can be operated by folks with a wide range of skills. The main personal quality you need is a high level of persistence. You will also need expertise in using computers and working with on-line date bases. Beyond that you won't need any special background, degrees, or education to succeed in this business.

Ethics and Judgment Recovery. As I stated in the beginning, the judgment recovery business is not for everyone. You may not feel comfortable enforcing judgment liens. I do believe you can be a high-integrity person and still make a living in this business. After all, you are dealing with a legal document created by a court where a professional (judge) has determined that the money is owed.

There may be a few cases where you truly wouldn't feel comfortable collecting the money if, for example, the debtor has a life-threatening illness or is facing some other tragic circumstance. In these rare circumstances you can make a case-by-case decision.

Marketing Strategy. Two main marketing tasks need to be done in this business: finding the judgment holders and finding the judgment debtors. In this section I want to offer a few ideas on finding good quality judgment liens to purchase.

The first way is to run small classified ads in newspapers around the counties where you would like to buy judgments. Generally the smaller papers, especially the free penny pincher or thrifty nickel type papers work best. The ads should be something like this:

Cash For Judgments: If you hold a judgment, we will buy that judgment for cash: call 555-7722.

We Buy Judgments: Fast cash today call: 555-7722

Can't Collect Your Judgment? Call for free message 24hrs: 555-7722.

Perhaps the best strategy for finding prospective judgment holders is to go down to the local small claims court and look at the files.

The method of indexing and filing judgments changes from county to county, but generally case files, especially for small claims court are open to the public. Usually there is an index book showing names, dates, and docket number. It is the docket number that you will need to have the clerk pull the file. In some offices the files may be accessible without a clerk's assistance. In any event, if a clerk ever gives you a problem ask to speak to a supervisor and or ask them to show you the specific state law showing the files are off limits. As a rule these files and other public records are accessible based on various freedom of information and public access laws.

After you do your research and gather your names from the courthouse you can mail the judgment holders a letter explaining that you have several arrangements where you buy judgments. In a good number of cases, you should at least receive a call back from the holder of the judgment.

Another way of finding judgments is to send flyers or letters to accountants, attorneys, and financial planners explaining the unique service you offer. This group of business people are the ones most likely to have clients who hold judgments. Try marketing to this database mailing list about four times a year. You will usually find your response rate increasing the more you market to the list.

The Top 3 Questions About Judgment Recovery. (1). Isn't there a lot of competition from lawyers in this business? No there isn't, because most lawyers have other specialties and bigger fish to fry—especially when you deal in the smaller judgments of $1,000 to $7,000. (2) Do I need a collection agency license to buy judgments? Generally you do not because you are not a collection agency, but an owner of the judgment who took an assignment of the lien. (3) Do I have to get in my car and physically track people down and pound on their door to collect money? No, because almost all of your research and skip tracing will be done with a computer and various on-line credit bureaus.

Hot Profit Tip: In almost all cases the person's current address will show up on their credit report. As the judgment owner, you are a formal creditor and are therefore allowed to check the debtor's credit report (of course, check all appropriate laws and get basic legal counsel). Furthermore, you will be using the telephone, letters, and the small claims court system to handle most of your collection work.

Pitfalls and Cautions. Of course any business opportunity has problems and legal pitfalls to avoid. In print anything sounds easy. This can be an excellent part-time or full-time venture, but it requires getting off your duff and making it happen. It also requires time and effort researching and checking various laws to make sure that all of your collection methods are legal.

Even though you are not a collection agency, you need to comply with fair debt collection laws. For example, you cannot call debtors before 8 a.m. or after 9 p.m. (their time zone, not yours). Do not use illegal debt collection techniques; debt collection regulations are covered by the Fair Debt Collection Act.

Another big pitfall is buying judgments against a debtor who has filed for bankruptcy protection. In many but not all of such cases, the judgments are not pursuable. This is because most unsecured debts get wiped out in bankruptcy proceedings. This shouldn't be a problem unless you actually have written a check for the judgment rather than setting up a contingency arrangement. In many cases bankruptcy information will appear on their credit report and on other on-line credit databases.

Another problem in the judgment business is dealing with folks who are continually on the run. I hesitate to label anyone as a hard-core deadbeat, but the facts are that a small percentage of folks are nomadic and have virtually made a business out of not paying their bills. The "skippers" can be tough to deal with since they use fake names and phony addresses. If you're in the business for any amount of time, you will learn to spot them. There are ways of handling people who have moved out of state. The Judicial Judgment Collections Association is a nationwide network of judgment recovery specialists who will partner with you on these deals if they are in their region. Find out more at www.jjca.org.

Additional Profit Centers. As mentioned earlier this type of business works very well as a supplemental or complimentary business. My preference in finding additional profit centers is to find related products or services that will work with the main business without distraction.

This judgment business could easily work in tandem with a tenant screening service or eviction service since both of these services involve knowledge of credit and debt laws. Property investors like this business because it provides additional cash flow just as note payments or rents do. In some cases, investors also get good leads on distressed properties for sale by judgment debtors. **Note:** many distressed property buyers have a good knowledge of lien and foreclosure law, which certainly helps when dealing with judgments.

Another related business that would work nicely with the judgment business would be a collection agency. The collection agency business can be highly lucrative; it also uses many of the same tools and collection methods that are used in judgment recovery. If you are interested in the collection agency business consider contacting American Collectors Association, Inc., 952.926.6547.

The judgment business also works well with the "paper" businesses discussed in this book. buy/sell installment house sellers, mortgage brokers, discounted note investors, and mobile home paper investors could use the judgment business as an ancillary business opportunity.

Resources and Additional Contacts. A great resource for judgment buyers is the Judicial Judgment Collectors' Association (JJCA)—web address **www.jjca.org.** Without a doubt I believe this is one of the most important organizations to join if you get into the judgment recovery business. Their web site has a special "members only" section which is a gold mine of resources and information. They also hold educational conferences and workshops which are great for getting the technical knowledge and networking contacts you will need. Groups like this are what you need to get educated. There is no need to pay $5,000 for a seminar to learn this business.

Opportunities in Discounted Mortgages. In this section we will review and explain, two high-profit opportunities in discounted mortgages. These opportunities are the major ones in the discounted mortgage business, although there are smaller niche markets within the cash flow industry that we will briefly review.

I will first provide a brief explanation of the discounted note and mortgage industry, and then we will get into some advanced money-making ideas which you should find fascinating. Although there are many questions you need to ask yourself before getting involved in this business, I believe that many of the general concepts of analyzing and discounting income streams can be valuable and instructive to any entrepreneur. You should read this section of the book even if you never want to personally buy mortgage notes.

The first opportunity we will review is buying notes and other debt instruments for your personal account. In other words—investing in discounted notes. The second opportunity is buying and selling discounted mortgages as a business. In other words—note brokerage.

There is a case to be made for both note investing and note brokerage. I will explain the pros and cons of each opportunity. In many cases investors will do best by working in both note investing and note brokerage.

What Are Discounted Mortgages? Before we get too deeply into this section let me state that I use the terms "discounted mortgages," "notes," "debt instruments," "trust deeds," and "income streams," to designate the same thing: cash flow from a real estate financing contract in which one party makes payments to another for a debt owed. These are all types of owner financing debt instruments.

Although there are dozens of different financing contracts used in real estate (notes, installment contracts, lease purchase, second mortgages, etc.) we will use a standard note and mortgage as the typical debt instrument since they are the easiest to understand.

In one respect there really isn't such a thing as a discounted mortgage. There are just mortgages where people sell them for less than the face value (principal balance) on the document. In most cases when we say "discounted mortgage," we mean a "private mortgage," or, more precisely, an "owner financed mortgage."

In most real estate transactions across North America people go to formal lending institutions for the money needed to buy real estate. In some cases sellers hold the mortgage or "paper" for the buyer by receiving monthly payments for all or part of the purchase price. In these situations, a note and mortgage (or trust deed) are signed by the buyer to the seller for the unpaid portion of the real estate purchase. A basic term for this is "owner financing."

These notes, secured by mortgages, become a valuable asset for note holders because they are income streams. Thirty or forty years ago there wasn't much of a market for these private party notes, but today, there are several loosely organized markets for these notes. Private investors and institutions will buy these notes for cash.

In many cases, sellers cannot sell their property for cash but can sell with owner financing and then sell the note to an investor for cash. In other cases sellers never plan to sell the note, but because of certain circumstances decide to liquidate the note, choosing a lump-sum cash payment over long-term monthly payments.

Why Notes Are Discounted. Without going into a long dissertation on the time value of money and opportunity cost theories, let me offer you a few reasons why notes are discounted.

In financial markets around the world debt instruments are bought and sold in packages for hundreds of millions of dollars. The various packages or blocks of notes are rarely bought for the face value of the documents. They are either sold at a discount or a premium depending on interest rates, risk, term, quality of collateral, credit rating of debtors, etc. It boils down to risk and rate of return analysis.

Owner-financed mortgages are also bought and sold. In almost all cases these mortgages are sold at a discount because this smaller marketplace is more disorganized and less structured than the big-time lending world. Furthermore, these mortgages can be riskier than ones underwritten with traditional banking rules and qualifying standards. Many privately held notes are what the banking industry calls "Non-Conforming," meaning they don't meet standard lending standards. While this can mean more risk, in many cases the risk is manageable by knowledgeable note buyers. Again, it boils down to a more closed and disorganized market and more risk factors. Because of these factors, private party notes are sold at hefty discounts that create handsome opportunities for investors.

Buying Mortgage Paper for Personal Investment.

Buying discounted mortgage notes can be a unique opportunity for investors to earn high yields without a lot of on-going management needed to service the investment. In most cases, buying paper requires far less day-to-day management then buying rental property or other real estate. Yields of 18, 20 and 25 percent are typical in the discounted note business, which is why many investors are attracted to it. In fact, many investors are earning even higher returns by rescheduling and "remodeling" notes.

The Business Model.

In paper investments, the paper buyer is looking to find motivated note holders who for whatever reason want to convert the payments they are receiving into cash. The investor then trades his cash for the note, which provides a superior yield over competing investment vehicles. After coming to an agreement on the price of the note, the note holder transfers (assigns) the note to the note buyer. Next, the new note holder will begin receiving the payments from the real estate buyer/debtor.

As mentioned earlier these notes are almost always discounted (sold for less than the actual principal balance). For example, a private party mortgage might have a $20,000 balance written with a 9 percent interest rate. If the investor buys this note with a discounted price of $16,000, the yield will shoot up much higher than the stated interest rate on the note. The discount combined with the interest rate, create a blended rate, which is the overall yield (discount and interest) on the investment.

Buy and hold paper investors are looking to build a portfolio of high yield notes. Building a portfolio can be done using either your own cash or using leverage. In most cases, paper investors use lines of credit or private lender's money to buy notes, since this business by nature is very cash intensive. I will show you examples of using your own funds and using OPM.

The number one tool used by paper buyers is the financial calculator. I won't take up valuable space here to explain how to operate one, but I can give you a basic review of what income streams look like.

A typical income stream is composed of four factors or charting categories. These are the number of payments, amount financed, interest rate, and monthly payments. A financial calculator has these categories as its keys.

N % PMT PV (present value—loan amount)

A typical $20,000 note at 10 percent for 10 years would like this:

120 (months)   0.83 $264 $20,000

When an investor buys one of these notes he does not offer face value or full price for the note. The investor's cash is too valuable to buy into a note at only a 10 percent yield. Instead, a discounted offer is made based on various risk and note grading factors. In most cases, an 18 percent yield or greater is desired. Keep in mind, the note buyer should NOT discuss his desired yield to the note seller. Everything is kept in terms of dollars. Sellers will not understand yield and risk analysis; besides, they will think you're greedy if you tell them you need a double digit yield.

In order to determine how much to pay for the note in order to achieve a desired yield we need a financial calculator. We first enter into the machine all of the known data. Let's use the above figures again. We have a $20,000 note at 10 percent interest for 120 months with payments of $264 per month. With this data entered into the calculator we next punch in the new yield we want into the interest category button where we previously had entered 10 percent. We enter 18 percent, or more precisely 1.5 percent, the monthly rate for an 18 percent annual rate. We then ask the machine how much to pay in order to get our new higher yield. Remember in the calculator's brain is all of the original data, and the machine will discount

cerned. Properly purchased, high quality notes are desirable and can be quite lucrative.

The only negative aspect of note investing is that you can run out of capital relatively quickly—unless, of course, you find lenders willing to lend you money to buy notes. I have seen some successful note investors use private lenders, who tend to be more flexible than banks. If you can learn where to find capital to buy these notes you can make a lot of money.

The other possible negative is for extremely young investors. Notes don't appreciate like real estate does, although I know many note aficionados would argue this point (due to compound interest). I personally like note investing for older investors who don't have the time or enthusiasm for rental properties. But this is my personal preference, and I'll admit that skilled note buyers do make high returns ranging from 20 to 40 percent annually, and its hard to argue with those kind of rates.

If you are a younger paper buyer I'd like to see you purchase these investments inside tax sheltered plans such as self-directed IRAs. A few companies handle the administration of these. One such company is Mid Ohio Securities at **www.midoh.com** or 440.323.5491.

Licensing Issues. As a general rule you do not need a license to buy notes into your investment portfolio. In most cases investors are considered just that—investors—not mortgage lenders or agents.

Resources and Contacts. A good primer that provides a lot of details, sample offers, contracts and forms for the note business is *Making Money Trading Mortgages* by author Delbert Ashby. You can contact him at: The Wellington Company, 2579 Rutland Rd., Davidsonville, MD, 21035 or email him at money-man@moneypatch.com.

Another resource is a monthly journal about the cash flow industry called the *Paper Source* and edited by Bill Mencarow, an authority in the note industry. *The Paper Source* also has conferences, seminars, and trade shows. Be sure to visit their web site at **www.papersourceonline.com** for excellent information and news about notes.

Another important resource is *NoteWorthy Newsletter*, a key publication within the note business. *NoteWorthy's* editor, Jon Richards, is a respected authority on debt instruments. They, too, hold conferences, seminars, and workshops on the cash flow industry. Their web address is **www.noteworthyusa.com,** or you can call them at 800.487.1864.

Discounted Note Brokering Opportunities. In

the last section we focused on buying discounted paper as an investment. In this section we will explore buying and selling notes as a business opportunity. The term for this is note brokering or cash flow brokering.

Many of the same principles for buying and holding notes apply to discount note brokering. Even if you lack interest or capital to buy notes for your portfolio, I highly recommend you study the prior chapter carefully, since the general concepts and ideas work in both the investment and brokerage markets.

In the past ten or fifteen years we have seen a lot of changes in the discounted note business. In the past there was very little consumer or real estate industry knowledge of the note buying field. Only a few elite investors knew that owner financed notes could even be bought and sold—and these few investors had a wide-open market to themselves. This has all changed with a throng of new note brokers coming and going through the business. Today the business is more competitive than ever, but there are also more opportunities now than ever before.

If you are going to survive and even prosper in the note business today, you must be more than a note broker. You must be a diversified cash flow broker who is able to broker more than just mortgage notes.

This business originally was just about buying real estate notes. Today, innovative brokers are buying and selling all kinds of income streams. If it consists of a series of payments, it is brokerable. The key is to understand brokerable cash flows and have relationships with the institutional buyers to whom you will broker your notes.

Assignability. Almost all income streams are brokerable

because they are, in essence, written contracts, and contracts, according to common law, are assignable. Just as you can sell any type of personal property for cash, you can also sell contractual rights for a cash payment. unless the contract forbids assignment. These intangible contract rights are transferred with an assignment contract. An assignment contract is like a bill of sale, which both sells and transfers ownership in the subject contract to the new owner.

Types of Income Streams Being Bought and Sold: Mortgages, Installment Land Contracts, Judgments, Business Notes, Insurance Annuities, Lease Payments, Mobile Home Notes, Accounts Receivables, Medical Notes, Defaulted Notes, Car Paper, Cellular Tower Lease Payments, Land Leases, Lottery Winnings, structured legal settlements, and more.

This business has come along way since the early days of just brokering house notes! Since this business is competitive, you need to be ready to deal in several types of cash flows. This means having multiple outlets for selling your notes and cash flow instruments.

Even though this is a competitive business, there still are a number of advantages of this type of business opportunity. It can be easily operated from a small home office since a good deal of the work is done using phone, fax, computer, and FedEx. The business, like note investing, is very portable since most of the work is done by phone, fax, and the post office. As a friend of mine says, "All I need is my laptop, my phone, and my post office box!"

You don't need much cash or capital since you will be selling cash flow contracts to institutions and corporations who have tens of millions of dollars to fund your deals. In most cases, you will sell before you buy. Furthermore, you never have to worry about running out of capital when flipping notes because these large investors literally have more capital than there are good notes to sell.

The note brokering business works well as a complimentary business to other real estate business, especially other real estate paper businesses, like mortgage brokering, judgment recovery, or other real estate services. In fact, most of the expert brokers have other businesses they are running in conjunction with their note business.

The money you can earn from brokering fees will really be up to you and your ability to contact a large number of note sellers and make win-win deals. Typical fees per transaction range anywhere from $1,000 to $15,000 with an average of about $4,000 per note.

Another advantage of this business opportunity over note investing is you don't typically have to be as picky or demanding on the yield since you won't be holding the note. Whereas you probably would require at least an 18 percent discounted yield, an institutional buyer will be happy with a lower rate, which means more of your offers will be accepted by note sellers. As a broker you will also have many more outlets for the notes you would never personally have interest in. You can keep the gold nuggets yourself and sell the silver ones.

Note: Brokers who sell their notes do not have to worry about the note going into default since they are essentially out of the loop. In other words, the note and all of its worries go to the investor, which usually is an institution.

The Business Model. In this business you find note holders and other people with marketable income streams. You can help them convert their payment stream (notes, contracts, leases) into a lump sum of cash. These folks, for whatever reason, need to liquidate their cash flow asset.

Since the average note holder is completely in the dark about how to sell a note, you as the broker can arbitrage the note. In other words, you can buy at wholesale and then resell at a higher price to an outside investor. These outside investors aren't small investors but are pension funds, insurance companies, and private corporations.

Suppose, for example, you find a $70,000 owner-financed note with a fifteen-year amortization and a 10 percent interest rate. You negotiate the price of the note at a yield of 16 percent, which equates to $51,216. Then before actually buying the note you offer it to your institutional cash flow buyer who agrees to buy it at a 13 percent yield. The lender will pay $59,453 for the note. For your efforts you make a tidy $8,237 brokerage profit.

You can buy and sell partial mortgages, too, just as you can when you buy notes for investment purposes. Create the deal by buying as much note as the seller wants to sell and then resell it at a lower rate to your investor contact.

There are differences between the process of buying and reselling compared with regular investing. In note brokerage, the investor has a required documentation package that needs to be completed by you before they will fund the deal. In fact, these are things you as a private note investor should have, too, but many investors don't do a careful due diligence rundown.

Typical Requirements to Sell Notes to Funding Sources. You will need copies of the promissory note, mortgages—junior and senior, deeds, original closing sheet, title report, title policy if there was one, insurance declaration, drive-by appraisal, social security, number of debtors, last 12 months of payment history from note owner (if possible), and other supporting documentation.

Alternative Cash Flow Vehicles.
As we stated earlier there are a number of different cash flow instruments that can be brokered. If you plan to survive in the cash flow industry you will need a variety of funding sources for selling your deals. For instance, if a note seller who owns a business note which was created from the sale of their business calls, you need to have funding sources for business notes. Suppose you get a call from a party who receives payments from a lawsuit settlement. It would be to your advantage to have a contact that buys this type of payment contracts. The point is you can't just specialize in notes created from real estate. If you do, you will be missing a lot of other opportunities.

Tools, Funding Sources, and Skills.
For starters you need all of the traditional small business tools such as multiple phone lines, fax, computer, copy machines, and a business name. Beyond these basic tools the number one tool needed is a good financial calculator like the ones described in the note investment chapter.

Not only do you need a good financial calculator, but you also need to understand how to structure offers and analyze unusual cash flow streams. The owners' manuals help, but you may need specialized books put out by the various cash flow industry publishing houses like The Paper Source or NoteWorthy.

There are literally scores upon scores of different funding sources for different types of income streams. Again, I would direct you to The Paper Source or NoteWorthy's various publications and the internet. Remember, in most cases, you do not want to sell to other brokers. You want to deal directly with the funding source. Many groups on the internet are just brokers like you—not wholesale debt buyers. Avoid them if they are not end buyers who hold notes in their own portfolio.

The two qualities of a successful paper broker are persistence and patience. The failure rate in note and paper brokerage is high because most folks believe it to be a get-rich-easy-and-fast type business. Another problem happens when folks quit their jobs or other businesses to give note brokerage a full-time effort. In most cases this is a mistake.

The people who survive usually have a parallel business they are running to provide them with the capital and cash flow to survive the initial year or two of startup. In addition, by keeping others sources of income flowing the note buyer is able to fund his or her marketing programs which will help drive business into their company.

You should be a detail-oriented person who is able to track down not only note sellers, but also the large amount of required documentation. If you tend to be disorganized and more of a big picture type, than paper brokering may not be for you.

Another key skill or trait of a successful paper broker is the ability to structure problem-solving offers to note sellers and note funders. This means being a good listener and asking good questions and going beyond merely doing phone quotes and getting into what we call consultative selling. You need to be a problem solving advisor-consultant.

Lastly, to be successful in this business you need to be a good marketer. If you are going to buy and sell notes as a business you need more than just advertising to drive business to your phones. You will need a full mix marketing mix.

Marketing Strategy. Although classified advertising can be a nice passive way to generate selling traffic, you will need more fishing lines in the water to make a living brokering cash flows.

Networking and Referrals. Many top brokers in the country generate a substantial amount of note business through networking and referrals. This won't happen overnight, but it is cheaper and more effective than advertising. In a nutshell you need to get exposure and publicity.

Creating a networking referral base requires you to meet as many people in related fields and professions and let them know about your service. Here is a list of people who you should network and market to:

Realtors: You can greatly increase an agent's income by educating them about the note selling business. The biggest resistance real estate sellers have to holding the financing is that they want their money right away. You can solve this problem for them.

Rehabbers. In most towns and cities there are dozens of full-time real estate rehabbers who buy and sell houses. In many cases these folks end up with a lot of paper. These folks also have a great need for cash. You can solve this problem by converting their paper to cash.

Mortgage Brokers. Traditional mortgage brokers are involved in hundreds of transactions every year. A percentage of these transactions involve a combination of traditional financing and owner financing. The broker can aid his or her clients by letting them know you will buy their paper. Furthermore, they can possibly earn some extra referral fees through you.

Attorneys. Attorneys are another professional group that is involved in countless real estate closings. Again you can be of great service by providing an outlet for the various real estate and business notes that are frequently generated by their clients. By helping their clients get cash for their notes you make them look good.

Builders. Ah, another fine source of notes! Builders, like rehabbers, need to put deals together which often means doing what ever it takes to get the deal closed. They also need lots of cash, which means they don't like holding notes. In fact, I know one such builder who sells all of his trade-in homes (he trades people's existing home as down payment for a new one he has built) on-owner financed installment contracts.

Investment Clubs. Although these groups are mainly landlord types, members of investment clubs do in fact generate notes when they buy and sell their properties. Work them into your marketing mix with ads, mini-seminars, direct mails, etc.

Accountants and Tax Preparers. Now here's a group of people who know who is holding notes. After all, almost all note holders have a tax preparer handle their income tax. Why not keep these folks on your mailing list, letting them know of your service? These tax professionals are often the first ones who know their note holding clients need money (to pay taxes).

Financial Planners. These folks are constantly trying to get their clients to invest money with them. They would be thrilled to have their client liquidate their notes so they can invest the money in the stock and bond markets!

For Sale By Owners (FSBOs). Some note brokers have developed programs to help FSBOs sell their home with owner financing and then cash the note out at the closing table. This can be especially appealing because homes advertised with owner financing terms sell fast and for full price. In many cases they won't even feel your discount since they already have saved on the sales commission.

Business Brokers. Now here is a great source of paper. Almost ALL business sales involve at least some seller financing. A good bit of this paper is secured by real estate. Many of these business sellers would love to convert all or some of their paper to cash.

The Key to Effective Networking. You must keep in contact with your networking database. You can't just mail one letter or take them for a brief lunch. You must repeatedly remind them and ask for leads and referrals. People are busy and have a lot on their minds. If you're not making contact at least once every few months, you will be forgotten. Also, you must allow these planted seeds time to grow. The local attorney or accountant might not have any clients holding paper this month who need to sell, but six months from now they might. If you mail them a post card reminder every other month, who do you think they will call?

Advertising and Direct Mail. Ads can be extremely effective depending on the area where you are advertising and how many other ads are running. But don't let other ads scare you off. The turnover rate in this business is huge. Chances are, four months from now their ad will disappear.

If you are buying for resale you don't have to be concerned with geographic location. You can buy notes in and out of state since you won't be holding them. From my experience buying notes as investments I have found smaller, sleepy towns to be good areas to run ads since there isn't much competition. Again, stick with the thrifty nickel and small town type papers where folks read the ads for the fun of it.

Direct mail can be expensive. My suggestion would be to build a networking database of about 500 people. These would include many of the people and professions listed earlier plus others you can think of.

Another direct mail gambit that may be good is to rent mailing lists comprised of note holders. There are some companies in the cash flow industry that have compiled databases of note holders. This may be worth experimenting with. Keep in mind, a typical direct mail piece costs about 50 cents each when you factor list costs, printing, and postage. Use this method cautiously since many of these lists are of poor quality.

Putting Deals Together. After you negotiate an acceptable note purchase you will need to get some form of agreement signed. This essentially keeps the seller from continuing to shop your offer and prevents the seller from backing out once you have invested a lot of time preparing the deal.

Note and Mortgage purchase agreements are essentially short-term option agreements since they allow the note buyer (broker) wiggle room in the event the note proves unsatisfactory. In other words, the purchase is subject to the examination and approval of all related documents and credit of the note payer before any monies are paid. This affords you some protection in the event you can't get the resale funded. A good purchase agreement should probably be structured like an option to buy.

The Note Closing. Let's say that you have found and negotiated the note and even have an agreement to resell it. Now you need to have a closing. In most cases this will be a double closing, also known as a simultaneous closing. You buy the note and at the same table resell it to the investor. The investor is almost never physically present, but has a lawyer or title company handle the closing by following their written closing instructions.

Caution: You should NOT resell the notes with recourse (a personal guarantee). Check with your lawyer to make sure you don't sell the note to the investor with recourse. You basically want to sell the note "as-is". This is usually not a problem since most institutions don't require recourse. Review with legal counsel until you know what you are doing.

Additional Profit Centers. We have already said this business seems to work nicely in conjunction with ancillary business opportunities. On the other hand, you must give it enough time and energy or it won't take off. Probably the best bet is to work it with a similar business such as mortgage brokering, judgment recovery, or even landlording for a year or two while you're getting established.

One related business opportunity could be a note servicing and payment collection business where you act as a third party loan servicer for note holders and people in the buy/sell installment house business. This basic service works by collecting payments from debtors and dispersing payments to note holders. The process works the same way big commercial lenders service tens of thousands of notes for institutions. They receive payments from debtors and disperse payments to the big-money investors (FNMA, etc.). Note holders appreciate this since you handle all of the interest and late fee collections and calculations. You also save them the headache of having to mail 1098 interest statements at the end of the year.

You might even create a hybrid service whereby you collect and receive payments from tenants and disburse them to landlords and their mortgage companies. Who knows? Maybe you could create a professional bookkeeping service for landlords whereby you handle every single piece of paper flowing from the ownership of the property. This really wouldn't be property management, but more of a bookkeeping accounting type service.

Drawbacks to Note Brokerage. You can find negative aspects to almost any business, but I feel that I need to highlight a few negative aspects of note brokerage. For one thing, good quality cash flows are not always easy to find. Make no mistake about it—this takes work. The amount of paper in the marketplace often depends on the economy and interest rates. Back in the early 1980s when rates were high and the economy was slow, there was a huge amount of owner financing paper created. In many cases a slow economy and high interest rates help the paper business.

The next drawback some investors have is that you probably will have to self-employment tax (like any business) on the proceeds of these deals. In other words, this is business activity, not investing. Note investing (holding long-term) is usually not subject to self-employment tax. Keep in mind, the self-employment tax rate is 15 percent (plus all of the other income taxes).

Finally, some investors feel that a good note is so incredibly valuable that they would never want to sell it. Instead, these people try to find ways to buy these notes with leverage (OPM) and hold them for their long term interest and early payoff profits.

Resources. The same resources mentioned in the note investing section are appropriate here as well. Metropolitan Mortgage is a big-time institutional buyer. Consider contacting them and asking for their wholesale note buying department. Call 800.268.9184 or go to **www.metmtg.com** and ask for their brokers' packet.

If you are interested in selling unusual cash flow instruments such as insurance settlements, lottery winnings, annuities, legal settlements, cell-tower leases, or any other off-the-wall income streams, I suggest you go to **www.settlementcapital.com** or call them at 800.959.0006.

10

Independent Title Examiner

The real estate world would come to a grinding halt if it weren't for title examiners. Title examiners, also known as abstractors or title searchers, serve as behind-the-scenes people who perform a "quality control" function in real estate. In the same way that a home inspector checks out the mechanical elements of a building for soundness, a title examiner checks out the title to real estate for soundness.

Without a thorough inspection of the title and the various liens, clouds, and encumbrances, title insurance companies and attorneys will not be able to issue title insurance. In fact, the entire title insurance industry could not exist without a quality title examination.

It's important to point out that there some title professionals perform title searches and provide a written summary or abstract of the title. These folks are called title abstractors, title searchers or title clerks. Generally speaking these folks don't make a judgment as to the state of title, but merely report their research. There are title professionals who not only perform the title search and abstract but also the examination, which really is an analysis or determination of the current state of the real estate title. In this section we will use the term, "title examiner," although the depth of services you perform will be for you to decide based on the level of training and experience you develop.

The Business Model. There are basically two ways one can go about becoming a title examiner. You can work as an employee for a title company or law firm, or you can be an independent title examiner. Since this book is essentially about creating your own business, we will explain the independent title examiner from a business opportunity standpoint.

Being an independent title examiner is about being an independent contractor. In almost all cases you will be providing services to title insurance companies, law firms, mortgage lenders, and real estate brokers.

Although performing a title search is not a simple matter, the general business plan to operate this business is. Basically, your client will give you the property addresses and owners' names from which you will trace out, verify, and document the real estate's current title and limitations.

Your clients will then take your abstract report and photocopied documentation to their office to create a case file. From here a risk analysis is performed, and your client attorney or title company draws up title insurance and conveyancing documents such as deeds and mortgages.

You can profit from this since there always is a need for competent title searchers. As a rule, title companies, banks, law firms, and real estate brokers do not like having employees handle this work. Most would rather find conscientious title examiners to outsource this work to. You can be that outsource contractor.

How a Title Search is Performed. The general process of searching a title is the same in most states, but finer details and office names within states and courthouses may vary.

A variety of offices and records departments within a county must be searched to perform a title search. As a big picture overview, following are the offices and records that must be searched to perform an accurate abstract. Keep in mind that I am being overly simplistic. An entire how-to manual would be needed to explain the process in its entirety.

The Recorder of Deeds: In this office you will verify who the current owners are by copying the most recent deed on file. If you do not have the current owner's name you can either trace that through a courthouse computer or from one of the many index books. You will search out prior owners by tracing them back through the recital portions of the deeds, which pass from owner to owner. Each deed will have a recital, which typically lists the prior owners/sellers (grantors). In many cases this tracing back will b0e done for a period of 50 to 60 years.

> Usually in this same office you will be able to search current and past mortgages against the property. You will be looking for active (unpaid) mortgages along with satisfied (released/paid) mortgages against the current property. In addition you will back search and document

past mortgages against the property and confirm they have been discharged.

In this same office you will be seeking any conveyancing documents such as easements, right-of-ways, or recorded liens affecting the parcel.

Office of Court Records. In this office you search for judgments against the names of the current and past owners of the property. Like most of the other records, this information is contained in index books, which generally makes the process easy to follow.

This office may also record other pertinent liens or claims against the property. For instance, mechanic's liens may be indexed here. Federal and state tax liens (not property tax) may be filed here.

You need to learn which types of liens are filed in these various offices. Liens are usually indexed in books (many courthouses are changing to computers) by the name of the debtor or defendant as in the case of a judgment. In the index book a case or file number will typically be noted along with the type of lien and amount. This number will then be used in either another book or given to a clerk so the actual copy of the documents can be read and photocopied. Also, be on the lookout for a miscellaneous lien index where more obscure liens are indexed. Tens of thousands of dollars are at risk, so it is critical that you know this process thoroughly for your state and county.

Tax Claim Bureau. The next county office worth searching is the tax claim office. Typically this office houses the records of unpaid property taxes that townships and boroughs have turned over to them as unpaid. These unpaid taxes create a lien–a dangerous lien to be sure, because these liens typically take priority over all other liens (mortgages, judgments, etc.).

Tax liens are either searched by computer or by the clerk working for the tax claim bureau. In most cases you will need to pay for a written confirmation of the tax lien status on the property. Local tax offices will provide certification for the current tax year payment status, but typically a clerk within the title company handles this part of the search.

Probate Office and Bankruptcy. Other offices may need to be searched depending on the circumstances around the property. For example, if the property is being sold by an estate, the probate office records will typically be searched to ensure that the property in the estate has been formally probated. Another office possibly needing to be worked (perhaps via an on-line database) would be federal bankruptcy records. In the case of a known bankruptcy you will be checking to make sure the property seller's bankruptcy has been finalized and discharged.

You can see that even my basic overview shows this is work requiring full attention to detail. You probably should avoid this work if you have problems focusing your attention or in being a systematic, methodical thinker.

Fees and Income Potential. The income you will make as an independent title examiner depends to a large extent on the economy and amount of real estate transactions. For instance, a few years back I was talking with an independent researcher who said real estate sales were slow but his business was thriving due to the low-interest refinancing boom.

The typical title search these days can run anywhere from $75 to $125, with single item searches (e.g., judgments) running around $20. The best in this business develop a system of handling multiple cases at once. For example, if they have four title searches that day, they can do a judgment search on all four owners during the same visit to that particular records office. By bulk searching you can end up doing three or four full searches per day, which can be quite lucrative. Three $125 searches per day is $1,875 a week.

Additional Profit Centers. There are several possible profit centers or parallel businesses that you could operate in the course of being a title examiner. One possibility could be working the distressed real estate markets. By being extremely knowledgeable about liens, judgments, and foreclosures you could build a rental business or buy/sell business in the distressed real estate market. In fact, many professional real estate buyers would give their eyeteeth to know the ins and outs of liens, judgments, foreclosure

and title law. Since you would be an expert from your title searching business, you would know precisely what liens are attaching to the property and how to handle them. In fact, you would have a tremendous advantage with all of the "insider" knowledge a good title examiner knows. Remember, most distressed real estate deals involve liens, judgments, back taxes, divorces, and other messy title problems. As a title "technician" you could snap up a lot more deals by having the right knowledge.

The judgment recovery business as discussed in an earlier chapter could be a great opportunity since you are already hanging around the courthouse. Furthermore, you could quickly and easily find out which judgments and liens are attached to real estate since these are the real cherry deals in the judgment recovery business. You could also expand into buying other bad debts and liens. In most counties countless liens and mortgages are in default, but the holders of this bad paper haven't the foggiest idea how to recover their money. You might be able to work out a no-money-down deal where you'll option the debt instrument, recover or foreclosure the property, and split the money! There's opportunity all around, but to paraphrase Thomas Edison—it looks more like work than it does opportunity!

Skills and Tools. The main skill you need is knowledge. You must learn the specific art and science of title searching. A good law library would probably be a good start. You could pay someone outside of the county you choose to work in to mentor and teach you. In most cases the local searchers (especially independents) won't help you since they fear your competition.

Another option for learning is to get hired by a title company and let them train you. Work for a year, gain experience, then go out on your own as an independent searcher. Be wary of signing restrictive covenants with employers that forbid you going into business for yourself.

Lastly, every state has some kind of land title association where most of the title and escrow companies are members. In most cases, these associations have in-depth how-to manuals that provide state-specific title searching methods and procedures. To find a local association check with the American Land Title Association at **www.alta.org** or 800.787.ALTA.

As far as tools go most searchers use worksheets grids to chart their searches. Many new searchers are using laptop computers to help organize their work. In addition, most courthouses supply special copiers for the exclusive use of title searchers.

A copy of your state's real property law is also required. Your best bet is to find the book that is considered your state's legal authority in the matter. For example, in Pennsylvania the book is *Ladner on Conveyancing;* each state usually has a respected book considered the authority on real estate conveyancing.

11

Income Property: Professional Landlording

In this chapter I will explain income property investments in detail. This is one chapter you won't want to miss. We will review the many forgotten benefits and advantages of owning rental investments. When finished, I think you'll agree that the case for owning rental property is strong. In addition, you will learn about a host of alternative rental opportunities beyond apartment properties.

Few investments or businesses can offer the multiplicity of benefits that rental property offers. The rental property business can be comfortably squeezed into most lifestyles and competing opportunities. In fact, if you polled rental property owners you would find about 90 percent of them have another business or work at a full-time job.

Even though most folks choose to keep rental investing as a complementary or supplemental opportunity, there's no reason it can't be built into a full-time business opportunity. While rental properties can require a lot of hands-on-management, the general workload throughout a given year is relatively light compared to most jobs or business opportunities.

Why Many People Have a Low Opinion of Rental Property. You often hear people talk rental properties down. They will say things like, "I never want to be a landlord," or "rental property is not worth owning," or, "you can't find any good tenants," or similar statements. While some of this negativity is deserved, most of it comes from people who either never owned real estate or who never learned how to be a professional landlord.

Make no mistake about it, this business—like most of the opportunities in this book—is not for everyone. Being a real estate entrepreneur is no walk in the park. It takes a determined and hard-working individual to survive and prosper in the competitive marketplace of self-employment. I have yet to find a business (and I have looked at many) that is easy. Nothing is ever as easy or as profitable as it may appear. It usually takes several years until genuine prosperity catches up with your efforts.

There are several common reasons people quit the rental property business: 1) They are too impatient; 2) They never learned the craft of professional property management; 3) They are easily frustrated and not given to problem solving; 4) They paid too much for their properties.

If you are a patient, problem solving person with good property managing abilities and experience as a highly skilled real estate buyer, you can do extremely well in this business. And these are all learnable skills.

The Unique Nature of Rental Assets. If you make

a line-by-line comparison of rental assets to other investments or businesses, you will find that rental property offers a unique set of advantages that is virtually unmatchable among other opportunities.

People frequently buy rental property to solve some underlying cash flow problem in their life. The tendency to buy rental property primarily for cash flow causes many people to become disenchanted with the business. They buy property thinking they will have some incredible cash flow next month only to be disappointed, possibly even ending up in a worse cash position. This is due to a fundamental misapplication or misunderstanding of rental property investing.

Capital Builder. Here is the principle: Rental property is the

finest capital building investment you will ever find. There are few if any businesses or investments that will build a large block of equity or capital as easily or quickly as income property will. Rental property is the master of this universe, crushing nearly all competitors in the equity building arena.

Rental investing is a lot like farming. Remember the old folk saying, "Don't eat your seed corn?" If a farmer planted seeds and then kept uprooting and eating his sprouts every month he would feed himself, but it would be a tough way to make a living or fill his belly. Amateur landlords are no different. If you buy a property and expect to reap a harvest next month or even next year then you are playing this game wrong. This isn't to say you shouldn't look for monthly or annual growth, but you can't harvest the crop yet—it is too soon.

Cash flow will come. In fact, if you're a sharp buyer it can start happening within a few months, but you need to save and reinvest this, not eat it! This is the proverbial seed corn spoken of by the wise folk of yesteryear. You need to save and reinvest this so you can plant more moneymaking plants. Eventually, you will have so many plants producing so much harvest you can start eating the fruit without ever having to plant another tree. In fact, after several hard working years you'll have more harvest than you can eat, and you will have created a perpetual income.

Perpetual Income. The second unique characteristic of rental property is its ability to generate what I call perpetual income. Again, there are few, if any businesses or investments that can match this. The Principle: After rental investments become free and clear (deleveraged) they generate a cash flow that will last for decades into the future and provide a liberating freedom for its owners.

High Leverage. Another characteristic of rental investments is its ability to be purchased with leverage. Leverage is the concept of owning and controlling an asset with very little cash of your own. The principle: Rental property is the easiest and safest of all businesses or investments you can purchase with financing. There isn't even a close second! Rental houses, apartment buildings, rooming houses, trailer parks, land, storage space are all exceptionally easy to acquire with a little knowledge and skills. Banks love lending on property, and if you don't like banks there are countless sellers who will hold the financing if you ask them. It is ironic that rental property can be one of the most cash-intensive businesses one can enter, but yet one of the easiest businesses to build with minimal start-up cash. This is precisely why it is covered in this book of low-cost business start-ups.

When we compare rental investments against other investments or business opportunities, we find a plethora of unique advantages that are virtually unmatchable. I ask you this: What investment do you know of that can be acquired using very little of your own money, will grow in a matter of years into a large amount of equity and produce cash flow, and, if maintained and managed, can last for decades into the future? The answer is none.

Five More Powerful Reasons. Along with the previously mentioned advantages there are five additional benefits to buying and managing income properties.

Tax Advantages. Without going into a long dissertation on real estate tax law let me just say that rental real estate offers unique tax savings for investors. For starters, rental income is typically not subject to social security taxes or other self-employment taxes. This delivers an automatic savings of about 15 percent over regular business or working wages where do have to pay the required Social Security taxes.

Next, rental properties held as true investments can be sold and taxed on the much lower capital gains tax rates. This alone can be worth a tax savings of 30 to 50 percent over money earned in a regular business or from wages.

There's more. Investment property gets special tax treatment if sold on the installment method so that investors have to pay taxes only on the proceeds as they receive them rather than all up front. This enables owners to earn interest on their mortgage notes based on the gross selling price *before* taxes. This is in stark contrast to earning money at a job when you pay taxes on the money you earn and then banking your net funds and earn interest on the net amount—a lot slower way to accumulate wealth!

Let's also not forget that any equity you create from buying distressed property at below-market prices is not taxed until the property is sold. The same tax deferral applies to equity created from fixing up property. In a nutshell, equity created from bargain purchases or property renovation is not taxed until sold. Your net worth grows tax deferred, compared with wage type income where your net worth grows only after taxes have been paid.

Additional benefits are offered for real estate exchanges (delayed rollover) making the sale effectively tax-free or tax deferred. For example, we can create tax-deferred wealth by buying distressed property, fixing it up and then essentially rolling it over into larger property via delayed exchanges with virtually no tax payments due.

Inflation Hedge. Rental property is called a hard asset because it is a real thing and not some intangible blip or pulse in a computer hard drive. You can literally kick the bricks! Due to the physical nature and increasingly scarce supply of land and housing, rental property acts as a hedge against inflation. As inflationary forces drive up the cost of raw building materials and land, it also drives up the value of rental property.

Dealmaker's Profit. Real estate is considered a disorganized market. Values are not fixed in stone as they are in many other investments. For example, if Microsoft's$^{®}$ stock is trading at $68 today, there's no way you can play deal maker and negotiate a better deal. The price is the price. By contrast, in real estate values and prices are not established by big institutions but by buyers and sellers. We might call these folks the "little guys." If you are a persistent bargain hunter you can find bargain properties that are worth far more than the price you will pay. It is very common for skilled buyers to pick up a solid $10,000 equity the day they buy a property. Not only is this new equity gain tax deferred, it is easy. You know I shy away from that word, "easy," but it's true that making big equity gains by smart deal making is relatively easy.

The User Pays For Your Asset. Again there are very few businesses where you can buy large quantities of assets and have other folks pay the bill for the asset. Rental properties work precisely this way.

Suppose you buy a six-unit apartment building with a $130,000 price for $8,000 down. Let us also suppose the building has a breakeven cash flow during the twelve years, and at the end of the twelve years the building is free and clear. Not an everyday deal, but realistic for a patient buyer. In this scenario by the end of twelve years you would have six different income streams paying you every month for decades into the future. Your $8,000 initial investment would have grown through loan amortization to at least $130,000 in equity. Although this property only showed a breakeven cash flow, it still produced an average yearly profit of $10,166 in the form of mortgage reduction. Tell me, what other business or investment will pay for itself and create this kind of solid equity and cash flow?

Forced Appreciation. The granddaddy of real estate books was old Bill Nickerson's book, *How I Turned $1000 into Five Million In Real Estate*. Nickerson often said you could force real estate to appreciate by buying fixer-upper properties and doing just that— fixing them up! The value you create through fixing up property is called forced appreciation. In most cases, for every $1 you spend cleaning and fixing you get back $2 in newly created value (forced equity). The bottom line is you don't have to wait years upon years for real estate to appreciate; just buy rundown property at bargain prices to speed up the process.

Adding Up The Benefits. In reality there are several more unique advantages to buying rental property. In summary they are as follows: (1) Properties work for you 24 hours a day even when you are sleeping or vacationing; (2) property doesn't care what your educational background or personal makeup may be; (3) property is color blind and totally oblivious to your past failures or successes; and (4) owning rental real estate comes with its own forcing function in helping you save money. Since property can't be "tapped" as easy as your MAC card you have a forcing function that will help you preserve your assets from tempting spending.

Finally, I want to focus on the exciting opportunities within the rental industry. Every deal must be scrutinized for its ability to pay for itself and produce a cash flow, but we must not forget that rental property is above all else an equity-building vehicle. You must be patient. As properties grow in value and have their mortgages reduced or paid off they *will* produce a substantial income.

Income property brings you a unique investment and business opportunity that offers tax advantages and a host of profit making kickers along the way. Few businesses or investments on the planet offer the diverse advantages rental properties offer. So, if you look at rental property strictly from a cash flow standpoint you will not be viewing the entire spectrum of benefits.

The Nasty Management Factor. Of course everyone would want to buy rental properties if it wasn't for the "nasty" task of property management. The fact is that property management is not easy. If it were, everyone would be doing it.

I am convinced that property management comes down to two things: learning professional landlording skills and being in business. Professional management is a skill and a craft just like being a carpenter or baseball player. You wouldn't expect to be an expert the first day you tried to be a carpenter or baseball player. It takes time to learn any skill. In addition, rental properties must be treated like a business. I come from a retail business background where we are used to handling problems and consumer demands. For me, landlording really isn't any different: They are my customers and I do my best to solve problems and make their stay in my properties pleasant and long term.

The Uncommon Freedom. Before we get into the actual business model and specific rental opportunities let me close this introduction by talking just a bit about the freedom rental properties can provide you.

People work thirty to forty years to earn a paltry $1,200 social security check. Although social security is designed only as a supplemental source of income, many people find this to be their only income later in life. Rental investments offer industrious people a unique opportunity to build an income stream of $3,000 to $20,000 per month. Best of all you don't have to wait twenty-five years to start collecting the money. In most cases, five to ten years is all that is needed to build a good base of income.

The income stream from rental investments is similar to a life annuity from an insurance company. Although there will always be some work involved in managing rental properties, the money comes in like an annuity check. Best of all, it can quite literally last a lifetime. This income stream creates the freedom to work if and when you want, plus the ability to travel or just kick back and do the things you enjoy. Not to beat an already dead pony, but again, few businesses can do this for you.

In the next section we will explain and review a plethora of income property opportunities. Although regular houses and apartment buildings make fine investments we will also cover rooming houses, shared rental units, storage rentals, executive home-away-from-home rentals, handicap ready units, and insurance company rentals.

The Business Model. While there are a host of different rental opportunities within the rental industry, it is worth noting that the business models and principals are generally the same within the income property arena.

The investor's business plan is first to acquire rental properties using leverage and then to take these properties—primary residential housing—and offer renters the use of the property for a fee. The investor may not realize it, but he or she is primarily in the bedroom leasing business. Allow me to explain. The prospective user (tenant) either doesn't have the money (credit or down payment) to buy the property or for some other reason does not choose to purchase property at the time. The renter needs a place to live and sleep. The investor fills this need in the market by acquiring buildings with bedrooms and living rooms and leases them out to tenants. As primitive as it sounds, people need a place to sleep. If they just needed shelter they could hang out at the mall, but what people really need is a place to sleep. In case you've forgotten, motel living is a little pricey.

The investor is therefore acquiring capital at a wholesale rate by buying and structuring great deals and re-lending it to the tenant/user at a retail rate. The spread between what it costs to own and operate the building and the gross rent is the leasing profit.

The key to making money with rental properties is to acquire properties at the best price and terms so that the investor can produce equity and cash flow as rapidly as possibly. The best way to do this is to buy right. If you buy right—well below market—you can make mistakes and still make a profit. Buying properties well below market is like increasing your profit margin. The higher the profit margin, the safer the business endeavor and the more room for error.

The next step in the rental model is to be able to repair, rehabilitate, and maintain properties. This doesn't mean you have to do this yourself, but you need to know the methods and techniques used to cost effectively handle this part of the business. This is an area many investors don't take seriously enough. In many cases, investors don't know the great profits that can be saved or created by knowing fix-up trade secrets. Like buying right, knowing how to repair and maintain properties can make you a bundle of money; and it can help produce a larger profit margin and more fat in the deal.

An experienced investor once told me he noticed that skilled rehab investors rarely get into financial trouble in this business. They are able to operate properties with greatly reduced costs compared to investors who hire out all of the work to high-priced contractors.

Don't be afraid of the repair and fix-up part of the business since this is very learnable and with the help of some good trades people you won't be alone.

The third critical aspect to the rental business model is managing the people who rent your properties. This skill is a matter of developing and following a system for tenant selection and rent collection. Fact: the vast majority of problems landlords encounter is because of their own faulty tenant selection methods. In most cases, bad tenants are a preventable problem that can be avoided with thorough screening and good judgment.

The last major critical factor is what I call administrative detail. With each property you acquire comes a large volume of paperwork, documents, files, and bills. If you expect to buy a lot of property, you must develop a system of organizing, paying, and dispatching this paperwork.

The Housing Industry. Whatever you call yourself (landlord, manager, property owner) you are in the housing industry. You are providing people with shelter. Begin to view yourself as a housing entrepreneur, not a "landlord."

The Ultimate Goal Of Rental Investors. The ultimate goal of investors in rental assets should be to retire the debt against the property. In other words—get the asset free and clear.

The time needed to get a property free and clear depends a lot on how good of a financial manager you are. In addition, you can use specific strategies and plans to accelerate the paydown pace on the mortgage. A good goal for investors is ten years. This doesn't mean you will only take on ten-year mortgages, but if possible you will strategize to have the asset debt free in ten years.

After properties become free and clear the rental business becomes very enjoyable. Instead of mailing out most of your rental income to lenders, you keep it. After ten or fifteen properties become free and clear the cash flow can be rich.

The Two Rental Markets. If you decide to become a housing provider you will have to decide which rental market you will serve. Generally speaking there are two primary markets: Middle income housing and lower income housing.

Middle Income Housing. Middle income housing is a broad market of housing that generally serves people in the middle income sector of society.

Lower Income Housing. Low income housing serves the market in the less desirable and lower rent areas. This type of property is often located in inner city and urban areas, although many suburban and rural areas also have lower income areas that need to be served.

Apartments and Houses.
Within the rental industry there are two primary types of housing products: apartments and houses. Each has its advantages and disadvantages, and each category has strong proponents who claim their investment vehicles are superior to the others. To be honest, the case is strong for each type of investment.

Multi-Unit Advantages.
Apartments are typically a better cash flow vehicle than houses due to the economies of scale and the ability to acquire a lower price per unit deal with larger properties. In general, the more units you have in a building the higher cash flow potential. Also, the more units a building, has the more proficient the owner manager must be manage it successfully. In most cases, the better the manager, the more demanding the manager/buyer will be in the purchase. More units equal more risk; therefore investors demand a better return on their investment, and larger buildings provide better cash flow.

Multi-unit properties have better cash flows because of something called "economies of scale." It works like this. Owning a twelve-unit apartment building involved maintaining only one roof, whereas, owning twelve houses requires maintaining twelve roofs. This same twelve-unit apartment building will also require just one mortgage, one set of tax bills, whereas, twelve houses will require twelve mortgages and twelve tax bills.

There are also logistical advantages of owning a multi-unit building versus a bunch of single houses. Let's use our twelve-unit example again. One twelve-unit building requires only one address to service the twelve tenants. Twelve houses would require twelve addresses located in different areas across town. You will have less travel and logistical effort in delivering service to a multi-unit structure compared to single dwellings across town. This same principle applies to larger multi-unit properties versus smaller multi-unit structures. Logistically, wouldn't it be better to own one 36 unit building rather than six, six-unit buildings?

Because of the economies of scale, logistical advantages, and declining purchase price per unit, multi units are considered better cash flow vehicles than houses. In addition, you have the ability to raise rents while simultaneously cutting expenses giving the building a rising cash flow trajectory.

Single Family House Advantages.

House investors have a much different case for their investment vehicle that they think is even better. I think it comes down to which type of property fits your needs, skills, and goals best. In many cases investors buy both vehicles to balance out their portfolio.

Houses have a smaller gross income than multi-unit buildings, but their offsetting expenses are also lower. Most house investors do a kind of net lease arrangement where the tenant pays all or most of the utilities separately to the utility provider, while apartment owners typically provide many of these services as part of the apartment rent. This arrangement means there fewer expenses and less paperwork for a given property with a single-family home.

Next, houses are extremely plentiful and easy to buy and sell. Apartment properties are not as plentiful and are generally more difficult to buy and sell. In fact, large multi-unit buildings are significantly more difficult to sell than houses are.

Houses, by contrast, are usually easy to sell. In most cases you can sell a house in two or three months offering conventional terms or you can sell it in less than thirty days if you decide to offer some form of creative financing such as a lease option or owner financing. Apartment properties can take six to twelve months to sell, sometimes even a year or two with the seller often having to hold some of the financing for the buyer.

When you buy a house, you usually buy from owner occupants. Then when you sell a house, you sell it to owner occupants. From whom do you buy apartment buildings? Investors. To whom do you sell apartment buildings? Investors. Which group of people would you rather buy and sell to—investors or homeowners? Investors purchase buildings based on financial numbers, whereas homeowners usually buy based on emotions and eye appeal. The point house investors make is they have a product that is both easier to buy and sell because homeowners are not as demanding and financially savvy as investors.

Houses are lower risk investments than multi-unit buildings. Think about this. Would it be safer to have twelve houses scattered through a town or have all of your money tied up in a single twelve unit building? It is obvious that twelve scattered properties would diversify and spread the risk.

Another attractive feature of houses is that they attract a more stable tenant than do apartments, although some serious apartment investors would disagree with that statement. Generally speaking though, houses attract more family units while apartments attract a more transient clientele. This can mean houses often have less vacancy, turnover, cleaning, advertising, and work.

Making the Decision. I there is a strong case for both types of properties. You can make better cash flow from well-selected multi-unit properties than you can houses. If you want more of a full time business/investment opportunity that you can make a living from I would steer you toward multi-unit properties. If you want a more passive investment requiring less time and over-all work, I recommend houses. In any event, if you're new at this business you may be advised to start out renting houses due to their ease of management and then as your skills increase move into multi-unit properties. If you live in an area of the country with particularly high house prices then you may be forced to start with multi-unit properties in order for the numbers to work for you.

Opportunities In Multi-Unit Properties. My personal opinion is that if you are buying multi-unit properties it will pay to be selective about location. This is even more important than with houses since multi-unit properties are harder to manage and often attract more unstable tenants.

When shopping for units look for properties where the current owners don't know how to manage the property. In most cases this profile will be matched with a rundown property. A rundown multi-unit property is an extremely hard sell and you should be able to negotiate some owner financing terms along with a wholesale price.

Be an extremely demanding buyer when shopping for rundown and mismanaged buildings because there are very few buyers who want these buildings. Many apartment investors are looking for a turnkey deal without a lot of work, but this is not were the money is. The big money is made turning bad properties around. Don't be afraid of bad tenants and lots of trash if you are buying at a bargain price.

Multi-unit properties are sold as a total unit, but your job should be to start analyzing deals based on the per-unit-price. For instance, a ten-unit building might be offered for $205,000. This amounts to $20,500 per unit. Shop and compare buildings based on the per unit price. Also, be sure to factor in unit price differences based on number of bedrooms. A building that has two-bedroom units will typically have a higher unit price than one-bedroom properties. Study past sales of apartment buildings and try to come up with unit prices based on the sales prices.

Before you make an offer on a building make sure you do a cash flow analysis. Include all of the costs that will be incurred. The possible list of expenses may include heat, water, sewer, trash, gas, electric, recycle fees, housing permits, licenses, property taxes, insurance, repairs (a big one), advertising, cleaning, mortgage payments, and a per unit profit to you.

When making your offer make sure the deal will provide you at least $50 to $100 per unit, per month, in management profit. This is above and beyond any of the projected tax benefits and profit from loan amortization.

Since mismanaged and rundown properties are difficult to sell, ask the owner to hold the financing on the deal. This is one advantage of apartment buildings, since these properties are routinely sold with owner financing. Keep your payments low to ensure your success. If the owner balks, explain you need this extra room to make the numbers work.

Hot Profit Tip. An owner with a mismanaged and neglected multi-unit property is often willing to carry some or all of the financing in order to get out a building full of problems. If you have fix-up skills and courage, you can buy these properties with very low down payments. Save your down money for fixing up the building and let the owner hold the entire note. If they balk, consider offering a six-month trial on an installment land contract where the title stays in their name. After you prove yourself, quickly get the seller to deed the property to you or a trustee. Get the deed out of the seller's name to protect you.

Best Building Size.
The ideal size of a building for an investment is, of course, a matter of opinion. You will cut your risks by starting out with smaller buildings of four or five units each. However, most of the pros prefer buildings with six to twelve units. Larger properties seem to have fewer buyers and can be purchased at a better price per unit. If you become skilled at the apartment

business consider buying buildings with 20 to 40 units since the cash flow can be even better.

How Many Bedrooms?

The number of bedrooms for a good investment depends on local supply and demand market conditions. Your options are efficiency units; and units with one, two, or three bedrooms. Most of the demand lies in the 1-2 bedroom market. Ask around at local management companies and investors to find what rents the slowest and fastest.

Clientele.

You have to careful to follow all of the anti-discrimination laws in effect. This is not just a racial issue. Age, gender, familial status, and religion can all be points of prejudice that are forbidden by law. Generally speaking you want to find people who have some stability in their life, either from work or past tenancy history. Many older folks make good tenants since they are usually mature and somewhat responsible.

Opportunities In Low-Income Housing.

Even though low-income rental property falls under the category of investing, it must be handled like a business because this type of property requires a lot more management.

You can buy houses or apartments in this segment of the market, but my personal preference is for house investments. Lower income houses in stable areas are still manageable, while low-income apartments will require more skill and work.

The Big Advantage of Lower Income Housing.

The number one advantage of investing in lower income housing is cash flow. Lower income properties can be bought at such good prices that they will usually provide a decent cash flow even with 100 percent financing. The downside, of course, is management. Most problems in managing lower income housing can be controlled with careful tenant selection and good management techniques.

The second advantage with lower income properties is that they can be bought with shorter term financing. In many cases, you can structure 7- 10-year, fully amortizing mortgages and get some extra cash flow to boot.

These buying advantages come about because there is less buyer demand in these areas, a more distressed market. Furthermore, less desirable areas are often physically distressed which compounds the matter. All of this means there are some incredible buys that can be made.

Hot Profit Tip. Seriously consider using the government's Section-8 housing program as a way of renting houses and apartments. In many cases they will pay higher rents with a better chance of getting your money than regular tenants.

The Number One Rule.
To be successful in this higher risk, higher management area, you must buy only the choicest of deals. This means never paying more than 50 cents on the dollar for houses in these areas. To be safer yet, don't pay more than about 35 to 40 percent of fair market value. If the deal isn't an absolute slam-dunk steal, don't buy it. If you are going to pay anything resembling retail prices you might as well buy in better locations.

Rule Number Two.
Marginal areas can be OK, but avoid anything remotely similar to a war zone or a bombed-out drug area. This can be hazardous to your health, both financially and physically. Plenty of areas are lower income but relatively stable and quiet. These are the areas where good tenants want to live, not areas with drug trafficking, high crime, and abandoned buildings.

Number of Bedrooms.
I have seen demand for houses with any number of bedrooms. Your best bet, however, will be for houses with three or four bedrooms. This size house seems to offer the highest rent and the most demand.

Once Again Fix-Up Properties.
A constant theme in real estate investment circles is "dirty, rundown, fixer-upper" properties. This is the type of property sellers can't sell and buyers don't want; therefore, you can make bargain purchases.

Additional Profit Center With Houses.
One of the great things about houses investments is you can decide to stop renting and sell it with your own financing. This is the flexibility you gain with houses. If a particular house has a high maintenance record you might just sell it on a land contract or lease option.

Depending on how you structure it, you could create an income stream for 15 to 30 years and get a good price for your house too.

Hot Profit Tip. Consider selling some of your marginal houses to your better paying tenants on some form of installment sale and generate cash flow without maintenance for years into the future.

Let's look at a typical deal. You buy a junker house for a distressed price of $24,000 that needs about $2000 in repairs. You rent out the house for $500 per month for six years and then decide to sell it. 72 months x $500 monthly = $36,000 in rents received (For clarity sake let's assume you paid cash even though that would not be the best move).

This means you had $26,000 invested and received gross rents of $36,000, leaving $10,000 in profit. But we can't forget the taxes, insurance, and repairs during the six-year period we rented it. Let's assume this washed away the $10,000 in additional rents. OK. We basically own the investment with zero money remaining in the deal. Now we sell the asset with owner financing.

Let's say we sell the house for a reasonable number of $40,000 at 10 percent interest for twenty years. Let's look at the numbers.

N I PMT PV

240 10 386. 40,000 240 months X 386. = $92,642 gross sales proceeds.

OK. We take our previous figures of $26,000 net rent combined with $92,642 in principal and interest and we get a whopping $118,642 cash return on our $26,000 initial investment.

I must stress that these numbers are realistic. I have seen many experienced investors sell dozens of houses on terms like this. One fellow I know sold a huge portfolio of rental houses over a period of about five years using a similar method.

Summary Of Low Income House Investments.
If you're a sharp buyer these kind of numbers are common. In fact, I have seen deals far better than the deal described above. In fact, the example just described would be considered marginal by most pro buyers I know.

The lower income rental and sales business can be highly lucrative if you take the time to learn the business. I have written a detailed business manual about lower income house investments. It goes into extreme detail on topics such as buying, fixing, management, and cash flow strategies. The book is called *Perpetual Income*. (See the appendix for details.)

The Rooming House Money Machine. When you
mention the topic of rooming houses people often think of rundown flophouses or fleabag hotels. The truth of the matter is that rooming houses can be operated in a clean and respectable fashion, not to mention the fact that they can be an extremely lucrative investment. Rooming houses can be money machines. I know several landlords who own them and wouldn't think of selling them. One investor I know actually has made a living just from one large rooming house alone. So if you're interested in making a great rental income you'd better listen up

---

Hot Profit Tip. Rooming houses are a real secret among professional investors. The fact is rooming house properties give one of the greatest bangs for the buck. Most pro landlords love them because the cash flow can be phenomenal!

Renting real estate by the room generates more rent per square foot than almost any other residential real estate. This is based on the principle of subdivision. Rather than rent a whole house by itself, why not divide it into rooms and rent it by the room? The general principal is that the smaller the unit of subdivision, the greater the profit.

Room Rental Profits. You could rent an old mansion for
probably about $850 per month (big, old homes are not in demand by consumers) to one family or you could break it into 10 rooms that each rent for $85 per week.

10 rooms X $85 = $850 per week

$850 per week X 4 weeks = $3,400 per month

Now there's some serious cash flow!

When you mention rooming house investments people often say something like, "Why would you want to own a rooming house?" My answer: Because of the cash flow. You can quite literally make a comfortable income off of one or two rooming houses.

Rooming House Myths. There are several myths and preconceived notions about rooming houses that are just flat wrong.

Myth #1: Rooming houses are flop houses. Not true. A well-run rooming house is not a flop house, but an affordable and private living area for a growing segment of the population that doesn't need or want a big house to be happy.

Myth #2: Rooming Houses Have Constant Turnover. Not true. The tenants of a well-run rooming house often keep their rooms for well over a year, sometimes many years. In fact, I have spoken with several rooming house investors who have had roomers stay for as long as fifteen and twenty years!

Myth #3: There is very little demand for rooms. Not true. There is a strong demand, and it increases each year due mainly to changing demographic and social conditions. As an example, the singles sector of the population is growing incredibly fast. Along with these social changes is the fact that people cannot afford traditional housing due to the high cost of real estate.

Myth # 4: People in rooming houses are deadbeats who don't pay their rent. Again, not true. If you screen people to make sure they have a job or pension check you will get your money. Most rooming house investors have very few payment problems. After all, if they can't pay a room rental where else will they live?

There's another point worth talking about this payment issue. If roomers don't pay, you can probably change the lock after about a week of time on their room and lock them out. Generally speaking, room rentals fall under motel tenancy laws, which are very favorable to the landlord. In most cases it is a private, non-judicial matter of evicting a tenant. In many states it is just a matter of giving notice and locking the door.

Services Offered to Roomers. The services you offer will depend on the level of service you decide to provide. Usually there is a basic package of services that comes standard with a room rental. A sample package will include cable hookup; basic furniture such as a dresser, bed, compact sofa, chair, nightstand, lamp, common bathroom facilities; and a common kitchen and laundry area. In addition, most rooming houses offer a weekly or bi-weekly, light duty cleaning of the rooms and hallway along with bath and kitchen cleaning.

Finding a Rooming House. Since most rooming houses are profitable ventures you probably won't see them offered for sale. Your best bet is to take several months or even a year or two and be on the lookout for one. You may want to find a real estate agent who is active in investment properties and make them your buyer's broker. An agent who is active with investment properties will be able to make weekly and monthly MLS searches for suitable properties.

The most profitable way to buy a rooming housing is to find one in decline because the owners either don't know how to manage it or are tired of trying. A rundown rooming house is a hard sell on the open market, so you probably can negotiate owner financing or a heavily discounted price.

Another advantage of buying a rundown rooming house is you already have the property zoned as a rooming house. In most cases, if the property has a prior history of being a rooming house it is grandfathered into that zoning classification. Conversely, it can be difficult to get a regular building rezoned as a rooming house. Local zoning people don't like these properties because some owners rent to trashy type tenants (drug dealers, etc.) Whatever the zoning situation, get a copy of the township zoning ordinances and read the zoning requirements.

Sometimes old ramshackle hotels and motels can be modified easily into long-term room rentals. Another possibility for creating a rooming house is to find an apartment building that is laid out in such a way as to accommodate room rentals. You might not be able to covert all of the apartments into rooms, but you might try it with a few units. Again, check with zoning ordinances.

Managing Rooming Houses. In most areas there is a big demand for room rentals, so you can be choosy in selecting your renter. Most investors want roomers who have a job or some sort of secure pension or retirement income. This requirement will help to keep drug addicts and prostitutes out of the property. Next, you should only take people who can pay a deposit and one or two weeks' rent paid in advance. This, too, will screen out people who are high risk. If they can't pay a few weeks of rent and deposit then they might be too close to the edge, financially speaking.

Rooms need to have their own locks and individual keys with you holding the master key that will open all of the rooms. You will want to allow your rooms a fair amount of privacy as long as the room isn't be used for illicit activities and partying.

Developing Rules. Owning room rentals will be a learning experience for you. Start out with an initial set of rules and add to them as you think of new ones. Explain the rules to each roomer and give them their own copy.

In your rules you will want to cover things like when rents are due, late charges, visitors, drinking, cooking in rooms, maid service, phone use, and policies for using common areas.

Most rooming house owners have a list of forbidden activities, which usually looks something like this: no booze, no pets, no visitors, no smoking in rooms, and no drugs. Of course you will have to create your own list, but think about things that affect building safety, noise levels, cleanliness, and overall harmony among the guests.

Make no mistake about it, room rentals will be a big thing in the future with the demographic changes in society and the problems of affordable housing. If you can learn to operate a clean and respectable rooming house, you will be providing a much needed service and make a good living doing it.

Tip: Since the term "rooming house" often conjures up negative images in people's minds, maybe we should come up with another term for this type of housing. Maybe something like: shared living quarters, guest rooms, sleeping rooms, compact housing, single room occupancy, inn rooms, etc.

The Rooming House Alternative. Since rooming houses don't pops up in the market every day, some investors use regular houses and large apartment units as a kind of de facto rooming house.

The actual zoning for creating a new rooming house sometimes is difficult to obtain (depending on the area), so some investors do a sort of low-profile room rental service.

The way this can work is by the loophole in certain civil rights and housing discrimination laws. Basically, people (investors, townships, codes, etc.) can't discriminate on who actually lives in a property. This is known as familial status. In other words, they can't tell you who you can or can't rent to based on the members of the group. If three or four unrelated folks want to share a house for rent the local government probably is not able to stop you. Of course, there are limits and some qualifications to this, but generally this is how it works.

As a result of these laws some investor will take a four bedroom house and rent out the rooms individually. Of course, there is a rent premium created because you will include various utilities and added services to the package. In addition, you might even furnish the rooms with basic furniture just like in the rooming house business.

In this arrangement your tenant might get cable TV, local phone service, heat, water, sewer, trash, and a furnished room. In turn, they pay a weekly or bi-weekly rent for the sleeping room. With three or four of the rooms rented, the house should rent for at least double what it would have rented as a whole unit.

Advertising Rooms. If you are running this type of service you need to be careful how you advertise the rooms. You probably don't want to advertise it as a rooming house since it really isn't one. It probably should be called a "shared living arrangement" or a "house to share." Whatever the case, be sure to research both local and federal zoning and discrimination laws to ensure compliance. Keep in mind that when you ask the typical governmental employee a question you often will be told No when they aren't sure of the answer. You need to educate yourself before you ask questions, and you need to be careful not to reveal too much information until you are fully educated. Consider taking a few months shopping the classified ads to see how others in your marketplace are doing this. Usually there are separate ad categories for this under "rooms for rent" or "house to share."

Hot Profit Tip. In this shared living arrangement be sure to use a rental contract that is titled Shared Apartment Arrangement or something similar that explains you are not renting a room, but a shared apartment or house.

Executive Apartment Service.

You might want to try this business opportunity with one of your smaller homes or larger apartment units. The service is an executive home-away-from home service.

For this service you take a property and completely furnish it with everything someone would need when away from home. It is like creating your own hotel suite, but you will be offering more services than a typical hotel room.

The target user for this service is corporations and government who don't want their traveling staff to live in hotels. The main advantage of this service is both price and convenience. A high quality hotel will easily cost upwards of $150 per day and won't include all of the services of a home away from home suite. A home away from home suite will charge $75 to $125 per day (about $2,500 monthly) depending on the area and level of services.

Basically you offer short-term rental stays ranging from one week to a few months. The price charged will depend on the local area, length of stay, and the amenities offered.

Services Offered.

Included in the rental are weekly maid service, cable TV, phone, dishes, cookware, utilities, ironing boards, hair dryers, shampoo, soap, coffee, soda pop, computer and Internet, Large TV, furniture, and towels.

If the client is willing to pay the price you could even provide a stocked refrigerator and a pantry full of food. Furthermore, you could arrange for added services like dry cleaning and laundry services. If that isn't enough, you could even arrange for other things like limo service to and from the airport.

Commercial Accounts.

Before you spend several thousand dollars experimenting with this service, you probably want to make sure there is a market for it. This will work best in an area with plenty of large corporations and industry that have traveling staff and out of town consultants.

Hidden Profits with Insurance Company Rentals.

Another great idea to add to the furnished executive, home-away-from-home service, is short-term housing for fire victims. Insurance companies are desperate to find furnished accommodations for fire victims and will pay high rates for short-term rentals houses and large apartments that are furnished and available on a month-to-month basis.

It is not uncommon to find insurance companies willing to pay $2,000 to $3,500 per month for short-term rental of furnished houses. This could be work beautifully into your corporate suite business! Not only that, but many of these insurance victims are given up front cash vouchers which prepays the landlord rent for four or five months!

Opportunities with Handicapped Ready-Units.

In the past five or ten years there has been a big increase in making businesses and public places more handicap-friendly. Wheelchair ramps and other modifications have all made being handicapped a little easier that it used to be. But there still is a great shortage in residential house and apartment rentals that are equipped for handicapped folks.

You can profit greatly by filling the void in this market by making some of your rental units handicap accessible. Not only should you be able to charge a premium in the rent, but in many cases you will get a great tenant to boot. You will find that these tenants will remain in your units for many years into the future if you meet their special housing requirements.

Another benefit of serving this market is an untapped market without competing with other landlords. To prove the point—how many landlords do you know that actively seek out handicapped tenants?

How To Modify The Unit.

The type and degree of modification depends on the type of physical disability the person has. Wheelchair-bound folks clearly need a unit without steps or with an accessory ramp. They also might need lower kitchen cabinets and counters to make them accessible from their chair. Installing safety grab bars around the bathroom areas will also be required. People with vision problems may need a unit suited for their seeing eye dog. Whatever the situation, you will need to do a little research to see what these folks need in a property to make it work. In many cases it shouldn't cost more than about $1,000 in materials to modify a property. Contact various private and governmental social agencies that work with these people to see what is needed to accommodate these special needs.

Finding Resident Clients. Most phone books include sections called Guide to Human Services. Simply contact the many social agencies that work with these folks. Consider contacting your local Section-8 housing office to see if they have any tenants needing housing with handicapped accessories. This will require some research and a lot of phone calls until you find the right contacts, but will be worth in from a rent premium and a quality of tenant standpoint.

Additional Profit Center. If you own a larger single family property with four to six bedrooms and the rooming house or shared living quarters arrangement won't work for you, consider renting your house out to one of the many agencies that operate a group home. A number of group home programs that house five to six people per home. These homes are typically operated by non-profit businesses. The clients are usually mentally handicapped or other people who need 24-hour supervision. In my area there are a number of group homes operated for delinquent boys. In many cases these group homes are the last attempt before the kids end up in prison. As stated, if you own a large house this could be a way to charge higher than market rents since a business is being operated out of the property.

Storage Space Rental Opportunities. You can't help but notice, as you drive around you can see new storage rental facilities being built in almost every town. The reason is the big demand for storage space.

I'm not advocating that you borrow hundreds of thousands of dollars to build one of the state-of-the-art storage facilities you may have seen. But I do believe there is a big demand for affordable storage without all of the frills many modern storage facilities offer.

Many investors have done extremely well just renting out garages. Many times these garages are older, but there still is a sizable demand for them when the rents are competitively priced. You might seriously consider building or buying garages or other cheap buildings that can be sectioned off as rental space. Depending on the area, low-cost storage is in big demand.

I have even seen clever investors take old barns and section them off with framing and wire to create separate units. On other occasions I have seen investors take old warehouses and outdated industrial buildings and create low-cost storage space for contractors or small businesses. The key seems to be pricing the space under market rates—and finding the right user. For example, my dad has a tenant in one of his storage units who rents the basement of an old building for his surplus merchandise business. He basically is a flea market vendor who sells distressed and surplus merchandise. His surplus vending business is prosperous but would not justify high rent storage space. He gets cheap rent, and my dad gets a good tenant.

While I like the idea of buying used garages units as investments, it isn't that hard to build simple cement block garages with concrete floors. If you do a lot of the work yourself (or play general contractor) you can typically build one of these cement block garages for about $4,000.

A $4,000 cement block garage will rent for about $100 to $125 per month. That's $1,200 per year in rent. In a little over three years you will have all of your money back and will have created a little money pump. The maintenance factor is super low on these structures, too!

Advantages of Renting Storage Space. One big
advantage of renting storage space is that you don't have to go through lengthy eviction proceedings if renters don't pay. In most cases, you simply send them a letter, post the notice on the unit, and wait for them to reinstate the rent. If they still don't pay, you can change the lock and hold their belongings. The process is much easier and faster than evicting people.

The second advantage is low maintenance and repair expenses. Regular residential rentals have heating, plumbing, and electrical systems that need maintenance and repair. Storage garages have doors and a roof, without a plumbing system.

The last big advantage is the cost factor. Because there aren't the normal mechanical systems needed in these storage garages you are able to buy or build them affordably. If you don't want used buildings, seriously consider building a few units yourself. To make it worth it, you probably should build a triplex or fourplex garage.

If you do most of the work yourself or act as the general contractor, you probably can build the units for around $16,000. Three or four hundred dollars per month return on a $16,000 investment isn't chopped liver.

Tools For Income Property Investments. A variety of tools are needed for the property rental business. Let's start with the paperwork.

First you need a good rental contract and a good rental application. Your first source for these documents should either be the local real estate investment club or a local real estate lawyer. A third source could be a real estate legal software programs on the market. The advantage of software is its ease of use and flexibility. If at all possible, look for software designed around your state's laws. For instance, in my state there is an attorney who produces real estate lease software specifically for my state. This state-specific software will be better than a generalized program, although Parson's Technology produces a number of legal software programs that are made for all of the states.

Next, I recommend you have a complete copy of your state's landlord-tenant law. This can be obtained either from the law library or from your local state representative. Just send the state rep a letter requesting a complete up to date and copy of the rental law. Last, visit the law library and see what books have been written specifically on your state's landlording laws.

After you start with rental property investing I recommend you get your properties computerized with a tenant/property management software program. There are several programs on the market like Tenant File or Tenant Pro. (If your cash is tight there's no need to spend money until you have at least five or six properties. On the other hand, most of this software is inexpensive.)

A company name is advisable to help you create a slightly more business-like relationship rather than just using your personal name. A business name allows you to operate more as the property manager and not the "rich" landlord. See chapter on company names.

Repair and Rehab Tools. The tools you need will depend on how much of the repair and maintenance work you actually intend to handle yourself. If you intend to do all or most of the work yourself, obtain as many tools as you can afford. Having a

great tool collection will make all of this work a lot easier. Here's a good starter list: a complete set of hand tools (hammer, utility knife, screwdrivers, etc.), a reciprocating saw, a circular saw, a cordless power screw driver/drill, a small sledge hammer, a wrecking pry bar, a shop vacuum, painting supplies, an airless power sprayer, a staple gun, a miter box, a 50 foot drain-cleaning snake, spackle knives, a plumbing torch, a pipe wrench, dust masks, goggles, tin snips, a ladder, flashlights, and work gloves. There are many other tools you could purchase, but these are a good start. The cost for a basic tool collection is about $1,000, but it will pay for itself in the first remodeling job.

Investing Knowledge Needed. You need a good knowledge base in three areas in order to be successful with income property: buying knowledge; knowledge about repair, renovation, and maintenance; and tenant management knowledge. In order to profit in this business you must become proficient in each of these three areas. If you have major weakness in any of these areas it will reduce your investment returns. In many ways it is like a three-legged stool; if any of the legs are broken or missing the stool will not hold weight.

There are many ways you can learn the rental craft. First, make friends with other landlords. Offer to help them with their properties if they will help you along the way with your questions. Next, read as many books on landlording and buying real estate as you can. As mentioned earlier, my book, *Perpetual Income,* is a good in-depth how-to manual on income property. Join a real estate investment club. If I were you would travel up to an hour or more to attend these meetings. On average I get one good idea per meeting.

The Big Repair-Maintenance Question. One of the biggest questions you will have to answer is, Who will handle your repairs and property maintenance?

The answer depends a lot on your current level of skills and knowledge in this area. In my opinion, if you have a lot of skills and time, then you should handle much of your own maintenance, repairs, and property remodeling. This is especially true in the early capital building years when you have more time than money.

If you don't have the skills or knowledge, then it comes down to time. If you have the time, I believe it is worth learning to handle this work.

Other factors are involved in deciding whether or not to do rental investing as a full or part-time business. If you plan to do this as a full-time business, I believe you should handle as much of this yourself as you can—at least until you build a good cash flow and a lot of skill as a professional manager.

My Irrefutable Repair/Maintenance Law: In the professional income property business the more knowledge you have about, repairing, renovating, remodeling, refurbishing, painting, patching, troubleshooting, diagnosing, tools, shortcuts, and salvaging, the more money you will make.

After investing for nearly 20 years I believe this above principle is irrefutable. From personal experience I have found that the more shortcuts, trade skills, repair tricks, problem diagnosis, maintenance and general construction knowledge I learn, the more confident and successful I become.

I don't do all of my own repair and maintenance work, but I have made a constant effort to learn all I can about these areas of the rental business. Properties do need repairs and maintenance—if you remain ignorant it will cost you money.

From my many years of watching investors, I have observed that the most successful ones, the ones who last, are the ones who know a lot about repairing and fixing up properties. The ones who choose to remain ignorant are invariably the ones who end up quitting or are driven out of the business out of sheer frustration.

Don't worry about any of this repair and maintenance stuff. When I started I had a negative IQ in this area. I was totally baffled about remodeling. In fact, I wanted nothing to do with the repair and maintenance end. Then I got smart. I took an interest in learning everything I could and let me tell you, the tricks and fixup secrets I learned have saved me a small fortune. It is all very learnable.

Hot Profit Tip. I learned most of what I know about maintenance and repairs from the contractor handymen who have serviced my properties over the years. I also learned tons from my investor friends. Don't be afraid of this area—you can run ads for a handyman to help you!

If you want to do the rental business full-time (which I don't recommend unless you first own at least ten properties) you probably will have to do at least some of the repair, maintenance, and unit prep work yourself. The profit margin in the early years of the business demands it. Otherwise you probably won't survive doing it full-time.

Full-Time or Part-Time. Rental properties are ideal as a sideline or complementary business, a part-time endeavor.

If you are really gutsy (or crazy) you might make a go of full-time income property investing. If so, I have several observations and suggestions. First, I would say think seriously and hard before you jump into it full-time. Understand that you will consume much of your rental profits on living expenses, and you won't grow as fast compared to doing it as a parallel business. Doing it as a parallel business (part-time) will enable you to plow all of the profits back into the rental business, and you will grow like a weed in cow manure. You also will be more bankable if you have other income or employment.

If you insist on full-time investing I recommend taking one of several steps to enhance your cash flow. I would get into one of these opportunities: rooming houses, larger multi-unit buildings 6-12 units each), or low-income house rentals/installment sales.

Regular single family and small apartment (2 to 4 units) investments in middle class areas will be a tough ride as a full timer. These properties make fine investments, but are better as vehicles for equity growth. I would not recommend going full time until you have at least 15 to 20 properties in your portfolio.

Management Skills. Property management isn't the most exciting endeavor in the world, but it is a skill worth learning. In fact, being a skilled property manager will enable you to make a lot of money in rental investments. The world is full of sharp real estate buyers, but there are few sharp managers.

There have been large tomes written on property management, so I will only cover what I think are the main pointers about successful property management.

Stay Close To Home. Buy properties close to home. Properties require time and attention. If the property is too far from your home you won't be able to effectively manage it. As a rough rule, I would advise keeping your properties no more than 45 minutes from home. Fifteen to thirty minutes is even better.

Tight Control. Most good managers keep a tight control on their properties, tying in with the close-to-home principle. Tight control means screening tenants and making periodic inspections of the rental property. It also means quickly responding to tenant's repair and maintenance problems.

Do-It-Yourself. Handle the property management yourself. It is generally a mistake to hire a management company, especially in the early years of building your portfolio. No one will handle your money as well as you can. This isn't to say there aren't good management companies, but you are better off building your own management team and saving the fees.

Enemy Numero Uno. The number one enemy of rental investors is vacancy. Vacant properties kill cash flow, so do everything you can to get empty properties cleaned, repaired and rented.

There are two primary ways to avoid vacancy. One, select renters who will not only pay their rent, but who from past history will probably stay in the unit for several years. This selection process is indeed an art. If possible, avoid folks who seem unstable and move from place to place.

The second secret to avoiding vacancy is to respond promptly to repair and maintenance requests. Think like a wise business person here: By efficiently and cheerfully handling repairs and problems you will be making an investment in the property that will both preserve the value of the property and help retain the tenant.

You can take this one step further: Try to make minor improvements to the property every year or two. These would be things like adding a ceiling fan, installing a new storm door, replacing some shabby carpet, or whatever. This does wonders at keeping tenants in your buildings longer!

Avoid Emotions with Tenants. As a professional landlord, you will find numerous times when it is easy to get emotionally blinded when dealing with tenants. The easiest time is when you show properties to prospective tenants who practically beg you to let them rent the property. They often will be in a hurry and have a story as to why they need a place right away. This situation becomes tempting to new landlords because the empty property is costing them money. They give in to the desperate renter and usually end up regretting it.

The investing game must be treated like a business. You need to carefully screen prospective tenants with credit applications and keep a sharp eye out for deadbeats and folks with stability problems. Although most tenants are good folks, about 20 percent of them can make landlording tough. They may seem like nice people and will promise to pay you, but once they are in the property the whole relationship begins to change. You, as landlord, become the bad guy, and they will have all sorts of stories as to why they can't pay.

There will even be situations where you find yourself losing your cool when dealing with tenants. Always remember that this is a business and that these people are your customers. Treat them with respect, fairness, and firmness. In many cases, they will not be on equal footing with you financially or otherwise, so try your best to endure them. Remember, a good paying tenant is a valuable asset—do what you can to preserve the relationship.

The 10-Day Notice Rule. You must collect your rents or you can get into trouble quickly. Don't fool around with non-paying tenants, especially in the first year of a rental relationship. As a general rule, give non-paying tenants notice to move if they don't pay within ten days of a due date. If you let them slide, they will often begin to abuse you on a monthly basis with all kinds of excuses about the car being in the garage or some other unacceptable excuse.

Your tenants need to know that you come *first* when it comes to bill paying, because if they don't pay—they don't stay!

Tenant Screening Tips. Do a credit check on every prospective tenant. This doesn't necessarily mean you will require perfect credit, since many acceptable tenants have some bad credit, but you want to avoid tenants who have credit reports that are composed mainly of bad credit and chargeoffs.

Before you actually rent to someone make an unexpected visit where they now live. This is an effective way to see how they live and the condition you can expect your property to look like after a few months. Many professional landlords use this simple trick to get a close-up view of their prospective tenant.

Look for folks who seem to have some stability in their lives. Avoid folks who seem to be in major transition in their lives, bouncing from job to job and from property to property. This is a danger sign.

Rental Property Buying Secrets. In this section you will find tips and observations on making good real estate purchases. The general principles for buying rental properties are the same as for buying houses for resale except for a few differences. An entire book could be written on this subject so we will only skim over a few key concepts.

Buying Right is A-1 Critical. Let me tell you, it is no fun to pay full price for buildings and wait fifteen or twenty years until you see a profit.

By buying right you can shave ten or fifteen years off the profit curve and start making positive cash flow and equity within months. On the other hand, paying market value (full price) for houses and apartments may require holding the properties for ten years or more until you "feel" a profit.

You don't have to "steal" properties to do well in rental investing, but you should seek bargain properties giving you at least 20 to 25 percent off the fair market value. In lower income properties the rule is even tougher: you should not pay more than about 50 percent of fair market value.

Fixer-Uppers are Where the Money is. Just like in the buy/sell business, fixer uppers are where the money is. Fixup properties can easily be bought at a discount, and after repairs are worth a lot more than you paid. This "forced" appreciation can happen in a matter of months, creating rapid equity and cash flow.

Tip: Remember, dirty, rundown properties don't look like good deals—they look like work! Offer a deeply discounted price and then clean it up.

Interest Rates are Critical. In the fast buy/sell business, interest costs on the money are not as critical as they are in the long-term rental game. In rental investments where you hold properties for the long term, the rate of interest is critical. Low rates mean faster equity growth and ultimately more cash flow.

I have owned investments requiring me to pay 7 percent interest, and I have also owned properties with 10.5 percent. Let me assure you, the 7 percent mortgages pay off dramatically faster than the 10.5 percent mortgages.

In one situation I refinanced a 25-year, 12 percent mortgage down to a 15-year, 9 percent mortgage and not only lowered my payment by about $20 a month, but also cut 10 years off the payments. Let's just do some rough estimates of the savings on that refinance. I saved roughly 120 months of $300 payments—a whopping $36,000 savings—by lowering my debt costs!

In your income property business become very interest rate sensitive. Low interest rates will greatly speed up the debt reduction process. The rental business is no fun if you pay full price for properties and high interest rates

Developing Your Credit.
Good credit and a good personal reputation are valuable assets worth tens of thousands of dollars. Do whatever you can to keep your credit report clean. If your credit is poor, begin today to clean it up and rebuild it by making timely payments.

If your credit is good, banks and mortgage companies will lend you plenty of money on well-bought properties. By having this financing available you have a powerful tool to take advantage of good deals that other investors can't buy.

Credit Line Method.
One proven methods of buying is to buy properties for cash at extreme discounts using some sort of personal credit line such a home equity loan or a business credit line. After you own the property, fix it up and get it rented. By paying cash and buying at deep discount and then rehabbing the property, you will have created a tremendous bargain in terms of equity. Once your property has been rented and repaired, refinance it with a "non-owner occupied equity loan." This refinancing will enable you to pay off your short-term credit line and place a long-term mortgage on the rental property. With your credit line repaid you can repeat the process on the next deal.

Owner Financing.
Short-term (1 to 5 years) owner financing is relatively easy to obtain for rundown properties, but getting

owners to hold 15 to 20 year mortgages can become more difficult. If you want to buy properties strictly with owner financing, you will probably be forced to deal in lower-income houses. Neglected and mismanaged apartment buildings also are frequently sold with long-term owner financing. Higher end property can be bought with owner financing, especially rundown property, but it is harder to obtain. Frankly, this whole area of owner financing will be determined by your ability to make a lot of offers on property. If you are trying to build a large rental business based solely on owner financing you will probably end up dealing more in low-end properties. This can be workable if you make sure you avoid the tough drug and crime areas.

The Mistake of Good Terms. Generally we think of good terms as a deal we arrange with very little of our own cash. Although high leverage deals are nice because we don't need much money, never confuse a "no money down" deal with a good deal.

So-called "no money down" deals may or may not turn out to be good deals. I remember one house I bought with 100 percent financing and basically paid market value for the deal that hasn't made me any money in the 12 years I have owned it! No money down doesn't mean it is a good deal! *The price must be right!* You have to buy right—cheap!

Good Deals Take Time to Find. Finding a good deal is a lot like going hunting. It takes time and patience. One good deal is worth five so-so deals! Take your time and be a patient bargain hunter.

Remember, one excellent purchase can be worth $50,000-100,000 in net cash flow and equity over the next 10 to 15 years. It is worth being patient and waiting for the right deal. After all, most investors need to buy only one or two good deals per year to create an excellent sideline business.

Resources and Helpful Sources. Many folks cringe at the thought of owning rental properties, but if you treat it like a business and continue to get educated, rental properties can be *highly* rewarding. There are few businesses and almost no investments than can match the income and equity building capability of owning rental assets. In fact, I feel so strongly about rental assets that I would give this business-investment opportunity a 5-star rating for ambitious folks who aren't afraid to get their hands dirty and work hard.

Many helpful books are on the market about buying and managing real estate. My book, *Perpetual Income,* is a must read for both beginner or advanced investors. It is full of detailed and step-by-step information on buying and managing rental assets. This book goes beyond the typical book store investing book. The fix up and repair chapter alone is over 50 pages in length.

Perhaps the best web site on the Internet for landlords is Jeffrey Taylor's site at **www.mrlandlord.com.** This site features plenty of free resources and a goodly number books and reports which they sell. They also publish the Mr. Landlord newsletter. Call them at 800.950.2250.

Another helpful website is **www.infoleverage.com** which focuses on generating positive cash flow from smaller properties.

Creative Real Estate magazine is another resource that real estate investors will find helpful. Call them at 858.756.1441.

If you get into the housing business you will need to learn how to maintain and repair properties. An excellent resource is *The Family Handyman* magazine. Investors, don't let the title fool you. This magazine is full of great tips and ideas for repairing and maintaining property. You can reach them at 651.454.9200 or on the Internet at **www.familyhandyman.com.** Another source for repair and construction knowledge is **www.constructionbook.com.** Call them at 800.253.0541.

An absolute must is to join a real estate investment association. You can find a group in your area by contacting the national group NAREIA at **www.nareia.com.** You can make a lot of valuable contacts at these meetings and find answers to many of your questions. Based on my experience, I am certain that you will learn at least one good idea or profit making tip at each meeting you attend. One of the great aspects of these associations is that landlords do not view themselves as competitors, so there will be a lot of cooperation and information sharing!

Master Leasing Income Property. You don't need to
own rental properties to generate cash flow. You can control properties without ownership using a master lease. If you control the property with all of the rights of use and possession, you can garner cash flow by sandwiching in the leasing of these same units to sub-tenants. In this opportunity the entrepreneur is specifically looking for

income properties where he or she can gain control of the building via a master lease. Once the master lease is secured the hard-working entrepreneur can turn around the property and release the units. This is property management without ownership.

The Master Lease Property.

Although I have heard success stories of people using master leases to control single family homes I think the biggest opportunity for an upside profit margin is to acquire a master lease on multi-unit buildings or mobile homes parks. If you decide to work with single-family homes you are probably smart to go a little on the higher end of the scale. Low-end houses won't have as much rent spread and typically need more maintenance.

For all intents and purposes a master lease gives the entrepreneur virtually all of the benefits of owning a building except for the advantage of equity. The biggest plus of using a master or sandwich lease is the leverage.

In many cases a properly negotiated master lease can be acquired for little or no cash investment. This will require some skill and fix-up knowledge, but in most cases less than $2,000 to really get going.

The Business Model.

Generating income using master leases follows virtually the same business model as conventional rental property. Rather than repeat the same tools, techniques and resources, I will focus on the key points you need to know about finding and securing a master lease and negotiating it. Keep in mind that a master lease can sometimes be used as an effective tool for managing other people's property without a formal real estate license due to the leasehold rights in subleasing.

As always, be sure to research laws in effect in your state and consider getting legal counsel.

A master lease is a real estate contract giving the fee title-holder the ability to lease the entire property to a master tenant lessee who, in turn, has the right to sublease part or all of the building or property to sub-lessees. This concept is also known as sandwich leasing.

A properly drafted lease is a powerful interest in property known as a leasehold estate. This type of estate gives you the right to enjoy and possess the property along with the right to sublease the estate to others—unless subleasing is forbidden in the lease.

Generally speaking you will be master leasing a whole property at a "bulk discount" rate and then releasing the individual parts at retail market rates. The difference between wholesale leasing and retail releasing (sub-leasing) is your lease spread. This really isn't that much different from using a mortgage to buy and then leasing out your property, except you won't be gaining equity or tax benefits that go with property ownership.

The Perfect Master Lease Scenario. Your goal should be to find either mismanaged properties with high vacancy rates or out-of-town owners who are in way over their heads.

Whatever the case, as with most real estate investments you want to find people who are motivated and flexible because they have ownership problems. These ownership problems are typically tenant problems or simply neglected buildings. Owning a property that has bad tenants or neglected maintenance is a high stressor. If you can find these people by running ads or direct mail letters to owners of neglected buildings you can offer to solve all of these problems by taking over the building a giving them a "guaranteed income without headaches."

This of course, will require swift, hands-on management efforts on your part. You will need to get rid of the bad tenants and begin cleaning up the building. Then, using your professional management methods, you need to find good tenants.

Let's say the property has a total potential of $350 per month for each of six units. This is a potential rent of $2,100 per month. Let's say the owner currently is only getting rent on 2 units and the third tenant is a deadbeat. The owner is getting $700 per month plus all of the headaches. Your offer is to completely take the building off his hands for $800 per month and will handle all of the maintenance and repairs up to $200 per month with receipts to validate your expenses. While a lot of owners will not accept this offer, an owner who is sick of management will take it if you can assure him you will take much better care of the building then he will. You in turn clean up the building and sublease all of the units. Your potential spread is $1,300 before raising rents. Important: try to find buildings with low rents so you can boast your spread by raising rents higher than what the old owner was charging. Also, look for ways to cut expenses as explained in the chapter on rental cash-flow consulting.

Terms of the Master Lease. Like an artist, you can do anything your creative mind dreams up as long as the owner is willing to go along with it. There really isn't a standard master lease since so few master leases are used in small deals, although they are used in large commercial projects.

Consider negotiating any terms that you need to make the arrangement work for you. For example, work in a 2 to 3 month moratorium on master lease payments, transfer (assign) existing tenant security deposits to you, extend the duration of the lease, add rights to improve property, insert repair and expense caps with repayment agreement on improvements over a certain dollar, figure in a clause with a future option to buy and escape termination, add a legal exculpatory clause or limits, *include the right to sub-lease,* and possibly the right to convert the deal into an installment purchase if timely payments are made and the right to renew the lease at the existing rates and terms—and virtually anything else you can negotiate to your favor.

Hot Profit Tip. If possible consider basing your master lease on a performance basis so that you will share some of the rental income with the owner as you improve the property. The advantage is that your lease payments will remain low while you get the building cleaned up. The owner also benefits by gaining some of the rents when you get the property turned around. This method is like a partnering relationship with less risk on your part.

Critical Clauses. In a master lease a clause allowing you the freedom to sublease/release units or parts of the property out to others is vital. Your lease agreement must be very clear as to what duties you and your owner have. Unless things are totally spelled out, disputes are likely, especially on larger, more complicated properties.

Make sure your owner gives you a written letter showing you have the right to collect the rents on the existing leases. Also, consider getting an assignment of rents from the owner for the preexisting leases. It is also important to get a fairly long master lease term (with an escape clause for you) because you don't want the owner to terminate your lease after you have worked so hard to turn around the property. **Note:** Be sure to have the lease notarized and even recorded at the courthouse to ensure your leasehold estate is documented and protected.

Final Thoughts On Master Leases.
You are a landlord in this arrangement. You must follow current landlord tenant laws and practices for your state.

While most master lease deals are done on large commercial properties, you can create a nice business with smaller properties if you aren't afraid of working hard on turning around problem properties. Just make sure the problems are solvable before you take on the lease. If the location is horrible, for example, you may have the same problem the current owner has.

I know that master leasing is a workable business because I know one family who holds a 25-year, sandwich lease position on a commercial property (a single tenant) that generates over $20,000 in spread annually!

12

Opportunities With Mobile Homes

A book on real estate business opportunities would be incomplete without a section on mobile homes. The category of mobile homes, or, more accurately, manufactured housing, has great potential as a business opportunity.

The extremely high cost of site-built, new construction makes factory built homes a bargain. On average a manufactured home costs at least 50 percent less than a site-built home. If you really think about that, the factory built home makes a lot of sense.

With a factory built home you gain the economies of assembly line efficiency combined with bulk material purchasing power for the home factory. In addition, you gain efficiencies of using cookie cutter layouts and design plans, rather than custom built homes. You also don't lose construction days due to the weather. Furthermore, you have an overall higher level of quality control due to the repetitive nature of building the same basic home over and over.

Years ago mobile homes were considered to be mostly a low-income type of dwelling. In recent years though, mobile homes have become much more mainstream. In fact, many of the new manufactured homes are luxurious and beautiful.

They Aren't Trailers Anymore. Years ago mobile homes were called trailers. Today, the word "trailer" conjures an image of a dumpy metal box in a rundown trailer park. The housing entrepreneur does not use the word trailer—this is a turnoff.

You may not even want to use the term, mobile home, because this term is also going out of style. The new term is manufactured housing. Another big turn-off are the terms, trailer park or trailer court. These are totally out of date. Manufactured homes go into communities, not parks! (Even so, you'll catch me using these terms every now and then. Old habits die hard.)

Trends in Manufactured Homes. Manufactured
homes of the past ten years are far more energy efficient than the
homes of a few decades ago. The quality and construction has
improved greatly due to various federal and state construction
codes tailored specifically to the manufactured housing industry.

Manufactured homes are available in a variety of styles, sizes,
and layouts, a major change from the 12-by-70 foot industry standard of the 1970s.

Upgrades in all of these factors—price, quality, style, energy
efficiency, selection—make manufactured housing a big winner for
the coming decades.

Two Big Opportunities in Mobile Homes.
Although there are numerous opportunities within the manufactured housing industry I will focus on the two main opportunities
that fit the start-up entrepreneur best.

The first opportunity is in buying and selling used (pre-owned)
mobile homes. The second big opportunity is in buying and operating a mobile home community (remember, we don't call them
trailer parks anymore). There are also several spin-off businesses
and profit centers we will touch on lightly.

In this section I have merged these two opportunities into one
business model because for reasons I will explain later they work
best when worked together. You can buy and sell used mobile
homes without actually owning the mobile home park, but there are
several challenges and pitfalls in doing so.

The Geographical Situation. Mobile homes are more
common in some areas of the country than others. As a general rule,
there is more money to be made in those areas in your state or
region where mobile homes are welcome. For instance, in some
areas of the country any attempt to build a new mobile home park is
quickly killed by zoning officials. On the other hand, there are
many rural areas where mobile home communities and parks are
welcome. In fact, many rural areas have little or no zoning.

From this investor's experience and observation, the most
lucrative geographical areas tend to be moderately rural or areas
where you see mobile home parks as a common type of housing.
Trying to prosper in this business in area hostile to both parks and
mobile homes may be more difficult. If you are serious about this

opportunity, you will be shopping for a good business climate that might be an hour or more from your home.

The Business Model. There is a lot of money to be made buying and selling used mobile homes because this market has an exceptionally high level of distressed sellers who are unable to sell their homes. This creates a lopsided buyer's market with a lot of bargains.

To compound this buyer's market, there is very little in the way of financing for this used mobile home market. In fact, most banks won't touch a used mobile home loan.

This combination of factors creates opportunity for creative investors to buy distressed homes at a high discount and then resell them at retail prices by packaging the deal with seller financing. While there is a huge opportunity here, especially for the cash-poor investor, there also are some real problems associated with this business model. I will explain the basic model and many of the hidden problem areas inherent in this business. I will then propose some solutions that should eliminate most of the pitfalls.

Buy/Sell/Finance: Pre-owned Homes. Some investors have done well buying distressed mobile homes in mobile home parks for cash and then cleaning, repairing, and reselling them for a sizable markup.

The profits are created in ways that are similar to the methods used in buying and selling houses on installment contracts. You first make a profit by buying the mobile home at a deep cash discount. You then refurbish the home with new carpeting and vinyl, and make needed repairs. Your final profit building step is to offer the home for sale with owner/seller financing. All parts of this process (buying-cleaning-fixing-financing) create income that can make this business profitable.

The Big Snag Areas. Although the buy/sell-finance business is very profitable and workable, there are some legitimate pitfalls with this business model. I not trying to be negative on this opportunity, but you need to know the full picture before getting started. It is also important to know that these problems usually occur with the larger, more professionally operated mobile home parks. You may be able to work without a problem in smaller parks and areas where mobile homes are commonplace.

The first pitfall is in buying and selling used mobile homes in parks that are owned by other investors. In most cases you are free to buy a mobile home within a park, but the problem is that your resale buyer (or renter) must be approved by the park management. That's the snag. You might be able to sell the used home fairly easy, but while the park is deciding whether or not to give their stamp of approval on your buyer, you pay the lot rent on the vacant home.

The second pitfall of flipping in another investor's park is the lot rent factor. As just mentioned, you as the investor are responsible for making the lot rent payments during the fix-up and resale time. Since you are paying the lot rent, the park may not be in a hurry to get your buyer approved. Furthermore, if your buyer defaults on the lot rent payments, you, as the finance company, may be liable for the back rent and current rent payments once they have vacated the home. Since this process can take two to five months, this added time plus the time it takes to resell the home could reduce your income out of pocket by several thousand dollars in lot rent fees due to the park.

Key Cautionary Tip. Before handing over cash to a mobile home seller verify that their lot rent is paid in full. Most parks will not allow you to move the home out of the park until the back lot rent is up to date. (It is a common law lien.)

The third common problem associated with flipping mobile homes located in other people's park is what I call investor hostility. Many parks do not want mobile home investors buying used homes in their park. The park management knows how profitable all of this business can be, so they don't take kindly to investors who want to invest within their park. I have talked to many park owners who came right out and said—No investors in the park!

The fourth problem is the age factor. Many parks have age restrictions on mobile homes. For example, some parks will say no used homes over the age of 20 years can be in their park. You may unwittingly buy an older mobile home in a park and then be forced to move it out. Many parks will allow older homes inside the park as long as the existing home owner remains in the park. But, once the home owner decides to sell, the park may want the trailer moved out so they can upgrade the park with a nice new home. This is very common. **Note:** many park owners sell new homes so they jump on any chance to get a vacant spot so they can make a big profit selling a new mobile home.

One other potential snag is that many park owners do not allow mobile home owners to rent their trailers. In other words, no renting of homes within the park. In my area this is standard practice. Keep in mind, the park owners can rent out homes, but outsiders can not! Policies like this can increase risk and limit your options for generating income.

The Control Problem. All of these problem areas revolve around one central issue: Control. When you buy and sell used homes in other people's mobile home parks you are out of control. There are too many variables where other people get to decide your fate. I think there is a better way.

Note: Although these are very real problems I don't want you to get a roadblock mentality. If you have your own solutions for covering these problems or if the circumstances are different in your area, then by all means go for it.

The Solution: The best solution to cover the lack of control is to buy your own mobile home park and then you can make your own rules as to who buys, sells, rents, or finances the homes.

Mobile Home Parks as Investments. Although I can't say every mobile home park is a great investment, I can state that in general, mobile home parks can be a highly profitable business to those who learn how to succeed with this opportunity.

The beauty of owning a mobile home park is you not only generate a substantial cash flow, but can establish several ancillary profit centers that can be readily worked into the business mix.

Mobile home parks are considered stable investments. As a rule, the default rate on investor loans for parks is very low. This means most parks carry themselves from a cash flow standpoint, and the majority of investors like owning them.

The resale rate for used parks is also fairly low. Generally, there are not many parks for sale on the market. This again shows that park owners are relatively happy with their investment.

Mobile home parks command a fairly high price. This is mainly due to the predictable income stream that they provide. The income streams are steady and predictable; therefore, investors will pay a premium to place their money in them.

Lot rents are high and tend to rise because more and more people need a nice place to "park" their mobile home. This means steady and rising rental incomes for park owners.

Mobile home parks have a "captive audience." Due to the semi-permanent nature of mobile homes (they're really not very mobile) park owners generally do not have a lot of turnover within a park. If the community is maintained and operated cleanly, many of the lot renters will stay for five to twenty years, which again reflects on the overall stable nature of mobile home parks.

Mobile home parks are a type of income property. You have almost all of the advantages that go along with rental assets, as we have discussed in our section on rental assets. In a nutshell, you can buy a rental asset at a negotiated price, finance all or most of the purchase, improve it, raise rents, and have the tenant user over time buy the asset for you. In the end, you have a free and clear, growing income stream that can last for decades.

Lastly, in the park business you are only renting the ground and aren't responsible for leaky roofs, clogged toilets, or house maintenance. The bottom line is you have a nice, predictable income stream.

Leasing Lots and Selling Homes. The ideal business
model in my opinion is buying a mobile home park (preferably distressed in some way) and then buying and sell homes inside your own park. This marriage (lot renting and flipping) works exceptionally well because you gain the added control that was missing in our earlier examples, plus you make profits both from lot rents and the sales on used homes. You should also explore selling new homes inside the park as a dealer for one or more of the many manufactured housing companies that will be happy to make the arrangements with you.

Mobile Home Park Strategy. If you are a cash-poor
entrepreneur, your best bet is to look for a smaller to medium sized mobile home park that is somewhat rundown and distressed. You want to find a park that is either mismanaged or one whose owners just want out of the business and have let it go.

A mismanaged park sell at a reduced price with some form of owner financing. If the owner has existing financing, explore the options of assuming the mortgage or having the seller carry some form of installment contract.

After you purchase the park, one of the first things I advise you to do is to change the parks name. For example, let's say the rundown park's name is Smith's Trailer Court. You want to stop association with a negative image name that won't attract the type of residents you want. You might call it something like Summer Fields Community or Green Hills Community. The name should sound pleasant and warm.

Next you want to make an immediate effort to get the non-paying, bad residents out of the park. These are the folks who aren't paying their rent and probably have jacked-up cars and beer cans outside their home. These bad tenants will scare away the desirable folks you want in the community.

Along with purging some of the bad apples, start making improvements to the park by grading the roads with fresh stone. Also, paint all of the garages, maintenance sheds, and other buildings on the grounds. Clean the place up by gathering the trash and debris from the trailer park grounds. In many cases this alone will drive out the druggies and deadbeats.

Next, walk around and talk with the folks in the community and see what needs to be handled. Besides giving you their complaints, these folks will also tell you who is selling drugs or doing illegal activities inside the park.

Hot Profit Tip. If you see any homes with missing skirting this is a no-no that will make the park look trashy. Send out skirting notices to all of these residents.

Abandoned Home Pitfall. A problem area with mobile home parks is dealing with abandoned homes. In many older parks obsolete and worthless homes that are not salable because they are just plain junk take up space and degrade the appearance of your park. You will need to see what your legal options are and then dispose of them. In many cases, these abandoned homes will need to be dismantled with sledgehammers and burned or taken to a landfill. The metal framing can be sold for scrap.

After you begin turning around the park you should slowly begin raising lot rents. You will need to know the local market for lot rents and the current demand for spaces. Be judicious. After all, these folks are somewhat of a captive market, so don't take advantage of them.

The Buy/Sell Strategy.
If you own a park of 15 to 40 spaces you will have plenty of opportunity to buy some of the homes that come up for sale in the park by folks, who, for whatever reason, need to sell. Watch for repossessions from banks and finance companies. You can get excellent deals on these homes. You then clean, repair, install new floor coverings, and get the home ready for sale. Then sell the home and offer your in-house financing.

Here's a typical deal. You buy a 12 year old home in rundown condition. You determine it will need $2,500 in repairs. You buy it for $4,500 and pay cash. Upon completing the repairs and remodeling process, you will own the 12-year-old home for a total investment of $7,000—and your new appraised value should be about $16,000.

Next, sell the home with about $2,000 down and payments of $300 per month for 60 months. If the deal goes to term you will collect $18,000 in payments plus your initial $2,000 down payment. In total you should net about $13,000 in profit.

Guidelines For Buying and Selling.
Several tips and rules of thumb you need to know before buying a used mobile home include the following:

Age Rules. Avoid buying used homes older than about 15 years in age, and almost never buy a used mobile home older than twenty years.

Size Rules. Never buy less than a 3-bedroom mobile home. Avoid outdated styles and sizes (do your research).

Use Book Value Guides. Appraisal books are available that will give you retail and wholesale valuations on mobile homes. Use these books, but remember you must only buy wholesale. **Note:** The risk level is much higher in mobile homes due to the lower income nature of many of the buyers and various depreciation factors. Therefore, you must buy right to create enough profit to cover losses and note default.

Let the Buyer Repair it. In some cases if the home doesn't needing a lot of repairs, you can get away with just giving the home a good cleaning and letting the buyer fix up the home themselves. You won't get as high a sale price, but you will conserve your cash in the deal.

Profit Guidelines. Since the risk level is higher in holding this paper, you should shoot for a cost times 2 sales price. If you total costs in the deal are $6,000 shoot for at least $12,000 in sales price. (Holding the note should enable a good markup since this ads value to the deal).

Low-End Homes. Some investors have done well with older, lower priced homes in the $2,000 to $3,000 range. This seems to work well, but keep in mind you will often get a lower-scale buyer that may require swift attention when they don't make their payments. Also, keep in mind that there is a broad range of quality in manufactured homes. Educate yourself on the quality level of the various mobile home manufacturers.

Back Tax Pitfall. Many new buyers to mobile homes don't realize that in many areas of the country additional taxes go along with mobile homes owned within a park. This tax, in whatever form, is usually tied to the school system as a school tax. Be careful when buying because a distressed seller won't inform you about these back taxes and you may end up with an undisclosed lien on the mobile home, often $200 to $500 per year! Learn what taxes are associated with mobile homes in your area.

Unique Parts and Materials. Although most of the repairs needed for mobile homes can be done with regular hardware and building supplies, keep in mind that mobile homes have parts and hardware that are made just for manufactured housing. If you get involved you will want to set up a wholesale account with a mobile home supply company.

Mobile Home Rehab Advantage. One advantage of buying used mobile homes is you that can often refurbish them very economically. Most of the newer homes will only need a fresh roof coating and some skirting repairs for the outside. Inside you will probably need some basic repairs, cleaning, painting, fresh carpeting and vinyl.

Default Solutions. If you sell a used home and the buyer defaults on the payments, one option is to try to buy them out of the deal. Rather than go through the somewhat lengthy process of eviction or repossession you might try to offer them a few hundred dollars cash to vacate. In many cases this will work, especially if they have a drug or alcohol problem.

Remember the Learning Curve. If you get involved in this type of real estate remember the learning curve. You are bound to get burned now and then especially in the beginning. Try to stay involved long enough to break through the learning curve.

Hot Profit Tip. Some entrepreneurs buy used mobile homes that need to be moved at close to salvage prices. They then move them onto their own property where they do a complete refurbishment of the home. They then market the home as a "renewed" home. For instance, they might take a wholesale purchase of $3,500, renovate it for another $3,000, and resell it outright or on terms for $12,000-25,000. If they can package the home with a lot (well, septic, utilities) they can get a much higher dollar for the deal! I have even heard of some companies that have created an indoor assembly line team that rebuilds a high volume of used homes and then resells them.

Renting Mobile Homes. Renting mobile homes can be a high-profit business if you buy them at deeply discounted prices. Following many of the same guidelines used for buying mobile homes for resale you can end up with astounding cash flow yields. Remember, these homes typically won't appreciate, so cash flow is critical.

If at all possible try to buy used homes that sit on the owner's land. This gives you maximum control since you will own both the lot and the home. In many areas of the country you can buy the home and the land for $10,000 to $25,000. If you can't buy the land, you must get an extreme bargain because the risk level is higher. For example, you might have to move the home. **Note:** Do not buy used mobile homes (for resale or rent) unless you buy them at absolute fire-sale prices

Consider buying repossessed homes from finance companies. If you can buy a used mobile home following the guidelines previously mentioned for $3,000 to $10,000 and then rent that same home for $300 to $400 per month, you can see that will give you a high profit margin. You might even buy a used home and land with the intention of renting the home for the next 10 years and then haul it away and replace it. With numbers like these, who cares if they don't appreciate? **Note:** Mobile homes that have their own land (not rented land) do in fact appreciate at rates close to conventional housing!

Additional Profit Centers.

If you own a park you can provide additional services that can add to your bottom line. For example, many folks living in mobile homes desperately need additional storage space. Consider providing garages or storage units in your mobile home community. As mentioned in an earlier section, storage garages are relatively cheap to build.

Coin-operated Laundry Units. If you have a suitable building, consider installing some laundry machines. Shop your options. Some companies will install the machines with nothing down on a profit sharing arrangement. Vending machines are another possibility that might work well in the laundry center.

Satellite TV. Now here's a biggie. Consider giving the cable folks the boot and work a deal to buy satellite feeds in bulk and sub-meter the service to the residents with your own cable. Satellite dish programs like this are available.

RV Rentals. Depending on the nature and location of your mobile home park, you might provide an area where people can either store their RV (for a fee) or where they can set it up permanently as a home. If you have plenty of land this is a possibility.

Speculation Sales. If you find a suitable piece of land, you can buy it, install a new manufactured home on it and sell it for cash. Mobile homes permanently installed on a lot with footers, where the buyer gets a deed, are a very, salable package. Banks are not afraid to loan money on these. (In fact, mobile homes secured to land will appreciate almost as much as a regular home.) Consider getting a dealership with a new manufacturer and do these little land and home sale packages. A respectable profit is very likely.

Resources. My first recommendation is to join your state's manufactured housing association. At the very least find out about their meetings and pay them a visit. These state associations will provide you with countless contacts and inside information about the business.

Attend manufactured housing shows. These are typically for dealers only, so you may need to have a business card showing you are a mobile home investor in order to get into the show. These trade shows tend to be held annually so find the nearest one to you. These shows are excellent at giving you an education about the industry (You will be surprised at how easy it is to become a dealer!)

If you are interested in buying and selling used mobile homes you should read Lonnie Scruggs' books, *Deals on Wheels,* and, *Making Money with Mobile Homes* available through various on-line sources.

13

Real Estate Consulting Opportunities

Consulting can be an excellent business for those people who have developed specialized knowledge that other people need. Rather than giving away this hard-won knowledge and experience, you can create a consulting practice thereby selling—or let's say, renting—your mind to others for a nice fee.

Many people who have developed a large body of knowledge and expertise often fail to realize the value they possess between their ears. We all tend to take such talents for granted, but in reality they are a tremendous asset. We can't list them on a financial statement, but there are ways to convert our experience, knowledge, and wisdom into equity and income.

Consulting is an excellent way to convert your knowledge, experience, wisdom, and expertise into an income stream of fees and profits without needing a lot of capital to get started. Due to the very nature of consulting (selling time and advice) you have the ideal business, especially for the creative but cash poor person.

What is Consulting? Consulting is the business of helping people solve problems and optimize assets. In business consulting there seems to be three main thrusts: Problem solving, improving profits, and specialized task performance.

Consulting places you in an advisory role to guide and shepherd clients through problems with your expertise. A consultant's job also is to reveal hidden or overlooked profit centers within their business. Furthermore, a consultant's job is to act as a gentle critic of the client's current operation. It is that said a good consultant will get the client a little bit mad and bruise the ego—mildly painful yet very therapeutic. To paraphrase business writer Brian Tracy—a good consultant needs to be a little bit of an insultant.

Consulting's Key Requirement. One critical prerequisite is needed before even entertaining the idea of starting a consulting practice. The requirement is you *must* have some type of specialized knowledge that people want and need—and sufficient demand for this knowledge. For instance, you might be a world-class authority on the Australian Spotted Toad, but chances are there is only a few handful of folks in the entire world who need this type of knowledge. You must not only have a specialized body of knowledge, but also a large enough market that needs your knowledge.

To be an effective consultant you not only need to be knowledgeable—you also need to have a sizable base of business experience around the subject you plan to consult on. You cannot be all image, puff, and fluff—there must be a deep well of experience and expertise from which your clients can draw from. The old cliché of "fake it 'till you make it" won't cut it. You must have spent legitimate time in the trenches before you sell yourself to others.

The Six Consulting Opportunities. There are far more than six real estate consulting opportunities awaiting the real estate entrepreneur, but we will focus our attention on the six opportunities that seem most marketable.

Keep in mind, only you can ultimately determine which, if any, of these opportunities is right for you. You not only need experience and expertise to sell, but you also need a viable market in your given area of interest. Even if you have no interest in the consulting opportunities presented here, this section is replete with ideas to spawn your own ideas for a consulting business.

We will review consulting opportunities in foreclosure consulting, real estate agent consulting, real estate services coupon marketing, rental cash flow consulting, lease option consulting, and tax reduction consulting.

All of these consulting services are so similar in nature and in execution that I will begin with an explanation of the basic tools and skills required in consulting and then we'll get into specific business opportunities and ideas.

The Broad Business Model. Consulting is about building a trade or brand name that is, YOU Inc. You are selling yourself. You are the product. It follows that if you are selling you—you must be special.

Consulting is about specialized knowledge, but it also about image. This means you must be packaged cleanly and sharply. Consulting is about bringing value to the table so the client walks away with an abundance of usable and profitable advice. If the client doesn't make or save at least four times the fee they are paying you, you're probably not giving enough value to the client.

Consulting Skills.

A good consultant should not be a know-it-all expert, but rather an empathic and concerned partner in helping the client solve their problem and maximize their assets. A good consultant must be a good listener.

Client-Centered Consulting.

You and your company must be one hundred percent client-centered and client focused. Shape all of your discussions, presentations, marketing, advice, and attention to the client, not yourself.

Consulting Tools.

To start and operate a successful consulting practice you will need sharp communication and packaging tools. Since consulting is essentially selling intangible things like time and advice, you can get started with only a few thousand dollars.

For starters, a full array of communication tools are needed. These include a dual phone and fax lines, answering/voice mail service, a cell phone, and call forwarding services. In addition, a good computer with word processing software and a laser printer are mandatory since a consultant does a lot of communicating via letters, faxes, and business briefs.

Next, you will need to develop high-quality promotional marketing documents such as cards, brochures, stationery, envelopes, and direct mail pieces. Make these documents client centered—people only care about what you can do to help them. Don't go cheap in this area.

You will also need to invest in high quality business attire. This doesn't mean you need a couple of $500 suits, but you should have updated, clean and well-fitted business clothing. This means sport jackets, polished shoes, dress shirts and ties. Again, you don't need to look like Wall Street, but business casual or a step above is about right.

Office Needs.

If you do a lot of telephone consulting you can operate from a home office. Most of your consulting will be on site consulting, so a home office should work fine. If clients are coming to see you, work out an office sharing or renting arrangement using the conference room of your account, lawyer, or title company. If at all possible, avoid outright office leasing. Many of the nicer hotels and restaurants have conference rooms available for minimal day or half-day rates.

Consulting Contract.

In this business you can't work on a handshake or verbal commitment. You need a consulting agreement that spells out the services you will perform and how much you will be paid. There are numerous consulting agreements available from consulting books or from any number of general consulting software packages.

How Consultants are Paid.

There are numerous payment arrangements in consulting: Hourly fees, per-job fee, contingency percentage fees, monthly consulting retainers, speaking and workshop fees.

You will have to decide what types of payment arrangements will work best for you. The per-job fee is popular; for example, you might charge $750 to solve a particular problem.

One clever way to build income is to set up clients on a monthly retainer so that you provide unlimited advice for your clients during that month. Suppose for example, you set up 10 clients each on a $1,500 monthly retainer fee for your expertise. That's a comfy $15,000 per month!

The Irresistible Contingency Fee.

This is one of the most effective ways to find new clients. It tells them they have nothing to risk because they pay you nothing unless you solve their problem and get the desired results.

This works especially well in those situations where your services save the client money. The offer could sound like this: I guarantee you will save $5,000 in lost profit these next four months or you pay me nothing. Or, I charge half of whatever I either make or save you in profits. (**Note:** in these arrangements it is important you spell out in the consulting contract the client's obligation to cooperate and execute the plan you provide.)

Setting Your Fees.

Your fee structure depends on the level of advice and skill you bring to the table. You need to price your services high enough to cover the down time when you aren't consulting. On the other hand, you need to start out with lower fees in the beginning until you prove yourself and create a referral base. The general range for consulting is between $40 to $200 per hour. Some consultants prefer to mask their hourly fee by quoting only by the job or working on a contingency program with some form of profit split.

Hot Profit Tip. You don't actually have to meet clients to consult with them. Consider offering several levels of consulting. E-mail consulting is an excellent way to communicate with a large number of clients. Telephone consultations are another great way to consult without either the consultant or the client leaving their office to communicate. Last are audiotape consultations. Have the client fill out a detailed written brief of their problem and you mail them an audio taped response.

Real Estate Agent Marketing Consulting. In this opportunity you are a marketing consultant for real estate agents. More specifically, you will help agents build their own real estate brokerage business by doing professional and focused marketing programs.

The Agent's Problem. Real estate agents have two big problems that professional marketing consultants can help solve. First, agents all look the same. Real estate sales and brokerage is a me-too business. Pick up any real estate advertisement and all of the agents are saying the same thing; they all look the same, too. We call this becoming a commodity. Agent homogenization. Your typical agent not only is a me-too, but lacks the self-clarity to define who they are to the public

The second problem agents have is a lack of time and focus. The typical agent is so busy doing real estate that they can't develop a cogent and coherent niche message that breaks through marketplace noise. You can solve these problems by specializing in marketing for agents. You will partner with select agents in developing marketing campaigns and provide much needed time and focus to recast their marketplace image.

Required Skills and Experience. This opportunity is one of the few presented in this book that requires experience and

specific skills. To be an effective real estate marketing consultant you will first and foremost need a background in marketing. This doesn't mean you need a college degree, but you will need to fully understand the concepts of advertising, business branding, and positioning. Secondly, you will need prior experience in real estate so you understand the process of buying, selling, and financing real estate along with a good understanding of the business of being a real estate salesperson. The book you are reading can provide some of this knowledge, but not all.

Your Target Client. The type of clients you will be seeking are those agents who have broken through the first couple years of real estate sales—have tasted some success—and are generating enough income so they can afford your services.

These agents have proven themselves as being on the winning road, but not having arrived. You want agents who are willing to think outside of the normal pack mentality. Furthermore, you want agents who understand that real estate sales is building a business, not a job.

The Pitch to the Client. Before you can market *for* the client you are going to have *to* market to the client to sell your own services. This means high-quality, client-centered marketing documents (cards, brochures, letters, stationery, advertisements, etc.).

You will need to explain to the potential client their desperate need to break out of the pack mentality and create their own brand name in the business. Most agents are in the marketplace using scattered and inconsistent marketing methods.

Your job is to sell the client on allowing you to craft, sharpen, and retool their marketing image, methods and advertisements. In essence, you will develop a differentiation strategy for the agent, which will enable them to gain a competitive advantage in the marketplace. No longer will they be a me-too!

Actual Consulting Services. A consultant isn't someone with all the right answers, but rather someone who knows the right questions to ask. One of the first things you will do after taking on a new client will be to conduct a detailed interview using at least 100 questions so you can learn all you can about the current state of the business and the client's goals.

In this initial inquiry session you will also need to learn as much as possible about the problems, successes, strengths, weaknesses, and current marketing methods. Gather a file of past ads.

Differentiation Process. Next you should work with the agent in defining all of the things that they do that set them apart from other agents in the business. They may offer special services, free services, unusual services, or anything else that makes them unique. If the agent is not doing anything special, then help them create some special services, perhaps things like free tax appeal appraisals, discounted commissions, free home valuations, free help for FSBOs, internet services, free moving truck after closing, free stay at a bed and breakfast for referrals, free information on any listing in the county within thee hours of inquiry, or anything else that increases their value in the market.

Specialization Process. Next you need to help the agent create a specialty. This involved identifying a real estate niche that has worked well for the agent. If the agent doesn't have one—create one. Specialties include new construction, buyer's broker, upscale homes, inner city homes, condos, land, property management, farms, commercial property, income property specialist, business broker, and rural property.

By creating a specialty you create a centerpiece for your marketing around. The agent may list and sell outside the specialty, but marking a special service as a specialty will enable the agent to begin to break away from the me-too pack.

Once you have recast and retooled the agent's marketing program, it is time to roll out new advertisements, cards, flyers, and commercials.

Marketplace Domination. After you create your agent's list of unique marketing differentiation points along with choosing a specialty, you are ready to dominate the marketplace. Remember, most agents are simply copycats, so what you have done so far is highly strategic and valuable for the client. In fact, if you only performed this service it would be worth thousands of dollars to the agent.

By dominating the market I don't mean running more ads than all of the other agents. You will be running a lot of ads. The difference is you will be running bold and aggressive headlines combined with totally client-focused and benefit rich copy. Marketing domination is done by running cohesive, consistent, and coherent marketing campaigns that make the business standout from among its competitors. Market domination is measured as successful when the first thing the market thinks of is your business.

Headlines. Most agents are poor headline writers. Your task is to write bold headlines that will get your client's ads noticed. Don't be afraid to push the envelope; a little puff is okay as long as you are truthful. You want to avoid things like, "The Best Agent in Bradford County" or other boastful, agent-centered hype. Remember—client-centered sells. You want something like, "We List At 4.9 percent Commissions." Or, "I'll Sell Your Home In 90 days or I'll Buy It."

Good headlines should be interesting and arouse curiosity. Making headlines provocative and bordering on the outrageous can do this.

Advertising and Marketing Design. Choose a good graphic designer as a subcontractor to work with you in creating bold and different advertising pieces. You and the agent will be the idea people while the graphic designer will be the artist. Don't be afraid to make design changes or suggestions since many of these designers have more artistic talent than business savvy.

From my experience, the marketing message is more important than the artistry of the ad. Good headlines and benefit-rich copy sell better than fancy but dull ads. If you have a computer with a high quality color printer combined with desktop publishing software, you may be able to design your own marketing devices (cards, letters, flyers, ads, brochures).

Hot Profit Tip. Besides changing an ad's headline, the next best way to increase its effectiveness is to improve the location of the ad within the publication. Many business people accept whatever position the newspaper, magazine, or marketing medium gives them. Try to get the best positions within the marketing medium; simply request ahead of time where you want the ad placed. If you run a lot of ads within a certain publication your bargaining power will improve. Generally, inside front cover or inside/ outside back cover are good. Also, the first three or

four pages are best. The right side of the publication is preferred.

Consulting Tip. As a consultant, create a file and save every creative or different real estate advertisement that you find. I would save only those ads that have some creative or unique aspect to them. Most don't. These home advertisement booklets and ads are everywhere. It is an especially good idea to save those ads from outside your marketplace when you are traveling. These various ads will help generate ideas for your clients.

Direct Mail Management.

If you're not geared up for direct mail it can be a time-consuming distraction. As a marketing consultant you could offer to manage the direct mail program for your agent. This would entail the agent submitting all the names from call-ins and prospects so the agent can build a large data mine on his clients. This database can be worked via direct mail and joint ventures with other related service providers.

Additional Services.

There are several additional services you can offer in your consulting practice. One such service is competitor research where you "shop" the competition to see what they are offering in the way of services. This may require using a straw shopper to actually call and question your client's main competition. It may also require gathering and studying the competing agent's marketing devices.

Another service could be conducting marketing focus groups where you actually bring together past real estate consumers to see what they liked and disliked in the real estate agent they used. This may require some minor inducement or compensation for the participants.

These services can bring valuable market intelligence to the agent client you are working for. After the data is gathered you should produce a "confidential" report with a strategy for the client.

Trademarking and Copyrighting.

After you begin creating a brand and unique market position for your client, start copyrighting and trademarking all of the marketing pieces (ads, letters, logo, selling jingles) you and the client develop. This will also separate your client from the pack by making his marketing messages look professional.

Trademarks and copyrights are in most cases done with very little paperwork or filing. Typically, an acceptable common-law trademark or copyright is created by simply marking the document with © or a small TM symbol after a logo or trade jingle. (Also, place a name and date after the copyright symbol.)

Pricing Consulting. For the larger marketing jobs of retooling and differentiation I would suggest a pre-set monthly program with a minimum of six monthly periods. This must be in a contract form. After the initial six-month program you probably should create a maintenance program at a lower billing rate.

Creating Marketing Territories. One powerful way to sell your services is to create a protected territory for each agent client. This ensures them you won't be offering the same services to other clients in the immediate area. This can be used in your marketing presentation to create a sense of competition and scarcity of your valuable services.

Be careful though, not to place too many limits on taking new clients. One way around this might be to limit the "territories" by county and or specialty. For example, you could have several clients in a marketplace by making sure these various clients have different specialties. Suppose, for instance, you had a client that specialized in city homes. Couldn't you easily take on another marketing client within that market that specialized in upscale homes?

Client Duplication. Since a lot of consulting work can be done over the telephone, and by using email, fax, and teleconferencing, there's no reason you should limit clients based on where they live. In fact, taking on similar clients in different parts of your state will actually help you replicate and leverage your efforts. In many cases, the marketing strategies for an agent specializing in farm properties will be nearly the same on the other side of the state. If you had five or six similar clients you could even conduct monthly teleconferences where the specialty agents shared with each other what is and is not working.

Resources. See resources listed in marketing chapter.

Real Estate Service Marketing. If you understand marketing, advertising, and real estate enough to consult with real estate agents why couldn't you offer your consulting to other real estate services providers?

Don't you think you could offer many of these same services to mortgage brokers, real estate attorneys, home inspectors, appraisers, handyman repair companies, and title companies? The correct answer is yes.

You could easily duplicate the agent marketing consulting strategies for real estate service companies. In most cases, these business people are too close their own business to fully exploit the opportunities in the market.

Real Estate Coupon Consulting. I have shown how you can help real estate agents maximize their brokerage business using marketing consulting. In this opportunity I will explain some related opportunities helping real estate service companies maximize their marketing to attract new clients. This idea could possibly be worked in conjunction with the consulting opportunities just presented or perhaps alone. You can create a brand new marketing device and strategy for the real estate industry.

The Business Model. Coupons are a hot marketing device in today's economy. Folks love special offers and ways to save money. In this opportunity you will create a valuable coupon book or magazine centered around real estate related businesses. Your coupon book can be used by people who need to buy, sell, or rent property. It will provide legitimate, money saving certificates and special offers to real estate consumers.

Advertisers are vendors and service providers within the real estate marketplace. These select companies will create (with your help) special offers, dollars-off-coupons, and rebates available only through the coupon book.

Coupon Clients. Any company with a product or service a real estate buyer or seller would find helpful during their real estate transaction could be a prospect for your coupon marketing services. Here are some examples: Real estate brokers and agents, home inspection companies, title companies, mortgage brokers, attorneys, roofers, handyman services, carpet cleaners, painters, carpet sales, movers, relocation companies, insurance brokers, auctioneers, 1031 tax deferred exchange facilitators, property management firms, termite inspection services, water conditioning companies, interior decorators, and any other related service that is tied to the purchase or sale of real estate.

Allow one or two vendors within a given category or specialty. For instance, you probably would only allow one home inspection company per book issue. You can also use this policy as a selling point letting the vendor know they will be the exclusive vendor in their category.

The Critical Factors. It is important if you want to succeed that several things be done properly. First, you must make sure that the offers presented in the coupon book are legitimate money saving offers. This is critical. You cannot fill the booklet with junk offers that are nothing more than hype and advertisements. Many of the coupons I see being used in the general marketplace are of little value to the consumer. The offer should present true and inclusive savings for the consumer bearing the coupon.

The coupons must not be mere advertisements. They must be eye-catching, money saving offers with a high perceived value. If your coupon book doesn't deliver substantial value to the user, the program won't work. This will require helping the client in creating his or her coupon offers.

The second critical factor is the format and quality of the coupon book. You want the coupon certificate books to have a rich look about them. Newspaper print is definitely out! Glossy silver, gold, blue, and maroon colors convey a high-value image.

Design Considerations. You definitely will need to subcontract with a graphic designer who has a lot of ad design experience and top quality computer design equipment.

You will need to come up with a size format. A smaller book may appear thicker and improve the perceived value. Also, make sure the various ads are staggered on the pages so when the consumer tears out the certificate coupon it doesn't have another coupon on the other side.

Tip: Remember to copyright and trademark all of your proprietary work. If the program really takes off consider a formal registration of your coupon book's name. This gets more involved legally and financially, but may be worth it to guard your proprietary work.

A good headline or subtitle will be important in marketing your certificate book. For example—

Save $750, on your next real estate purchase or sale— guaranteed!

Name Consideration.
Develop a classy name for your product. Don't try to be too cute. Class and professionalism is the goal. Also, the term "certificate" sounds better than "coupon," doesn't it? Maybe the combination of terms sounds best: coupon certificate.

Idea Model.
In many areas of the country you will see coupon books called Entertainment Books®. Consumers pay about $30 for the book, but it offers substantial money saving offers like 2 for 1 dinner specials. Pick up one of these books and see if you can get some ideas.

Another consideration is frequency. Perhaps to start you will want to have two issues, although eventually you probably will have four issues (spring, winter, fall, summer).

Formatting Twist.
Along with savings certificates you may be able to bolster the salability and value of your product by including how-to sections or tips on the different aspects of buying, selling, or renting real estate—perhaps even a CD program with some special real estate software. Be creative.

Distribution and Pricing.
Perhaps the best way to make the deal work is to combine the interests of both advertisers and consumers. For example, you might charge each vendor $1,295 per coupon book run. If you have 30 vendors that would be $38,850 per book in revenue. Then you could sell the books for somewhere in $19.95 and $49.95 depending on the level of true savings offered to the consumer. **Note:** This is why it is important to offer legitimate savings to the consumer. Folks won't pay $29.95 for a book of worthless ads—the savings must be real and substantial.

This whole pricing area is tricky because there must be a balance of true savings for the consumer and a reasonable marketing charge to the vendor. Also, if the vendor doesn't see results you won't get repeat business.

The books could be distributed at newsstands, bookstores, real estate vendor offices, direct mail, telemarketers, fundraisers, and any other way that connects with buyers and sellers of real estate.

Internet Tie-In. We all know print media are expensive to produce and distribute. Start asking what if? questions. What if I sold a classy certificate with a password that tied into an Internet site allowing the certificate holder special printable certificates off the web that are guaranteed to save the consumer at least $500 to $750 off their next real estate transaction? The Internet certainly would lower your production and distribution charges, but you still need some tangible marketing device to put into the consumer's hands.

Partnering Twist. One idea worth considering is to joint venture with high-quality and reputable vendors for a percentage fee. For example, the vendor might pay a base fee to cover production and design costs, but all other fees would be based on the amount of business you bring them. This puts less risk on the vendor because they have nothing to lose in the event the marketing doesn't work.

The challenge with joint ventures is enforcing collection and tracing actual new business from the coupons. You might want to build a provision into the rebate arrangement that requires the consumer to qualify for a discount only by mailing or emailing you the proof of purchase. Then you rebate them the money saved and bill the vendor, who would pay the agreed upon percentage based on redemptions.

Foreclosure Consulting. Losing your property in a foreclosure can be a scary and troubling experience. In most cases property owners are too intimidated by the lender to take appropriate actions to stop the sale. A foreclosure consultant can educate the homeowner as to their options along with acting as a third party mediator to try to bring about agreement among the parties.

There are a variety of services and contacts a foreclosure consultant can provide that will justify a debtor's engaging their service. These services range from helping the foreclosure victim find a buyer for their home (via investor contacts or real estate agents) to arranging a bailout loan to negotiating a discounted debt settlement.

The business opportunity here is to help people save their home, credit, and equity by acting as a professional mediator and educator in the foreclosure process. For these services the foreclosure consultant is paid a fixed fee of somewhere in the range of $295 to $695 depending on the size of the loan and amount of work needed to save the property.

It is worth noting that there have been a fair amount of scams and rip-offs in this area of foreclosure consulting. Ignorant people are charged thousands of dollars (often secured by their home) by rip-off artists to "save" their property. This sort of price gouging is unethical and bad business. Don't confuse unethical services with one in which the lender settles a debt as paid-in-full and the consultant earns a fee as a percentage of the reduced debt settlement.

The Business Model. Thousands of people fall behind on their mortgage payments every month. Many of them have every intention of saving their home and stopping the foreclosure process. The problem is they wait too long to take action. They also aren't armed with the knowledge of how the process works and negotiating with the lender from a position of strength.

The foreclosure consultant's job is to act as an educator and a mediator to help the homeowner know their options and to assist them in talking with the lender. **Note:** The term foreclosure consultant sometimes conjures up a negative image. From here on out we will use the term Foreclosure Mediator or Mortgage Consultant.

The business model for being a foreclosure mediator is actually quite simple. You run various ads and use direct mail to contact people who are either in foreclosure or close to it. For a fee you will analyze their financial situation and loan default in an effort to present their best options to either save their home or gain the most time. As part of this job you will also work towards preserving and or restoring their credit and equity as much as possible.

Tools Needed. Along with all of the standard office tools such as a computer, fax, voice mail, and copier, there are several other things you will need. You must have the legal guidebooks written specifically on your state's foreclosure laws. You can find the titles and publishing house information by searching the larger law libraries within your state. In most cases you shouldn't have to look far since most counties have a law library.

These state-specific books are priceless at learning the nuts and bolts of your state's foreclosure laws and rules. In most cases there are several books authored by lawyers within your state.

Next, you will want to pick up several books on bankruptcy. Nolo Press has several good books written at a layperson's level. (Bankruptcy law changes about every five years so make sure the books you rely on are up to date.)

It's a good idea educate yourself on the subject of credit repair and credit laws since you will need to have information about how your clients can clean up their credit after the episode. Bookstores and libraries will be helpful.

Client Worksheet. You will need to create a client questionnaire or worksheet to help you discover and document the client's current financial status related to the property. It should have the following questions: lender's name, address, phone number, debt amount, number of mortgages against the property, judgments, liens, back payment info, social security number; client's address, phone, employment, current income amount, etc.

Client/Mediator Contract. This is an important document that you and the client both need to sign before you work on the client's mortgage mediation case. This document basically spells out the work that will be performed along with the fee being paid. This document will also authorize the lender to release all information regarding the loan to the mediator. (Without this release the lender won't talk with you.) The contract should also spell out possible options, stating clearly that the specific actions to fulfill such options are the responsibility of the debtor. Furthermore, you should explain that there are no guarantees as to the outcome of your mediation services. **Note:** some lenders may require a notary seal to verify this release document's authenticity.

Team Players for Your Mediation/Consulting.
It is wise to network with an attorney who you can work with those cases that get too complicated or involved. You will also need an attorney who you can refer cases to who need to file bankruptcy. Look for a newer and open-minded attorney who won't feel threatened by your services. Be careful not to reveal too many of your

marketing secrets since the lawyer might try to run away with your business idea.

A network of serious real estate investors (or yourself) is a good idea because the best thing for some of your clients will be to sell their home before the foreclosure sale. As the consultant you can refer your clients to a list of real estate buyers to make a fast sale.

In some cases your client won't be totally desperate, and a conventional real estate broker might be a good referral so your client can get the best dollar for the property and pay off the debt. A good working relationship with a real estate agent or broker will help the client sell the home for a better price than will the real estate investor route.

A mortgage broker is another team player you should have in your network to help your clients save their home. In many cases a second mortgage or complete refinancing will provide the client with the breathing room needed to save their credit and their property. Your client's credit will probably be on the rough side, so you need an equity or hard-money lender to handle the lower grade financing.

Additional Profit Center. Since many of your clients need money, it may be smart to become a mortgage broker or work under a mortgage broker in order to create additional revenues from loan placements. This could work nicely in conjunction with foreclosure mediation.

Referral Fees. Depending on laws in your state you may or may not be able to earn referral fees from the people in your network. You will need to research this yourself. If no fees can be taken, perhaps you can earn reciprocity referrals—with each of you referring to the other. (Another possibility might be charging a marketing/advertising fee per client. Be sure to obtain legal advice if you are considering this option.)

Licensing Laws. Most states do not have specific foreclosure consulting laws on the books. But it is still wise to research this matter. California does have a foreclosure consulting law as civil code section 2945-2945.11. Also be aware that some lawyers may think you are horning in on their territory in the practice of law (UPL: unauthorized practice of law). Be careful not to advertise in any manner that portrays you as an attorney or offering legal advice. You are a mortgage consultant who is an expert in mortgage financing and credit remediation. Again, this matter is subject to state laws and legal interpretation so get legal advice.

Financial Options for Delinquent Mortgages.

A debtor has a multitude of options to stop or slow down a foreclosure action. Following is a brief explanation of options available to someone behind on mortgage payments.

Sell the Property.

Your client may not like this, but outright sale of the property is a viable option if there is some equity in the property and the mortgage is delinquent. If you need a really fast sale, consider offering it to real estate investors. If you have more time use a real estate broker to help the client get a higher price. Whatever the case, let the lender know the property is on the market. This may require sending or faxing them copies of the listing agreement or pending sales contracts your client signs.

Payment Plan.

Many debtors don't realize it, but with a third party negotiating you can often work out a payment plan, which will eventually bring the debtor current. Make sure you know how much the debtor can afford before you negotiate. In most situations the lender will require a lump sum, good faith payment along with regularly scheduled payments with extra (25 percent) money to be applied to the arrearages.

Forbearance.

This term applies to a situation in which you negotiate with the lender to allow a month or two of non-payment until the debtor gets back on his feet and brings the mortgage current. For FHA or VA mortgages, programs are available that allow special repayment terms in true hardship cases. FNMA and other large institutions also have in-house "secret" deals that they make to help hardship cases such as a catastrophic illness after verifying the debtor's story. In other words, the lender may make special provisions for repayment.

Bankruptcy 7,13.

There are a variety of bankruptcy options available for debtors. Bankruptcy is among the most powerful cards you hold in this negotiating game. Lenders hate it because it stops them cold in their tracks. Be cautious not to use this too early in your negotiating because it may not be the best option for the debtor, and the lender might surprise you and ask you to go ahead. Save this card to be played later.

If other options don't work or if the lender doesn't seem agreeable to a reasonably repayment plan, then you can use one of the bankruptcy plans to stop the mortgage foreclosure. Your first choice might be to just use this lever in your negotiating as a way to persuade the lender to work with your client. In the event it doesn't help the matter you might refer the client to the attorney in your network.

Chapter 7. Chapter 7 Bankruptcy is total liquidation of the debtor's assets in order to pay creditors. As a rule, Chapter 7 is used when the debtor feels there is no way he or she can ever dig out of the financial pit. The debtor can choose to keep the home, although they must make the scheduled payments. In some cases this works since most of the other debts have been wiped out, enabling the debtor to make their mortgage payments.

Chapter 13. This is the form of bankruptcy known as the wage earner's plan or payment plan bankruptcy. In a nutshell this plan stops creditor collection efforts for a period of time while the courts determine the financial condition and ability of the debtor to repay the debts. Eventually a plan is developed for the debtor. Late payments are generally added to the debt balance, and all future payments must be kept current. (This plan is usually a restructured payment plan that lowers the various debt payments for the debtor. If the debtor defaults on the plan they can then consider filing a chapter 7 total liquidation that will drag out the process even more and provide more buying time.

Lenders and Bankruptcy. Typically, secured mortgage creditors (first mortgages) are not wiped out in a bankruptcy. The lender's problem is that during the bankruptcy process any foreclosure collection efforts must cease. The lender does have some options such as petitioning the court to have the stay lifted. Whatever the case, lenders don't like bankruptcy because it is costly in terms of legal fees, lost time, and a stalled mortgage loan.

Refinancing. If the debtor has a lot of equity and still has an income, one option is to encourage the debtor to seek refinancing. This could possibly be done through yourself serving as a mortgage broker or through a mortgage broker contact. This refinancing might enable the client to lower their payments or provide the lump sum needed to bring the mortgage current.

Refinancing someone who already has shaky credit can be difficult unless you deal with the right kind of lender. Generally speaking, a "hard" money lender is required. A hard money or equity lender makes loans based primarily upon the equity in the property. If there isn't much equity this probably won't be feasible.

Loan Modification.

This method works by negotiating with the lender to rewrite (recast) the loan terms. The goal, of course, is to lower the mortgage payments or to take the back payments and add them into the loan balance. Whatever the case, this option gives the debtor a fresh start. Lenders will not quickly agree to this option, and it may take effort and persistence on your part to make it happen (remember, foreclosure is expensive for lenders).

Deed in Lieu of Foreclosure.

The deed itself can be an excellent tool used to stop a lender from foreclosing a property. This basic strategy works by giving the property back to the lender and saving them the legal fees and time of doing a foreclosure. This strategy can work nicely when the client has no intention of keeping the property, but wants to spare their credit report from being totally trashed. It also works well when there is not much equity in the house.

The primary goal of this method is to keep the lender from marking the debtor's credit report with a foreclosure black mark. A foreclosure on a credit report will significantly damage it. When offering this option to the bank, try to get the lender to be gracious with the debtor's credit report.

This option may not work if the debtor has a lot of additional liens, mortgages, or judgments against their name. Unlike a foreclosure, a deed in lieu of foreclosure does not clear the title. A foreclosure will generally clean off all subordinate liens (except governmental) leaving a clear title for the lender.

When using this strategy make sure the lender agrees to accept the deed back as full satisfaction and payment for the mortgage. You do not want the lender pursuing the debtor for a deficiency judgment for their losses. Have your lawyer partner review the deed the mortgage company prepared before the client signs the deed back to the lender.

State and Federal Programs. If you get into this business you will need to learn the various state and federal programs that are available to help mortgage debtors who are in foreclosure. For instance, some states have an emergency loan program available to folks who are confronted with unforeseen medical problems or natural disasters.

One way to research this is to write a letter requesting information from your state or federal congress person. These office holders have staff who will do research on whatever question you ask them. In almost all cases you will get a response letter with some answers.

Negotiated Short Sale. This strategy works when the property is being sold for less than the value of the property, or when the amount of equity falls short of making the deal work due to closing costs, repairs, and legal fees.

Try to negotiate with the lender (especially second mortgage lenders) to discount the debt balance to enable the debtor to sell the house. Show the lender they will take a big loss if they foreclose on the property. Explain they are better off losing a few thousand dollars rather than paying thousands in legal fees and months of lost time (a foreclosure will often cost a lender $10,000 in legal fees, sales commissions, clean up fees, etc.). In the event it is a second mortgage, you will have even greater leverage in negotiating a short sale since they might get completely wiped out in a foreclosure sale.

If the mortgage was originally a low-money down loan there probably is mortgage insurance. If so, you may have to get the mortgage insurance company's approval of the short sale.

Hardball Strategy. In the event you aren't able to negotiate a workable payment plan or forbearance agreement with the lender you may have to resort to playing hardball with the lender. This will require the services of your partnering attorney.

This method involves looking for defects or improper or illegal practices surrounding the mortgage loan. There are several possibilities. For example, both federal and state laws are typically involved regulating mortgage lending. The attorney's job is to find violations that will give him bargaining power to get the lender to stop the foreclosure. Regulation Z, RESPA, FCRA, Truth-in-Lending Act, and state interest rate statutes are all possible problem spots for the lender. In some cases the violation of these laws can deem the transaction as defective, creating legal wiggle room for the debtor.

Another possibility is having an attorney file for an injunction. An injunction is an order issued by a judge to stop the legal proceeding until it can be reviewed by the courts. This probably won't work unless the debtor has a truly meritorious case such as something being done improperly or significant legal issues at stake.

Negotiating Tip. Banks have heard a lot of empty promises and stories from debtors who cannot pay. Your best results will occur by knowing that banks truly do not want to take back property in a foreclosure action. This is a losing proposition for them. Before you contact the lender, make sure you have a plan or strategy before you call them. Try to determine that the debtor can fulfill their promises, or you will lose credibility when you call back a few months from now with another "plan." Also, the sooner a delinquent debtor deals with the problem the better results you will have. In the event there isn't much time left, your client may not have many options left except bankruptcy.

Mediators are becoming a popular alternative to litigation due to the high cost of legal fees and the court system. Do your best to create win-win agreements. Act as a problem solver and not as the lender's adversary.

Advertising for Business. The best place to run ads for this business is the money-to-loan section of the paper. There are several types of ads that can be operated. Your best bet is to try several different headlines: Foreclosure Stopped, We Stop Foreclosure, Money To Loan, Cash For Homes, We Buy Homes, etc. The type of ad you run will be determined by what services you are able to provide. For instance, if you are a mortgage broker or work with a broker you possibly could run the "Money for Loan" ad. If you work this business in conjunction with other real estate business such as buying houses you will probably pick up some leads from a "We Buy Houses" ad since many people in foreclosure try to sell their homes. As mentioned throughout this book, the freebie papers are often excellent for running ads. Keep in mind that it often takes several months of running an ad to reach its full effectiveness. The reader may not need you today, but two months from now might be looking through the paper for your advertisement.

In most larger cities and metropolitan areas credit bureaus and legal reporting companies collect notices of default and mortgage foreclosures from the courthouse. You might be able to subscribe to a weekly list of default and foreclosure notices that will provide names and addresses for your marketing program.

Additional Profit Centers.
This business opportunity could work well with the judgment recovery business, mortgage brokering, discounted mortgages, and house flipping. These opportunities are similar in the fact that much of the same real estate knowledge is needed to operate them.

Resources.
Along with various legal publications from your local law library you should read as many of the "save your home from foreclosure" books on the market as possible. Check with your local library by searching books in print. With the title in hand you can then request they import the book to your library through interlibrary loan. In most cases they will do it.

Perhaps one of the best books is *The Homeowner's Guide to Foreclosure: How to Protect Your Home and Your Rights,* by James I. Wiedemer, published by Dearborn. This book is written by an attorney who does a good job explaining the foreclosure process and the various legal options for people in foreclosure. Also: see Nolo Press (appendix).

Rental Cash Flow Consultant.
One of the best ways to make money as a consultant is to find a business with a lot of dollars passing through it. The consultant then enters the business as an outside pair of eyes to study where the cash flow leaks and short-falls are occurring.

The consultant can offer the business owner a unique proposition: I will either make or save you at least twice my fee or you pay me nothing! This is an appealing offer since the client essentially will be getting free help thanks to the additional cash flow generated by the business. This pay-by-performance proposition puts all of the risk on the consultant.

In most businesses, especially rental property, there are dozens of ways the income stream can be maximized through revenue enhancements or by cutting expenses. Typically, business owner and property investors are too close to their own business to see where the gaps and leaks are occurring. In other cases, owners simply don't have the knowledge, resources, contacts, or business acumen to spot their lost opportunities.

As a cash flow consultant you can provide a great service to small and medium sized landlords who need your expertise and creativity to help them squeeze every drop of cash flow from their income property. Your reward for this terrific service will be a tidy consultant's fee ranging from $995 to $3,000, depending on the size of the project and the level of profit savings.

The Business Model. For this consulting service you market your services to real estate investors who want to make more money. Since all investors want to make more money, you will have a huge market of prospects.

Your ideal clients will be smaller and medium-sized landlords who are serious about their investments. Your service will be to analyze their portfolio both on paper and in person in order to constructively critique the manner in which they run their business. The bottom line of this service is you will help rental investors make more money from their properties, either by cutting waste, raising revenues, trimming expenses, reducing debt service, improving maintenance technique, and any other method that will improve cash flow.

Required Skills and Knowledge. Experience in rental property ownership or management is mandatory in this business in order to be credible and to have enough business savvy to consult effectively with landlords. Rental property management and ownership is not something one learns over night or even in a year. My suggestion is for you to have at least five years of profitable ownership before you entertain this business opportunity. Furthermore, you should be well read in the general fields of business, marketing, and real estate.

Conducting a Consultation. The very first thing a consultant does is conduct an in-depth interview with the client in order to size up the client's current methods of operation, goals, and problem areas. (This means you must develop a comprehensive questionnaire of at least 100 questions).

This questionnaire would contain questions like: Have you ever evicted a tenant? Describe in detail the process of preparing a vacant unit for rent. Where do you find tenants. What type of heating system does your building have? What is your biggest problem area? What problem area causes you to lose the most money? What is the highest rate of interest you are paying on a mortgage loan? Describe your typical tenant selection process. How long has your longest tenant been with you? When did you buy your first property? Who performs your tax preparation and why? Do you make any payments to a private mortgage holder? How do you handle repairs and maintenance issues? Where do you buy materials from? When was the last time you raised your rents? How much? (Make the questionnaire as long as possible, even if it takes 2-3 hours to get through it.)

The question list needs to be organized into topical areas such as maintenance, buying, selling, rent collection, taxes, insurance, banking/finance, type of buildings preferred, goals, biggest loss areas, best money making methods, procrastination areas, etc.

The interview needs to be conducted orally in order to get as much information from the client as possible. **Note:** It is very important at this stage of the process to focus mainly on gathering information. Do not make recommendations or voice your opinions yet. This is the time to let the client vent as much of their frustration and viewpoints as possible. Take extensive notes.

Next have the client take you to their largest properties in order to see how they are operating them. Make sure the client doesn't just show you the choice buildings, but the not so nice properties as well.

Property Evaluation. Make up a comprehensive flow chart or check list so you can inspect the properties in a consistent and logical way.

Energy Efficiency Analysis. The way a building is being operated from an energy consumption standpoint can be a major source of "found" money in terms of cost cutting. Some of these things may seem like common sense, but many owners neglect them. Take a hard look at the following:

Water Consumption. This can be a major cash flow killer, especially with multi-unit properties. Drips, running toilets, leaky plumbing, broken faucets, outdated water-wasting toilets, etc., can all run up high water bills. This is one of the easiest ways to improve a buildings cash flow. For instance, you can rebuild the washers in a faucet for around $3 in parts. If you have a 6-unit property with 3 dripping faucets you are probably losing about $15 per month. It doesn't sound like much until you multiply that over a year ($180).

Tightening up a six-unit apartment building so there is minimal water waste will cost about $400 (new water-saver toilets, shower heads, faucet repairs, etc.). This investment will save the owner about $30 per month in cash flow.

Insulation. Many older building were not insulated very well because years ago fuel was cheap. By simply insulating the roof or attic part of a building you will save at least a hundred dollars per month in the coldest winter months. In addition, the building will feel more comfortable for the tenants since the temperature fluctuations will be less frequent.

Weatherization. This is another basic, but cost effective way to save money. Study the properties to make sure they are airtight. Caulk and weather stripping is cheap.

One landlord I know installed new windows and attic insulation on a large 140-unit complex. He stated that these energy improvements paid for themselves in utility savings within one heating season. All of the future cash flow increases were pure profit.

Heating System. Study the heating system. In many cases you can install a new system that will use far less fuel and provide better heat. Not only could the heating system be updated, but the client could install separate heating units for each apartment unit. This will shift the heat costs to the tenant. This may require a rent reduction, but the bottom line should be improved. It is also worth noting, many of the larger heating contractors will install a new system and finance it over several years. In many cases the fuel savings will pay the loan payments.

Another aspect of fuel savings is the type of thermostats being used in the property. There are new Accustat thermostats that have a design that can save up to 10 percent on heat bills. This area is worth getting educated in since a simple recommendation to a client like this could alone save them hundreds of dollars per year.

Utility Metering. Some buildings are setup so the landlord pays the utilities. One sure way to increase the property's income is to install various utility metering systems. These devices measure and meter the precise amount of usage by each tenant. In turn the user is billed for their consumption.

A variety of devices and systems on the market are also worth learning about.

Maintenance And Repair Methods.
Analyze the property to see what type of improvements have been made. Did the owner over-improve or under-improve? In many cases the building will need improvements. You can advise the owner on what the most profitable improvements are and how they should be done. There is a definite art to doing economical unit preparations. Offer the property owner low-cost suggestions for spicing up their units without investing a lot of money. Clean and fresh looking units keep tenants longer. Create a checklist of ideas.

In several cases I have seen landlords replacing perfectly good ceiling tiles, floor coverings, and cabinets. I informed the landlords that what was needed was some cleaning and painting, not replacement. If one of the investors had taken my advice, he would have saved at least $1,000 in needless remodeling costs. If you are an experienced landlord who has been in this business for several years you probably don't realize how much knowledge you have, but this knowledge can be worth thousands to other investors.

Financial Analysis.
After your interview questionnaire and tour of properties, ask to see the financial data. This part of the consultation will be a financial checkup.

Interest Rates.
Study the financing currently on the client's property to see what options are available for saving money on interest rates your client is paying. This is critical. Income property increases in value as the net income is increased. If you increase the building's income, the building's value also increases. Some ways

to reduce interest costs include: refinancing to a lower interest rate and refinancing to lengthen the term, thereby reducing the payment. If it is a private party note, perhaps it can be paid off early at a discount worthy of a refinance? Does the mortgage have private mortgage insurance that can be eliminated? Could we shorten the term and lower the rate?

Property Taxes. I would wager that at least half of all newly assessed properties are overvalued in favor of the taxing authority. This is a solvable problem through a basic tax appeal. Analyze the tax figures and assessments to see if the properties are over taxed. This move can easily save the client between $500 to $1,000 per year even on a modest sized portfolio.

Insurance Issues. Are the properties adequately insured? In most cases, investment properties do not have enough fire insurance. Keep in mind, if the property is underinsured, and there is a fire, the client will be penalized by the insurance company and won't be paid for all of the loss! Having the building insured for its fair market value is not enough. IT MUST BE INSURED AT ITS REPLACEMENT COST—in other words, the cost to rebuild the structure. (Be careful not to incur any liability advising on replacement costs. Consider sitting down with the insurance agent to ensure the property has enough replacement cost coverage.)

Another issue is the price being paid for coverage. Study the rates to see what the client is paying. Perhaps you can refer them to someone in your network who will offer better pricing or better coverage.

Material and Labor. Find out where the client is buying their materials and building supplies. Are they getting the contractor discounts? For instance, in my area, a home supply store offers contractors 10 percent off one day each month. If you bunch your purchases for that day you can easily save $25 to $50 per month. Also, find out how much the client is paying for the work they are getting done. Is it high, low, or just right? Make suggestions if needed. If they are having trouble finding economical handymen show them how to find them.

Rents. Study the rent rates to see if there are any major weak spots here. Get the owner to raise all rents to market newly vacant units. Also, encourage even a modest raise like $10 per unit. In most cases tenants won't move over a $10 increase, especially if you are improving the property.

Unit Expansion/Creation. One of the finest ways to increase a property's value and cash flow is to increase the number of rentable units. For instance, look for areas within the building where another rental unit could be created. Are there any dormant or idle spaces that can be converted into an efficiency apartment or small office rental? Is there a garage on the property that could be rented for storage or converted to a living area? Any one of these recommendations could justify a $2,000 consulting fee. The more profit you create for the investor the more delighted they will be and the more referrals you will get.

Leases/Applications/Late Fees. Study the landlord's lease to see how good it is. If it is weak, offer him a better one. In many cases there are legal clauses and waivers allowable by state code, but landlords rarely use them. Fully maximize the legal code by using a strong lease. This can save investors money by speeding eviction proceedings and protecting their legal rights.

Strategic Planning. Figure out which properties are total losers and talk with the client about a plan to liquidate them. If they are homes, consider selling them on a long-term installment contract at a top price. If the owner wants to sell for cash consider hooking him up with a reputable 1031 exchange facilitator who will assist in doing a "tax deferred rollover."

Return on Investment. Ask the investor to give you the financial numbers from his tax returns and do a financial analysis. There is a number of software programs on the market. Crunch the numbers.

The Key to Success. You will have a very satisfied client if you can literally overwhelm him or her with practical ideas on improving their cash flow. Offer many solutions that can be immediately and cheaply implemented.

Your goal should be to offer at least ten money saving or profit generating ideas that the client can begin using. In most cases, you should be able to save the client at least double your fee within two years of the consultation.

Consultant's Work Agreement. You will need an agreement that spells out all the details of the analysis. You may consider offering a no-risk guarantee where the client can cancel at the end of the first day if they feel the consultation is of no value. Your cancellations should be minimal, especially if you work hard with the client and provide a lot of good ideas.

How Long it Will Take. A two-day consultation seems best since this enables you to do two to three clients per week. A two-day period also helps keep the price down to make it more affordable.

Fee Structure. I suggest a fee for your two-day consultation of $995 to $1,995 depending on the level of skill you have plus the size of properties you are competent to analyze.

The Written Report. The last thing you will do after doing the verbal consultation is to provide the client a written report. This report should review your findings and list the areas where there is money being lost. Next, you should list all of the suggestions on how the investor can optimize his cash-flow. This report should be at least 5-10 pages in length and be presented in a professional and bound manner (office supply stores sell these supplies).

Additional Profit Centers. Rental investing for your own portfolio is perhaps the best additional profit center to this cash flow consulting business. The advantage is twofold: you are diversifying within your same field, thereby not scattering your focus; and you are keeping sharp using your own properties as test models for your ideas and advice.

Marketing Strategy. For best results consider marketing to folks outside of your town. The old saying is true, "The definition of an expert is someone from at least 60 miles away."

Direct mail is probably the best way to market your services. Write at least a five-page letter with benefit-rich copy that at least gets the client picking up the phone. Have a toll-free number. Offer a high-value bonus tied with a dated response deadline. Lastly, make the offer irresistible by taking most of the risk as the consultant. If the client is not totally delighted after the first day of the consultation, they can cancel and get their money refunded.

Investment Clubs could also prove to be a good source of leads. In many cases you can either run ads in their newsletter or rent their mailing list. Keep in mind though, the local club is not the place to advertise—in their eyes you are not the expert, but a fellow club member.

Property Tax Consulting. Property taxes are a major source of income for most local governments. Local politicians like property owners because real estate taxes are easily collected, since the nonpayment becomes a lien, which will eventually force the sale of the property—they *will* get their money.

These taxes are levied against real estate based on the assessed value determined by the tax assessor. A high percentage of the time these property valuations are inaccurate.

In most cases, the valuations are done by non-real estate professionals doing what amounts to a drive-by appraisal. These tax assessors are often doing hundreds of "appraisals" a week, which contributes to a high error rate. To compound matters, the public property records are frequently incomplete and erroneous, making the valuation either too high or too low.

Property tax consulting is the business of helping property owners reduce their tax assessment and thereby reducing their property taxes.

The Business Model. Before we get into the business model let me explain who are the best candidates for doing property tax consulting as a business.

First of all, I believe property tax consulting makes a better ancillary profit center or value added service than a full-blown business opportunity. This is because most counties and states have time limitations and seasons for doing tax appeals. Therefore, the available time window for doing business may be too short to make it a full-time, sustainable business.

Secondly, many smaller properties to be appealed may not offer enough tax savings even if the appeal is successful to make the consultant enough money for a full-time business. This is only a generalization, and your particular area may be different.

Property tax consulting can be a nice client building or value-added service for real estate professionals such as a real estate agents or brokers. For instance, I know a title company that does tax consulting and appeals at a very nominal fee ($100 win-or-lose per appeal) for the very purpose of building good will and referrals. For the title company the service is not a business distraction, since they already have the tools and knowledge of using courthouse records and computer databases. This company does a lot of repeat business with investors who enjoy this low-cost, added value service.

Tax reduction consulting could be a nice ancillary profit center or goodwill builder for a real estate agent. In an effort to differentiate yourself from all of the cookie-cutter, me-too agents, you could provide this service to your best clients at a "cost only" basis.

Suppose, for instance, a sharp real estate agent tells all buyers or sellers they can receive a free property tax consultation on any home they buy or sell through the agent. The cost may be a nominal fee of $75 to $100. (Your costs would be only for a computer database, copies, research, and the filing fee.)

I think you'll agree this value-added service could greatly increase the amount of referrals, create tons of client loyalty, and give the agent a unique market advantage. Furthermore, the agent still could make some money providing the service for free (plus costs), since the agent could charge some minimal office expenses to the client as part of the hard costs.

High Profit Cases.
There are companies and individuals who do make a full-time business out of reducing property taxes. In most cases this involves doing high profit cases like large commercial properties, luxury homes, farms, mobile home parks, and other complex properties.

These large properties often involve tax bills going above $10,000 per year which means a large potential saving for the client, therefore a large potential contingency fee for the consultant.

Qualifications. When doing the smaller cases there isn't a lot of in depth knowledge beyond a broad knowledge of real estate and finding comparable properties. In these cases a good real estate agent has the tools and skills to handle the work. Larger commercial properties require more knowledge and skills, since they require several ways to analyze value (income, replacement cost, comparables).

The Tax Reduction Process.
Most states have a tax appeals time period of several months in the year. You will file the appeal application for the client and wait for a hearing appointment in the mail. In the meantime you develop your case file and backup

documentation. At the hearing you respectfully present why you believe the property is over taxed (over assessed). The board (usually three to five people) will notify you in writing as to the outcome of the hearing. If the facts are on your side, you probably will obtain a reduction. If you did not win a reduction in the assessment or if the reduction was not enough, you can then take the matter to the next level. This typically involves a court hearing in front of a judge and probably will require an attorney since non-lawyers cannot represent other people in court (you of course, can represent yourself if you are the owner of the real estate. You could possibly check into using a power of attorney—get legal advice).

Setting Fees. Most tax reduction consultants work on a contingency plus costs fee structure. This will range anywhere from half of the first year's savings to a portion of several years of savings. To research fees, consider shopping other consultants. Look in the yellow pages of a large city in your state.

Developing Your Case Documentation. Several areas need to be researched before going to the appeal hearing. The most common are the following:

Comparable sales to establish market value.

Public Assessment Records for accuracy.

Errors in lot size.

Errors in building size or description.

Errors in improvement valuation.

Errors in land valuation.

Locational defects: sewer plants, landfills, factories, prisons, toxic waste.

Factors unknown to drive-by-assessor, e.g., building is gutted.

There are countless factors that may come into play when developing your case documentation. Over-valuation can be proven by examining comparable sales within the area. Next, errors in the public assessment records (the assessment office or local borough will actually have a file on your property with amazing amounts of detail—much of it available on line). If any of the data in these records is wrong, this can help establish your case.

Lastly, don't be afraid of appearing before the appeal hearings. In most cases they are not real estate experts, just people trying to do a decent job. In many cases you will be more knowledgeable then they are. Just calmly present the facts and answer their questions.

Resources and Tools. The best tools are the public record databases and courthouse records. Depending on your county, much of this may be accessible on line from your home office. If you are a licensed real estate agent you definitely have an advantage with the MLS computer system for doing comparable sales research and analysis.

The number one requirement will be a knowledge of your state and county tax appeals law. You can obtain this information either from the county tax assessors office or from your local state representative by asking them in writing to send you copies of all the pertinent state laws regarding property tax assessment and appeals processes.

A plethora of books have been written on lowering real estate taxes. If you are serious, you probably should order some of these to get different opinions on the subject. Perhaps the greatest education will be actually going through the process yourself. In most cases it is simple—either the property is or is not assessed correctly. Consider appealing one of your own over assessed properties to learn the process.

Lease Option/Lease Purchase Consulting. The lease option or lease purchase agreement is a powerful selling and buying contract that essentially merges a rental agreement with an option to buy into one agreement.

Although this concept has been around for many decades, few buyers or sellers know how it works in detail. These circumstances create an opportunity for the real estate entrepreneur to offer a consulting service to both buyers and sellers.

The Business Model. There are several possibilities when it comes to doing lease purchase consulting. One involves consulting with investors and the other involves consulting with home sellers and home buyers.

Before we get into these ideas let's cover an important pitfall. As a home selling consultant you need to be aware of state licensing issues. As a general rule, you cannot be a home selling consultant without a real estate license. In most cases the state licensing statutes forbid helping buyers or sellers without a license. Fair or unfair, this is how they've set the rules.

Some folks conduct a lease purchase consulting business successfully without real estate licensing by simply flying under the radar screen so to speak. This low-profile approach sometimes works, but I am not advocating it. We will review several ideas about this licensing issue, but you must ultimately get your own legal advice.

The Licensee Approach. This first idea is for licensed real estate agents. In this consulting opportunity you will help three possible parties with your consulting: home sellers, investors, and marginal buyers.

Most licensed agents have some idea as to how a lease option or lease purchase arrangement works, but strikingly few know the finer details about putting one together. This creates opportunity for the creative agent to build a market niche.

In this case, you begin promoting yourself as the local expert in the area of lease purchase and lease optioning. Over time this will build your reputation as a creative player in the business. Let me ask you this: How many agents in your market advertise with ads dedicated to finding lease purchase buyers or sellers? Very few, I suspect. How many agents do you know who put on mini workshops for lease purchase buyers or sellers? Again—very few.

Most marketplaces are full of "marginal" buyers who would love to lease purchase a home because they lack sufficient down payment, credit, employment history, or other bank requirements for traditional financing. You as one of the few agents in your area with this specialty can help educate these folks and gain clients for life.

On the other side of the fence are home sellers who desperately need your help in marketing their house. You can serve these folks as well. For instance, don't you think in any given market there are at least a hundred highly motivated sellers within a county that desperately need someone to make their mortgage payments because their house is vacant? These sellers should be your clients.

Now you have two markets to work—buyers and sellers. You are marketing to both. *Voila!* You now have your own niche market of people who need your orchestration skills to bring them together. Your reward? You collect a portion of the option down money as your first payday, and if and when the house finally closes you get part two of your commission.

Pitfall Caution. As a licensee you have certain licensing liabilities and fiduciary requirements to protect the party you represent. It is important to create a legally tight disclosure form that outlines some of the risks for both the buyer and seller. For example, lease/option purchase agreements typically do not require the buyer to buy. If the buyer elects not to buy, you need to have covered yourself by disclosing this possibility to the seller/optionor. There is a higher level of risk in a lease/option situation, therefore disclose in writing the various risks.

Also, it is your job to thoroughly protect the seller's asset. Make sure you take every precaution on their behalf by screening out high-risk buyer/renters.

The Investor Approach. Since a license is often required, some investors have developed creative ways to work within the law. You will, of course, need to conduct your own legal research and counsel to ensure compliance.

This method, like the licensee method, involves marketing to both buyers and sellers. In the case of sellers, you are looking for motivated sellers who for whatever reason really need to sell. You also will be marketing to find motivated buyers who are anxious to buy but cannot because they are marginal in terms of down payment, credit, work history, income, or self-employment issues.

With this method you work with sellers to take over their properties by entering into a lease/option agreement. In this case, you will be both optionor and lessor. In turn, you will remarket the property to your buyer with a lease option. This will create a sandwich position for you. Your profit will come in the form of an upfront nonrefundable option-to-buy fee and a monthly spread of somewhere in the area of $100 to $300 in the wrap-around lease.

Rating the Lease Option Tool. In my opinion a lease option is one of the best selling/marketing tools a real estate seller can use. I also think that the lease option is somewhat overrated as an investor acquisition tool. In other words, lease options are a great way to sell or rent properties, but are over-hyped as an investor's buying tool.

In my opinion, you can achieve the same high-leverage and control with a good installment land contract. You will find that sellers will accept an installment contract more easily because they are truly selling the property, not renting it with an option to buy. Furthermore, you as the buyer will gain added control and protection as an equity-based owner rather than a prospective owner holding a lease with an option to purchase.

The typical motivated seller who has a moderately high mortgage balance will frequently allow an installment purchase with you simply agreeing to take over next month's mortgage payment (no cash down).

Once the property is controlled with an installment contract you then lease option the property to your buyer. You hold essentially the same sandwich position, but with added control.

As the owner of the property you can then work with the buyer without treading on the licensee issue, since you are a true principal to the deal. Remember, you do not need an agent's license to sell or rent your own real estate!

Lease Option Concepts. Your goal is to find underqualified buyers. This does not mean deadbeats or folks with horrendous credit. You want folks who are marginal because they are lacking some part of the qualifications such as income, credit history, stability (time on job), down payment shortfalls, mild to moderate credit problems, etc.

With the marginal buyer placed in the property they can begin working on obtaining financing. In some cases just developing a documented, on-time rental history combined with clearing up delinquent debts can transform them into qualified borrowers.

Down payment shortfalls can be cured by creating rental-option credits that go towards the purchase. This is typically limited to that portion of the rental payment above market rents. Try for at least $150 credit per month. Consult your mortgage broker for lender rules.

Investor Assignment Techniques. Another method investor use in doing lease purchases with other people's property is to set up the deal acting as the buyer/optionee. With the terms of the deal in place, the investor assigns the deal, lease and option, to his nominee or assignee. The fee earned is typically the difference between the option money negotiated on the "buy" side and the assignment fee collected on the "sell" side. Typically, no option fee is paid except a token $10 to $100 on the buy side (remember, these transactions are usually done with folks who have vacant houses and are motivated to sell). On the sell side of the deal a $2,000 assignment of contract fee is about average. By assigning your rights in the deal to another party you sell your position in the contract.

Potential Ethical Dilemma. Although this technique is fully workable there have been abuses by investors. Consider this: investors often don't care who they place in their position as nominee/assignee, since they make the upfront option fee. In these situations the buyer default rate is high. Amateur sellers can easily get burned, too, by not knowing how to deal with a non-paying lease-option buyer. In many cases the property ends up coming back in shambles six months to a year later. Ultimately, the seller may lose the property since they did not have the financial ability to make the mortgage payments while evicting the deadbeat lease purchase buyer.

If you put together a lot of these deals making your profit up front while the original owners are left cleaning up the buyer/renter defaults, I think your reputation will suffer. On a grand scale, sooner or later it will come back to bite you.

Lease Option/Purchase Pitfall. A critical issue you need to watch in a delayed closing deal is to make sure that the legal title holder can deliver a clear title when the ultimate buyer exercises the option to purchase. In many cases (especially distressed sellers) the seller has judgments or liens against their real estate. Since the typical lease option arrangement is not a secured position, liens and judgments can cloud the real estate title.

If you hold a sandwich lease/option position you must take precautions to ensure that the title will be transferable to your wrap around lessee/optionee. This may require your having the deed placed in escrow when you set up the deal. Another possibility is for the seller to deed the property to your trustee to keep future judgments from sticking to the property.

Lease Option Business Model or Tool. There's no doubt that lease option or lease purchase arrangements are a flexible and versatile real estate tool. They are especially helpful in selling homes to first-time home buyers.

The thing to remember is they are just one of many tools in a real estate entrepreneur's toolbox. To build an entire business around a lease option model is probably too limited.

As mentioned earlier, actual lease purchase consulting seems to be a good fit for licensed agents as a unique market niche or specialty. For non-licensees, the key opportunity may be in assisting sellers in the sale of their property in a sort of partner relationship, or where the investor buys a contractual interest (lease/option) in the property which is then remarketed in a sandwich position.

14

Making Money with Land

In this chapter we explore numerous opportunities in the land business. A good portion of these ideas we call mini-opportunities because most people would be hard pressed to make them into a full-time business. In any event I think you will find this subject quite intriguing.

We will look mainly at low-cost opportunities that can be operated with minimal cash. Large scale subdivisions and commercial development will not be reviewed because these businesses require extensive capital, credit, and risk analysis.

Some of the opportunities presented here will be useful for readers who already own land but haven't found ways to make money with it. Even if you don't find these ideas immediately useful, tuck them away in your toolbox of money making techniques.

We will also take a close look at land investments and review the advantages and disadvantages of buying and holding raw land. Trading in land can be a highly lucrative investment, especially for the patient investor who takes a year or two to learn and study the business before making costly mistakes. Much of this learning process will happen out in the field shopping parcels and sizing up the market.

Land trading can be a very comfortable business or hobby because it is well suited for the part-time investor. There is absolutely no reason why you need to quit your current employment or business in order to prosper with land investments.

The tools and skills needed to buy, sell, and rent land are basically the same, so we will only create one business model with each mini-opportunity falling inside of the general model.

The Business Model. Because this chapter presents a variety of small land businesses we will start by covering the basic tools and skills needed to make money trading in land.

One of the pluses of land investing is it can be operated strictly from a home office. There is absolutely no reason to have an on-site or rented office, since your clients will usually be meeting you on the property. On rare occasions when a more formal setting is required, you can use the methods presented in this book.

Although the land business can be complicated at times, the general business tools are the same as with other real estate investment or service businesses: fax, computer, voice mail, cell phone, company name, etc.

Many of the tools required for the land business can be found free of charge at the courthouse. Real estate maps and plot plans are typically housed in the map room or assessor's office. An updated county road map is another key tool to help you find tracts of land for sale.

Land as an Investment Vehicle. Investments are basically places where we park our money whether from our cash reserves or borrowed, and wait for a return on our investment. Return on investment can come in many forms: dividends, rents, interest, sale proceeds, etc.

Land has several advantages and disadvantages as an investment. You must understand these factors before you invest.

The Negative Aspects of Land Investments. The biggest negative to buying land as an investment is that land does not produce an income stream as other more typical real estate investments such as houses and apartments do.

In fact, land often creates a negative cash flow, since the owner must pay tax bills while holding the property. Furthermore, if you don't pay cash for the land, you will make mortgage payments, additional negative cash flow. And even if you did pay cash, you won't be receiving interest you could have earned had the money been placed in elsewhere.

Raw Land Return-on-Investment Rule. Because of the holding costs incurred with raw land you need to realize a higher than expected return on investment to make money with land. The general rule of thumb is land must appreciate at a rate of 15 to 20 percent per year to earn a worthwhile profit in land's buy and hold game. This may sound a bit high until you factor your holding costs for mortgage interest and property taxes.

Land is Higher Risk. Because land is a raw ingredient and not a finished product like a house, you are dealing with a higher risk commodity. After all, who really needs to buy a ten-acre parcel out in the middle of nowhere? Not many people.

It could take you five or ten years to find a buyer if you don't invest in the right land. Your land holdings are less liquid and therefore higher risk than other types of real estate. And, like most other real estate assets, raw land is a lot easier to buy than it is to sell.

The bottom line is that you as a land investor must make sure you are buying high-value deals at deep discounts, in order to compensate yourself for the risk.

The Pluses of Land Investments. Land is virtually a passive investment. You don't have roof leaks or broken plumbing calls from tenants. Because it is more passive then owning a rental building you will spend very little time maintaining your investment.

Fewer buyers means more bargain properties on the market waiting to be discovered. As a general rule, land is a buyer's market because there usually are far more sellers than available buyers, and more motivated sellers. As one author put it, "Land investing is like treasure hunting."

Although land is harder to sell, thereby less liquid, you have the converse advantage that land values are generally very stable. Paper assets like stocks, bonds, or stock market derivatives are highly volatile, and values can swing wildly. On the other hand, land prices move slowly upwards or downwards. The land market is safer than it is for many types of investments.

Another big plus is the fact that land can be purchased with high leverage. Owner financing is the norm in land deals since most banks won't lend more than about 50 percent of the purchase price.

Land trading—buying, selling, renting—can be an extremely high profit business. Depending on how well you buy, you can often earn ten times the purchase price either by waiting for the area to become developed or by subdividing it yourself.

Now that we explained the investment nature of land let's review some of the actual business opportunities.

Cellular Phone Tower Leases. Here's an opportunity for people who already own land but haven't found any ways to make money from it. I would not advise someone to buy land strictly for this purpose, but it is definitely worth knowing how this opportunity works.

With the communications explosion, telecommunication companies need land for the placement of their cellular telephone antennas. These are the metal towers you see while driving across the countryside.

These companies will pay a monthly land lease for their tower placement. Rates vary depending on the location and price of land. Rural areas with lower land costs typically bring a lease payment of $300 to $400 per month from the cell phone company. More expensive areas like those near cities typically command lease fees of $700 to $800 per month. The average fee is around $500 $600 per month.

Antenna leases typically run for five years with four renewal periods (potentially a 25-year term). When you add up the potential dollars, you can see how profitable and secure a cell tower lease can be. From a security standpoint, what are the chances a company like Sprint, Verizon, or Nextel will default on their lease payments?

Lease Terms. First you need a parcel of land with an installation base area about 50 by 50 feet. Years ago these tower sites needed to be placed high on a hillside or mountain. Today, with the new digital technology, the towers are placed on regular land sites.

In most cases the telecommunications company will outsource the tower design and lease acquisition to a contractor company. The contractor will then find three suitable sites and notify the landowners of the opportunity. These sites are rated in terms of desirability, and the contractor will negotiate with the property owner of the highest quality site first.

In most of these leasing arrangements the telecommunication's contractor handles all of the zoning, permits, legal issues, and tower construction at no charge to the property owner. In essence: it is a work-free and hands-off deal for the landowner.

Negotiation Pitfall. The cell companies who lease these sites say the biggest problem they have working with landowners is that owner negotiates too hard. In most cases, the contractor working on behalf of the phone company establishes a fair lease rate and then selects target sites. When they begin talking with the owner they find that owners are too greedy. In most cases, the rate being offered is the best rate. Besides, the company usually has two other acceptable site prospects to negotiate with. It also must be considered this is found money. If the property owner takes the deal they will have an extra $5,000 a year for doing nothing!

Billboard Rental.
Now here's another idea for those readers who own some land that is sitting idle along the roadside. Consider contacting a billboard company to see about leasing your land for a billboard placement. If there are zoning limitations let the billboard company's lawyers address that problem.

In the event you can't find an interested billboard company, consider contacting larger businesses to see if they have interest in a placing a sign on your property. If you can't find any takers advertise your own business! Again, check zoning.

Flea Markets, Parking Lots, RV Storage.
In this smattering of ideas are creative ways to rent out land while you wait to market the parcel some time down the line. These ideas are also good ways to generate income off land that is part of another investment property.

Suppose, for instance, you have bought a farm property with road frontage in a well-trafficked area at a bargain price. You could rent the farmhouse out to a tenant and rent out the land to nearby farmers for crop growing. In the meantime you could work on subdividing the land for lot sales.

Now here's the idea: Take a part of your road frontage land and consider creating a weekend flea market, also known in some parts of the country as swap meets. In most cases you will only need a gravel lot and some wooden tables. You might want to place a few small pavilions on the lot as well.

With your gravel lot and tables along a well traveled road you will have a nice flea market which can be rented out by the table or selling area. The amount of table space will depend on the amount of traffic and market demand in the area. It's probably smart to be on the low side on your rental rates until you build up a lot of traffic and public interest.

Table and space rates also depend on the competition of other flea market areas. In most cases tables are rented by the day or weekend. Shop all of the flea markets within a half hour of your location. Also, consider contacting a food vendor to see if you can rent out space for a refreshment stand. This wonderful business idea of course is subject to local zoning restrictions and existing competitors. Lastly, you will need to rent a couple of port-a-potties to take care of the restroom needs.

Parking Lots Opportunities. If you own a parcel of land located in more of an urban or business district consider paving it and renting out parking. Depending on the conditions, parking lots can be an excellent profit center because there is very little in offsetting expenses.

Many times empty "junk" lots can be bought at tax sales for extreme bargain prices. If these lots are next to businesses or apartment properties, take a serious look at this parking lot idea. Be careful of lots in rundown neighborhoods since these frequently become dumping grounds for old tires and junk furniture.

If you ever get the opportunity to buy a bargain piece of land near a car dealership consider offering it for sale or rent as extra parking for the dealership's new cars. Car dealers in northern states where it snows a lot desperately need places to park cars before snowstorms so they can easily plow their regular lots after the storm ends.

RV Storage. One small idea is to fence off an area of land where folks with boats, RVs, tractor-trailers, and other large items can be stored for the winter. This is typically done at storage facilities, but you could try it on an accessible piece of fenced in land. Rates will probably be around $15 to $30 per month, per vehicle.

Recreational Land Opportunities. The American dream is to own a nice piece of vacation property where you can get away for hiking, fishing, camping, or hunting. You can create a business of buying large parcels of wooded country land with owner financing and selling off on installment contracts multiple acres to people wanting vacation property.

One excellent idea is to create a hunting camp. For example, let's say you can buy a mountain tract of wooded land that is accessible by a road (road access is critical). You can create a beautiful hunting camp by simply placing an old mobile home or small shell cabin on your property. You can find plans and kits for shelter shanties that can be built for around $3,000. Don't worry about a bathroom or septic tank unless zoning requires it. (Very rural country areas typically have little or no zoning.) You can use other options such as a portable chemical toilet or an outhouse.

Make sure the area is known as a good place for deer hunting or other popular game animals. Streams, ponds, lakes, mountains, rolling hills, and other natural beauty will boost the camp's marketability.

Next, place classified ads in newspapers in your town or city. Advertise the property as a beautiful hunting camp with easy owner financing: 20-acre hunting camp with mobile home, $4,000 down/ $225 per month. Create a sales brochure with clear directions. Send out the brochure to all callers.

Distressed Junk Land Strategy.

Seasoned real estate investors know that tax sales can be a phenomenal place to buy land cheap. Land frequently is sold for 10 to 20 percent of its appraised value at these sales. Of course, a good bit of it is "junk" property on the side of a steep hill or on rocky desert slopes, but there are junk parcels that have value when marketed correctly. Believe it or not, a lot of obscure lots can be bought for $500 to $1,000 at tax sales.

First of all, there are parcels sold at distressed land auctions that are total junk and possibly a legal liability, such as a tire dump. You want to avoid all parcels that have anything remotely related to hazardous waste on them. You also want to avoid tiny landlocked parcels on a mountain because you will have great difficulty finding a buyer. Caution: At all costs avoid cheap lots in slum areas even though you can buy one for $100.

This basic strategy is to only buy severely discounted land that can be acquired for around $100 to $1,500. Then look for potential buyers, who for whatever reason would like to own it. For instance, a quarter acre parcel of land may be too small to build upon, but when added to the lot next door it could create a buildable lot. Or, a small unbuildable lot could be sold to a neighbor who would like to make their yard bigger for a garden or recreational area.

This "junk" strategy is a numbers game. Buy enough cheap lots throughout the county and eventually you will get calls and offers to sell them. With $5,000 invested and a few years, you could easily acquire fifteen or twenty parcels scattered throughout the county. With creative marketing you probably could sell them for a tidy profit.

Tip: The key is to buy cheap so you can sell cheap— don't get greedy.

Tip: Try offering owner financing.

Tip: Buy properties near towns, neighborhoods, and business areas.

Tip: Consider placing a small for-sale sign on the lot.

Tip: Send for-sale flyers to neighbors or nearby business owners.

Tip: Consider listing the lot with a broker so it gets in the MLS system.

Tip: Contact landscapers who need a place to dump branches, grass clipping etc. They might pay $2,000 for a suitable composting lot.

Junk Lot Story. An investor buddy of mine bought a two-acre parcel in a very rural setting along a paved road at a tax sale for $1,700. After the sale we drove up to see it. It was on top of a small mountain area at the intersection of two paved roads. Upon inspection we saw it had a partially built house foundation on it. We spoke to a neighbor, who said the original owner had been denied a building permit because the land failed the perk (percolation) test. In most areas land cannot be built upon until it passes certain minimal drainage and percolation standards for septic and waste water. We did see several perk test holes across the lot. Apparently the owner, being so distraught, committed suicide, and eventually the land went to tax sale. I thought my friend had really blown it this time— buying an unbuildable "junk" parcel of land.

Two years went by, and my friend sold his "junk" land through a broker for $35,000 with $2,000 down and monthly payments of $500. I couldn't believe it! The buyer managed to build an acceptable sand mound sewer system that the state approved. This investment turned out to be a good example of buying a seemingly "junk" parcel at a very cheap price and making a colossal profit. By the way, this same investor has done similar deals over the years, but he has also bought a few that haven't sold.

Profits Subdividing Land. The business of buying land in large wholesale parcels and subdividing it into smaller lots at retail prices can be one of the best opportunities in the land business.

The business of subdividing property is based on the principle that large land parcels can be bought at a bulk discount and broken down in small parts that will sell for a premium. There's an old saying in real estate that goes like this, "The two best businesses in the world are buying whiskey by the bottle and selling it by the shot, or buy land by the acre and sell it by the lot." While I certainly wouldn't sell whiskey either by the shot or the bottle, the rhyme certainly is a good picture of how subdivision works.

A hundred years ago people flocked to cities as the best way to live because of the conveniences and services located there. Today, the exact opposite is happening. Because of crime, high taxes, and high levels of governmental restrictions many folks are leaving the city for the country life. Another factor worth mentioning is that many employers allow employees to work from a home office using the internet, fax lines, and email, so people don't need to live near their jobs. In this opportunity you will be taking advantage of this trend, buying large parcels of country land (6 to 25 acres) and subdividing them into lots for building homes.

The Advantages of Country Land. There is a growing demand for country land due to the high cost of living in metropolitan areas. Second, rural areas have fewer zoning regulations, so subdivision and building problems are greatly reduced. Next, country land is relatively cheap, and you can buy fairly large parcels of land for a low price per acre. In addition, country land can typically be bought with owner financing.

Country Land Strategy. You want to find a semi-rural area within an hour of your home where you can scout out land for sale. You also want to buy land with owner financing and no more than about 10 to 15 percent down. Land that can be cut into parcels of one or two acres is preferred because country buyers don't want to be crowded.

As a rule you want land that has easy access from a road, preferably, land with plenty of road frontage. In fact, road frontage is a major factor that boosts value. Next, you want land that is near public utilities like electricity. Public water and sewer is also a huge plus because you will have fewer complications from township officials regarding on-site sewer and well systems. Flat parcels or land on gently rolling land are best.

Subdivision Tip: You will need a good real estate attorney along with a professional surveyor (usually a civil engineer) to help you complete your subdivision. The surveyor may be your best bet for recommending a lawyer to handle the legal documents of the subdivision.

Your next step after buying (or optioning) the land is to have a professional surveyor verify and stake off the property. The surveyor can also prepare a subdivision plan to be presented to the county for approval. This subdivision plan should cut the land into uniform lots (avoid irregular shaped lots like triangles or narrow and deep lots). If you place lots behind other lots there must be easy access to them.

After you price your lots begin marketing them with signs on the property and classified ads. In most cases providing your own in-house owner financing is the easiest way to sell land. Most land investors use an installment land contract where the full legal title stays in the investor's name.

Tip: Consider tying up property with a 6-month option before you buy it. This will allow you to complete research and feasibility studies before committing to the purchase.

Tip: Always build a lot release clause into your mortgage when you buy the land. This will enable you to pay chunks of the principal, which will create free and clear lots so that you can pass legal title clear of liens to your buyer if they pay for the lot before your mortgage is paid off.

Tip: Buy land from private individuals, not investors who are trying to do what you are doing. People who inherit land are good sellers since they have less emotional attachment and more profit is possible.

Tip: Begin marketing your land as soon as possible since in most cases your project will have a negative cash flow until you start selling. Make sure your payments on the buy side are low and fully amortizing—no balloon payments.

Tip: If you can't get an option, try writing up a purchase contract with a contingency clauses to provide a way out if the project isn't feasible. Sometimes a purchase contract with a contingency escape clause is more acceptable to a seller than an option contract.

Tip: Try to persuade the seller not to start the interest clock for six or twelve months. This will buy you time to get some of the lots sold.

Creating Cash Flow from Trees. In the event you own land that is heavily wooded you may be able to tap one or more profit centers.

Tree Sales to Paper Companies. If your property has a lot of smaller trees (5 to 10 inches in diameter) there's a good chance you can sell them to a paper company. Paper companies typically will walk your land and give you a quote. They handle all of the lumbering; you basically do nothing but collect a check.

Lumber Sales. If your land has a lot of mature trees over 12 inches in diameter there's a good chance these too can be sold. The preferred trees are oak, popular, and maple. You can sell them yourself, getting bids from sawmills, or hire a forestry consultant/broker, who in most cases will get you a higher price and will also supervise the cutting process to prevent excessive cutting and property damage. If you have interest in selling trees through a forestry consultant you can obtain consultant contacts from the Society of American Foresters at 301.897.8720.

Firewood Options. If you own a tract of land that is too small to be harvested by either paper or lumber companies you can consider the firewood business. This is hard work, but it can be a good way to make some cash on the side. Consult with a woodstove dealer for the most saleable wood types.

> **TIP: avoid pine. It has a high soot by-product.**
>
> **TIP: If the firewood business begins to work well for you consider buying a heavy-duty firewood processor. This machine can cut and split 2 to 3 cords of wood per hour. Also, keep in mind, all wood must be seasoned one year for it to burn efficiently—don't sell green wood, it's too wet.**

Wood delivery and stacking can be very labor intensive. Consider letting the buyer pick up the wood at a discounted price by the pickup truck load—for example, $45 per load. Another option is to package your firewood into small packages and offer them at a premium price for the occasional fireplace user. You have probably seen packaged firewood for sale in grocery stores, home supply centers, and even convenience stores.

Tree Farming. Depending on the type of soil and land you have purchased, tree farming might be a good opportunity. You might consider everything from raising Christmas trees to trees that will eventually be harvested by large lumber companies.

> **Tip: over the years there have been various tree farming programs where the government either gives you the seedlings or will pay you a per acre price to grow them. Also consider contacting large lumber companies to see if they have any programs for planting trees on your land.**

Summary and Conclusion. So there you have it—plenty of creative ideas for making money from land investments. There certainly are fewer investors in land than there are in other investments, but this can be a high-profit area. In fact, many insiders believe land to be among the highest profit real estate investments in the industry. Take a close look at it.

Section 3—Nuts and Bolts of Managing Your Real Estate Business

15

Design Your Company Name to Create the Image You Want

In this chapter you will learn tips and concepts for designing an effective company name. The name you create for your company is the easiest—and most cost-effective—way to tell the marketplace who you are and what you do. Of course, a good company name will not ensure that you are successful. The world is full of successful businesses that have weak company names and companies with great names but lousy service and products. My point is that you must do more than come up with a superb name.

You Are Your Brand Name. People in small one- or two-person companies often fail to realize that their business has a brand name just like Maytag, Ford, Remax, FedEx, KFC, or any other recognized brand.

Your brand name is the name of your company combined with all of the thoughts, feelings, and image people think of when they see or hear it. Your goal should be to design your company brand name and logo around the image and unique market niche you want. This won't happen overnight. In most cases, this will take several months of revising and tweaking it, the same way a food company reworks and experiments with a recipe before introducing a new food product to the public.

Naming Your Baby. My first bit of advice is to take at least thirty days to form a new company name. You won't work on naming your business eight hours a day, but a 30-day incubation period will let your creative mind mull over the possibilities. The last thing you want is to create a company name on a whim, print business cards and stationery and then realize it was the wrong name.

Your company's brand name is important. Automobile and drug companies spend hundreds of thousands of dollars in developing names for their products. Major book publishers take great pains to formulate book titles. Entertainers often change their names to create a more appealing "brand" name. Larry King, George Burns, and scores of other public figure types have all reworked their names into something smoother, shorter, and more memorable than their real names.

When possible try to build into your name something that conveys what you do. A name like Richardson Corp. doesn't really communicate any meaning. Suppose, for instance, this Richardson Corp., is in the business of selling homes to people on installment contracts (owner financing) with flexible terms but at premium prices premium. Wouldn't names like OwnerMaker Inc., Easy-Dream Properties, or Better Life Homes, work better than Richardson Corp.?

When you develop a name it's sometimes good to combine words to create a unique name. To illustrate, look at the names created by drug companies. Most of the time, these are made up words that are combinations of other words. One of the best known appliance brands is a word combination: KitchenAid, an almost perfect brand name. Another excellent company name that is a combination of words is the wireless phone company VoiceStream.

Don't try to be too clever. You don't want your name to sound "homemade" or amateurish. Another good tip is to avoid names that would be embarrassing for your clients to say, think, or read. Think about this one from personal experience. Have you ever wanted to buy a book but were just a little bit embarrassed to bring it to the counter because of its title? I have seen several restaurants use names that rhyme with vulgar words in order to sound tricky and catchy. The problem is, a fair portion of the public is turned off by this cheap tactic.

Another valuable tip worth mentioning is that shorter names are preferred over long names. Al Ries and Jack Trout, marketing experts and the authors of the book, *22 Immutable Laws of Business Branding,* explain this in great detail. In a nutshell, they say that most successful companies use shorter names because it is easier to remember and advertise. In fact, they show that many companies with long names have shortened their names. Remember, Federal Express? Well, now it's FedEx. How about Atlantic

Telegraph and Telephone? Now it's AT&T. These are just two of many successful firms that have shortened their business names for greater market appeal.

Long names may sound impressive, but are harder to remember and use in marketing. For instance, a name like North Eastern Executive Acquisition Group may sound big and powerful, but it is too wordy. Besides, the word order in a name like this makes the company hard to locate in the phone book or other directory service.

Should You Use Your Own Name? Generally I

would avoid it, but there is no hard and fast rule about it. Real estate agents use their own name as their brand name even while they are working for a real estate brokerage house. This has worked well within that field, so we shouldn't argue with success.

Two drawbacks to using your own name as the company name should be considered. First, ten years from now you may want to sell your company and you probably wouldn't want someone else trading with your name as their brand name. The last thing you want is someone trashing your reputation and name by giving poor service or filing for bankruptcy.

Second, in the event your company falls on hard times and is forced into bankruptcy or business closure, it may be harder to create a fresh brand name since your personal name was soiled by the business failure. If you use a company name and have problems, your personal name will escape the negative linkage.

Avoid "Enterprises" in your business name. According to some marketing experts, the word "enterprises" shouts that the company is run by amateurs who aren't well established. The word may not convey the professional image you want.

Helping a Less than Great Name. If you already

own a company and aren't happy with your company's name you have two options. First, you could scrap the current name and start over. Second, if the problem is that your name is not descriptive, consider adding a subtitle. Suppose, for instance, your company is a management company named Roger Properties, Inc. Not a strong name by any measure. Perhaps you could beef up the name by adding a subtitle—something like: Roger Properties, Inc., Residential Management Specialists.

Creating a Unique Marketing Phrase. While you are creating a company name you should also be crafting a unique marketing phrase. This phrase basically is a one-line marketing statement that gives more detail about what you do. You will use this one-line statement in all of your ads and marketing correspondence, including business cards, fliers, and advertising.

For instance, your business might specialize in helping landlords prepare vacant units for rental and with maintenance needs. Your unique marketing phrase might be something like, "Guaranteed Unit Turnaround in 72 Hours or We Work for Free."

Whatever business you are in, spend considerable time working and reworking a short and benefit-laden marketing phrase. Make sure you think about this from the client's viewpoint, not your own. Assume the client does not know or care about you— only what's in it for them.

Creating a Business Logo. A logo is your company name designed with letters and symbols in a professional and eye appealing way. You can handle this yourself by experimenting with desktop publishing software and various fonts.

A better option is to hire graphic designer to create a logo for you. Sketch out ideas of the image you want and ask the designer for at least 10 samples. If you don't like the ones presented ask for more samples. I had about 15 shown to me until I found what I liked. The going price for a professional logo design starts at $200, although the top design firms will pull fees of thousands of dollars to design a logo for their major clients.

Protecting Your Work. After you create a name, logo, and marketing phrase you should trademark some or all of your work. A non-registered trademark does give you local protection for your name, logo, and marketing statement without any cost by common law. However, a non-registered trademark is more of a local trading area protection and not a nationwide protection. To have nationwide protection you typically must have the company name registered (as shown by the symbol ®), which is quite expensive. In most cases, the trademark™ symbol above your name or unique marketing phrase will work nicely at no cost except the energy to hit the symbol button on your computer.

Putting it All Together. Okay, you have created your company name, logo, and unique marketing phrase. Now, you must begin using these tools in your marketing devices. The key here is consistency.

Be sure to back up all of your advertising and marketing efforts with high value service that matches the image you want to project. In the end, if you meet or exceed your client's expectations you will be well on your way to creating a valuable brand name for You, Inc.

16

Street Smart Business Tips, Strategies, and Success Secrets

In this chapter you will be on the receiving end of a full blast of business strategies and highly opinionated viewpoints on a variety of subjects. Between subjects and paragraphs, I will salt the chapter with business tips and rules.

Disinformation Dangers. In business and investing you will encounter folks who are eager to give you their opinion on just about any matter. While this may make for great chatter and small talk, be careful who influences you. Much of the advice and opinions handed out by well meaning folk is total garbage. If you end up following their philosophy or advice you will most likely end up in a ditch. In this part of the chapter I will give you several tips and red flags for spotting generalized nonsense.

John Doe Opinions. Let's start with the class of opinions that is probably the most worthless in terms of accuracy and value. Average folks down at the barber shop or local diner freely share their opinions on any topic under the sun. Even though they are experts in nothing, these folks often wield a strong influence over us.

TIP: Before you swallow someone's advice or opinion on a financial or business matter, find out their credentials and experience within the subject.

A good example is what I hear "John Doe's" saying about landlording and tenants. Just the other week someone said to me, "You just can't find any good tenants anymore." While there may be a kernel of truth to the fact that people aren't as honorable as they were twenty or thirty years ago, there are plenty of good tenants. The truth of the matter is you need to develop the knowledge and skills to prepare the property, so good folks will want to live there—then carefully weed out the high-risk applicants.

Avoid listening to typical negative advice and opinions from the John Doe crowd. If they don't have extensive experience and or success in the area under discussion, your best bet is to ignore the advice.

We Love to Exaggerate Problems. We seem to enjoy wringing our hands and talking about how bad certain problems are. While business and life are full of problems, most are blown out of proportion.

When you are new to a business don't let folks scare you into thinking that a certain business or investment has too many problems. There may be some truth to what they are saying, but in most cases there are ways to solve the problem if you just have the right information. As a general rule, most problems are grossly exaggerated.

It has been said, "responsibility is the price of success" and the more responsibility one has, the greater volume of problems you will encounter. In life, the people who earn the most are usually the ones who tackle the biggest problems. It is simple. Who do you think has more problems on a day-to-day basis: a person who owns 50 rental properties or the person who works at the local grocery store? Which one earns more money?

Competitor Disinformation Tactics. You might think I'm getting too paranoid with this one, so allow me to explain. In business you need to be careful who you listen to and who you share your business ideas with.

While you frequently will get misinformation and exaggerations from the John Doe types, you also must be careful about the information you get from rivals and competitors within your marketplace or field. In many cases these folks are already using the same idea and are steering you away with disinformation.

In several situations I have volunteered information to local competitors only to have them tell me it "won't work" or that there's no money doing that. When I was young and naïve, I would listen to these nay-sayers and give up on my idea. To my distress I later discovered the same folks who were negative about my idea had started doing precisely what I had told them I wanted to do. It's hard to say whether they purposely misled me or not, but I do know they gave me a healthy dose of disinformation.

TIP: In most cases it pays to keep quiet about your business plans and personal success. It may be OK to share with business colleagues as long as they aren't competitors who live within your market. If you are doing well, talking about your success tends to make people feel bad that they aren't doing well also. Avoid any talk that could sound to someone else like bragging.

TIP: Be careful about sharing proprietary business information with people who aren't competitors but may interact with your competitors. For instance, you might tell your mortgage broker a wonderful business method that is really working for you. While the actual information may be useless to the mortgage broker, he may innocently share it with your competitor who will steal your proprietary business secret.

Be Careful of "Experts."

This bit of advice sounds paranoid. In my experience experts are usually right. That's right—they are usually right. But there comes a time when you need to follow your gut feeling and go against the advice of experts. I can think of several times when I relied on an expert for advice only to find out years later how wrong they were. The "expert" cost me money in lost opportunity.

Face it, experts are mere mortals subject to error just like you and I. We need to be careful not to follow an expert's advice during those times when our knowledge or experience gives us better guidance. In my earlier years of investing I tended to put a lot of real estate experts on a pedestal and followed everything they said. In fact, I had done some investing which proved very profitable, but in the books and seminars the experts said to stay away from the particular type of deals that had been so successful for me. For several years I followed the experts' advice, but it didn't fit in my area. Eventually I went back to the methods that had worked for me.

TIP: If you find a certain method or type of investment (or business) that makes you money—keep doing it. Forget about what the experts say—even me. If you read something in this book or another book that contradicts what has worked for you—then keep doing it.

Who Should You Listen To? By now you may be thinking how arrogant the author of this book is to suggest that nobody is worth listening to. That is not what I mean to say. As a guiding rule, ignore advice of people who are not successful in the field you are involved with. Next, be cautious of rivals who will intentionally smokescreen you with disinformation. Third, remember that all people tend to blow problems out of proportion and exaggerate, so their negativity may be unwarranted. Fourth, although experts are good, remember they, too, can be misinformed. If it works for you forget the experts who say it won't.

TIP: Develop friendships and business relationships with people who are successful within the field you are involved in. Humbly ask them for advice. Ask them why they are successful. Study their way of conducting business. Most importantly, give them something of value to ensure that it is a two-way relationship. Freely give of your time—become their servant to do whatever they want done. Over the years I have worked for free for smart investors who have taught me a lot.

The Marketplace Concept. Although I have attended countless real estate seminars and have read dozens of real estate books, nothing replaces the education you get from getting out into the marketplace and doing business.

From my experience, the more you get busy doing business—making offers, buying, selling, renting, prospecting, networking, failing, succeeding, meeting associates, asking questions, and chasing leads, the more knowledge you will accumulate that will teach how business works.

Specialize Only to a Point. Although I'm a big advocate of becoming a specialist in your given field, I must also caution you to not over specialize. You can specialize yourself out of business!

I recently was talking to some investor friends who told me about a real estate agent in their market who specialized only in million dollar homes. For several years she made a high income selling million dollar houses—she was a very high-end specialist. She had no time for small listings. Then a funny thing happened—a whole year went by, and she didn't sell a single million-dollar house. With no income coming in, and virtually no "normal" client base, she ended up getting out of the real estate business.

Specializing will help you become excellent at what you do, but don't turn down additional profit opportunities if they are ripe for the picking. Some diversification of income is smart. Especially be open to opportunities that don't water down or clash with your current business. Remember: complementary business opportunities can be good as long as they don't scatter your personal focus.

A perfect example of adding complimentary profit centers to your business is that of Cracker Barrel. As you probably know, Cracker Barrel is a great restaurant chain with a country theme. It has a big fireplace and country antiques and decorations. The food is good old country fixin's too. The great marketing lesson here is the country gift shop that is an absolute perfect complimentary business. While people wait to be seated they don't need to be bored because they can enjoy the gift store and be entertained. I can't think of a better example of getting into a complementary business to reinforce the existing business image and profits!

TIP: Smart business people innovate their business by investing in the new tools, equipment, and technology that will save them time and money. The right tools give you leverage over tasks and are cheaper than labor. Short-sighted business people are afraid to invest money because it costs too much, not knowing how much not upgrading their tools and technology is costing them.

Weeds in Your Business Garden.
If you have ever grown a garden you know how quickly a nice garden can become overgrown with weeds.

Are there weeds growing in your business garden? A business is like a garden; it must be cared for on a daily basis. If you slack off on the routine and boring tasks of operating your business, it will become full of weeds. Weeds in a business garden include failing to call people back, being delinquent with payments, disorganized office environment, failure to keep current with product knowledge, broken promises, unresolved problems, etc.

TIP: Develop the habit of paying all contract workers within 48-hours of receiving the bill. The faster you pay, the better service you will receive—and you will get lower rates.

TIP: Avoid paying workers up front for jobs. Prepayment tends to slow performance since the reward is already received. Keep the carrot out front.

The Business Journal Idea.

I keep several notebooks where I write down ideas for my business. They are on a variety of subjects and areas, but especially ways to make my services more attractive (faster, better, cheaper) to my clients. The improvement journal is also a place for money-saving ideas for my business. I try to get whatever ideas I have into the notebook as soon as possible, otherwise they will be forgotten.

TIP: Your minimum goal should be to have one good idea added to the journal a week. Also, try to implement one good idea per week.

Problem Solving Mentality.

Effective business people are problem solvers who don't cave in as soon as problems appear. Many folks don't become self-employed because they have a low tolerance for problems. The more people you serve and bigger the problems you solve, the more money you will make. The problem is that serving people and trying to solve their problems creates even more problems. In my business endeavors I find that the busier I am, the more problems I encounter—and the more money I make during these hectic and problem filled months!

When I encountered problems associated with serving people, I used to think I had it extra tough and that other people in business have it a lot easier. Then I started becoming friends with a lot of business people. I discovered that they have many of the same problems. No one is exempt from problems, hassles, adversity, unreasonable people, mechanical failures, cash flow shortages, and on and on. Stop complaining and realize this is normal.

TIP: Use colored markers in your business. I have a red marker I use every day to underscore and highlight important points in messages and notes to myself and colleagues. The red pen works also nicely for underlining key points in books and reading material.

Find and Exploit Your Unique Business Advantage.

Over the years I have noticed that many successful entrepreneurs have what I call a Unique Business Advantage (not to be confused with market niche, position, or unique selling proposition, which are marketing concepts).

A unique business advantage is a special set of skills, circumstances, or conditions that other competing entrepreneurs do not have. This unique advantage gives the entrepreneur an added competitive edge that provides extra profit margin and reduced costs. By finding and developing your unique business advantage you will gain financial strength in your business.

For example, I know a man in my area who invests heavily in coin-operated laundromats. He has managed to dominate this business within his city. People can't figure out how he has managed to buy so many laundromats and make so much money.

One day he told our real estate investment club his secret. He buys laundromats only when there were apartment rental units in the building. In most cases, he bought laundromats that had three to four apartment rental units on the second floor. After buying a laundromat apartment building he would upgrade and refurbish the rental units. He said in most cases the cash flow from the rental apartments was enough to cover his entire mortgage payment leaving tons of profit from the coin operated washers and dryers. This simple strategy gave him so much cash flow that within ten years he was able to eventually buy practically every laundromat in town. His expertise at buying and managing apartment units gave him what I call a special business advantage for his combined laundromat and apartment business.

Another fellow I met was an expert contractor in the various building trades. After about twenty years of working for other people as a maintenance man and electrician, he began real estate investing. He specialized in buying lower income houses and apartment building that were fixer uppers.

With his expertise in the trades he was able to buy about 60 units in three to four years by purchasing rundown properties. Most folks could not have created the large cash flow that he created because they did not have his fix up skills and expertise. They could have done the same thing, but it would have taken longer and their cash flow wouldn't be what his was since he had very few labor costs. His contracting expertise was a unique business advantage.

A third great example of a unique business advantage is a large grocery store in my area called Shady Maple. This huge country grocery store has another business next door called Shady Maple Smorgasbord. This restaurant offers one of the best buffet style eating places on the east coast. The food is mostly homemade and people come from other states to try it. The restaurant has a unique business advantage because its owners also have the giant supermarket. This combination creates multiple advantages such as wholesale food sources, quantity supply purchases and the ability to liquidate various foods that my be getting dated or simply using up overstocks and inventory imbalances. Too many ripe bananas? Let's make a batch of banana cream pies!

Some possible unique business advantages might include the following. An established business with employees could start another business using some of the same staff to operate the new business. A printer could launch a publishing company using his own facilities to produce the books, newsletters, and reports. A real estate investor could begin his or her own management company since they already have the framework in place from their own property management.

TIP: Try to determine what unique business advantages you might have so you have an added competitive edge in the marketplace.

Competitor Surveillance. One of the best ways to sharpen your business is to find out what other competitors are doing in the marketplace. My family is involved in retail appliances. About once a year I visit various competitors to see how their showrooms are merchandised and what their prices are. This two-day process provides highly valuable competitor research. In addition I gain a lot of ideas while out in the marketplace. In some cases I see opportunities I am missing just by getting outside my own little business world.

Consider hiring a "spy" to shop your competitors (or potential competitors) to see what they are offering in terms of services and prices. Develop a research list for your shopper. This is a great idea for any of the real estate service businesses listed in this book. Even landlords should take a few weeks every few years and shop rents by calling as a "mystery renter".

Classified Ad Power.

One trick I have used effectively is to use classified ads as a way of finding people or things for your business. Whatever or whoever you need to help your business consider using classified ads to find them. I have been surprised at how many folks looking for part-time work will respond to ads. Try using short ads in several papers, especially the free ones. What knowledge, expertise, or labor are you lacking? Place a classified ad and you'll be pleasantly surprises out the talented people willing to help you.

Join Associations, Industry Groups, Dinner Clubs.

Some folks overdo going to seminars and conferences and never seem to take action with the ideas they learn. However, I am a big advocate of attending industry meetings.

In most industries there state and national associations serve and support people within the given fields they represent. From my experience, having worked within several industries, these association meetings are highly profitable. Whatever your business or investment involvement, I urge you to find, join, and attend these meetings.

Although the speakers and educators presented by these associations are usually good, I learn as much or more from the people I meet. Make it a point to keep in casual contact with the people you meet. Over the years, I have developed several long-term friendships with people from these meetings.

Another idea is to organize a small dinner club of like-minded business colleagues that will meet on a given time each week or month. I attend one such real estate dinner meeting and find it enjoyable and helpful.

TIP: The only downfall of attending these meetings is you will meet a lot of folks making money in a lot of different opportunities. Be careful not to lose focus on your own business. We are all looking for faster and easier ways to make money. It always looks easier looking from the outside. The key point is to not get lured away from what is working or could be working for you. As entrepreneurs it is our nature to try new and exciting things! (One fellow I know spent years deliberating over what real estate opportunity he was going to get into.)

Use Systems, Policies, Checklists, Forms. You can maximize you and your workers' efforts by creating as many systems, forms, checklists and policies in your business as possible. These are all ways of simplifying the way your business operates and multiplying your efforts. Most of these things are just instructions put into written flowchart form. These tools reduce the amount of thinking and remembering needed because the procedural flow is written down for reference. Although these simple tools require some effort to compile and create, your payback comes quickly.

Start creating your system by finding the most efficient way of performing a job and making it as idiot-proof as possible. Then put that system down into a written form so your workers can follow it until it is learned. Systems help ensure consistency and quality.

No worker can make excuses for failing to complete a series of tasks if the tasks are put into a checklist form where each step requires a checkmark or their initials followed by a bottom-page signature upon completion. This also creates accountability.

Preprinted forms are a time-saving tool because they reduce document preparation time. Using a word-processing tool try to create as many forms for your business as possible. Create a form file with your master copies ready for duplication.

A policy booklet is helpful at reducing worker questions because procedures and problematic issues are explained in writing.

Building Your Team. Most businesses are systems combined with teams. Your "team" does not have to be actual employees as discussed earlier, but you will have a multitude of people who work with you. Generally speaking, the best companies are the ones with the best team. The same way that the best athletic teams

win the most games, the best companies have the best talent working for them. The better the talent you have working for you, the more successful you will become.

You can help build a great team by being willing to share your success with them in some way. Usually this is money. When possible, tie their success into yours by paying with incentives and various commission (performance pay) programs.

Selecting the Right Business Form

An important decision you will have to make early on is the choice of business structure for operating your business. While this business decision could become complicated I will provide a fairly simple viewpoint.

There are four main business structures, I will provide you a basic briefing on each. The key word here is brief. I am neither an account nor an attorney. If you want a 500-page book on business entities I suggest a visit to the local law library.

From my experience and from watching dozens of start-up entrepreneurs, I can state with some certainty that most new entrepreneur worry too much about liability, taxation, and other legal minutia. All of this stuff is important—very important—but as a start-up entrepreneur, with limited cash and assets, you need to spend most of your time developing cash flow and a viable business, not lawsuit paranoia. This will come later.

The Four Structures/Forms. Generally speaking there are four basic business structures: Corporations, Partnerships, Sole Proprietorships, and Limited Liability Companies (LLC). Each of these entities or structures has pros and cons related to their formation, usage, and taxation.

The Sole Proprietorship. The most commonly used business structure is the sole proprietorship. This basically means that everything, including all profits and losses, are under your personal name and go on your personal tax return under Schedule C.

The advantages of using the simple sole proprietorship structure include, first, that a sole proprietorship requires virtually no special filings other than your regular income tax reporting and scheduled tax payments. It can be created and operated in most cases by simply doing business (unless you are using a trade name) in your name. No special business meetings or minutes are required for record keeping. Furthermore, an abundance of simple bookkeeping and business software is available to assist you in running a sole proprietorship. Keep in mind, you can still operate under a DBA name (doing business as).

The Corporation.

This is a hugely popular business entity which is used by almost all mid-sized and larger businesses. A corporation is a separate entity from the people who have created it. It has its own name and can last indefinitely. When operated and formed correctly it can offer liability protection for its stockholders and directors. In most cases, creditors cannot go beyond the assets of the corporation to satisfy business debts and judgments. In many cases a corporation offers additional tax perks and benefits not available to sole proprietors. Most of the tax perks consist of allowable tax deductions that sole proprietors are not entitled to.

The main drawbacks are the costs associated with forming a corporation and maintaining records. There also are additional accounting fees required for annual state filings and separate tax return preparation, since the profits from this entity are taxed on a corporate, rather than an individual's tax return.

When you form a corporation you have to file articles of incorporation with the department of state. Typically this requires an initial filing fee of several hundred dollars. Furthermore, you will have annual corporate fees and minimum taxes due to the state. In Pennsylvania, the minimum annual fee is around $300 even if you don't conduct any business that year.

There are some additional negatives related to double taxations where profits can be taxed on a corporate return and again on the individual's tax return if the accounting is not handled correctly.

Partnerships.

General partnerships result when two people decide to start a business venture. Minimal business filings are required. The main drawback is that each partner is fully liable for the other partner's actions.

TIP: In almost all cases I would avoid starting a business with a partner. In most cases you don't need one. A multitude of problems in partnering center around equality of effort, time, and investment. In many cases, one partner will contribute more than the other and resentment will build. It's tough when you have two individuals with different values, goals, viewpoints, and ideas.

The Limited Liability Company. This new business entity/device is a blended form of the other three business structures and is legal in all states. Although there are no uniform laws from state to state, most state laws pertaining to LLCs are similar.

In many respects the LLC is most like a corporation in the liability protection it offers to the owners. It also is created much like a corporation since you must file articles of organization with your department of state. Again, like corporations there is an initial filing fee along with annual reporting and fees.

The owner or owners of an LLC are not called stockholders; they are called "members." The LLCs form and method of management are controlled by a contract. This contract is called the "operating agreement." This contract can remain private and can be drafted with a lot of individuality. State law will dictate what must be covered in the written operating contract.

Profits and losses can flow to the individual members in much the same way a partnership would work with the added benefit of liability protection. The taxation issue is governed by IRS code and must meet several tests. If it does not meet the standard, profits and losses will not pass through, but be taxed like a corporation.

The overall advantage of an LLC is its relative ease of formation, liability protection afforded to members, reduced paperwork over that of a corporation, and flow-through taxation. I would seriously check out the LLC method for your state since this is great hybrid structure for a business.

How to Learn More About LLC. Since this entity is relatively new and since laws change from state to state you should call your department of state and ask them to send you information on creating an LLC. Also, ask for a copy of the LLC state law. If the state department doesn't have the law call your state representative or Legislative Reference Bureau.

What is the Best Choice? If you are starting a business with very little cash, my suggestion is to begin operating as a sole proprietor. After a few years of doing business you can convert to a corporation or LLC entity to gain liability protection.

Although corporations and LLCs are excellent entity choices, additional accounting fees and annual state filing fees that go along with them are drawbacks. In most cases even a simple corporation will cost $600 to form, plus additional filings and minimum state taxes each year. You also will have ongoing, annual accounting fees since you will need to file state and federal corporate tax returns: It's fair to say that a typical corporation will require at least $1,000 a year in various accounting, filing, registration, and minimum taxation costs.

Create a Fictitious Name. In most cases you should file with your state or county for a DBA (doing business as name). You will pay a small fee and register your company name. This enables you to receive checks and open a checking account with a business name.

If you go the DBA route you can always convert over to an LLC or Corporation by simply filing articles of incorporation or articles of organization (LLC) and using your old name with the added LLC or INC., attached—if the name is not already being used within your state.

The Exceptions. There always exceptions. If you are starting a business with a lot of risk and liability, you should seriously consider an asset protective entity like a corporation or LLC. For example, the home inspection business has a high amount of liability, therefore, it may be wise to start out operating within a corporate business structure, especially if you have assets.

What About Landlording? While landlording can carry a fair amount of liability, landlords need to be cautious about using a corporation or LLC to buy and actually own the real estate inside it. In many cases, you will lose many of the tax advantages of real estate investing. For instance, rental income is not subject to self-employment taxes (social security) in most cases. While a corporation does not pay self-employment tax on its earnings, it does pay it on salaries paid to employees. As a general rule, do not buy real estate in a corporate name unless you are in the buy/sell (dealer) business in a big way.

If you own more than a handful of rental assets you should consider getting a DBA name for management of the investments. This creates a more professional atmosphere rather than having tenants make checks out to you personally.

There are several ways to reduce the risk inherent in rental assets. Above all, be sure you have both fire insurance and liability insurance in the policy to help shelter your assets from lawsuits. Most personal injury lawyers go after insurance policies, not individuals or their assets. Land trusts are another way to reduce exposure, mainly by concealing ownership, since the raw title is held by a straw party (trustee). Court judgments can be obtained against trust property, but the owner's total holding are kept private as long as they are held by different trustees.

18

Shrewd Marketing Secrets

When you mention the word "marketing," people automatically think of advertising. While this is about half right, there's a lot more to it than that. Marketing is much broader than most people realize.

Marketing is anything you do as a business that influences—impacts, affects, motivates—clients to do business with you. As marketing expert and author Jay Levinson says, "Marketing can be anything from the way you answer the phone—the way you dress—to the way your office looks." Marketing can be virtually anything that affects the way a customer perceives you or influences them to do business with you.

We discovered a good example illustrating that marketing is more than just advertising in one of our businesses. We learned that red price tags seemed to have a subtle, but perceivably negative influence on customers. We stopped using red price tags and starting using a lively green color. (Remember, stop signs are red; green lights are "go.") Although this was a minor change, we found these new green tags increased sales! Best of all, many of these marketing changes and tweaks cost little or nothing to implement.

As a real estate entrepreneur who is building a business with very little cash you must use as many marketing techniques and strategies as possible. Although you may not be as well financed as your competitors, there's no reason why you can't run circles around them in the marketing department.

From my experience, a good portion of business people are weak in marketing. If you make it a point to master marketing and business positioning (niches), you will be ahead of 90 percent of your competitors.

Rule #1: The study of marketing is really the study of business because business is marketing. Develop your primary business craft, but spend as much time as possible learning about marketing. It's safe to say that every $1.00 you invest in your marketing education (books, newsletters, seminars) will pay you back tenfold in increased sales and profits.

Business is about one thing—getting as many consumers to buy your product or service at the highest profit margins with as many repeat sales and referrals as possible. That is the primary goal of business.

Rule #2: Do not turn over your business marketing to an outsider. You are the best person to create and implement your own business marketing strategy and plans. You have a much keener knowledge of your marketplace and industry than does your average marketing consultant or advertising agency.

Note: This is not to disparage marketing consultants. In fact, it can be a great business to get into, helping the many folks who don't have the time or knowledge to market their business. There are excellent marketing consultants who can create marketing strategies and write good ad copy. But I still believe you should be your own marketing specialist and write your own ad copy.

Marketing is a critical task. You are the best person to take charge of this aspect of your business. Besides, as a startup entrepreneur you will need to save as much money as possible for your business. I believe in this so strongly that I recommend reading and studying at least one book per month on marketing. A little further along I will give you names and resources for further study.

TIP: In your business journal jot down all the marketing ideas you come across. Don't leave them in your mind or you'll forget them. Write down tips you read about in business books and also those great ideas you get from other business people.

Break into the Market with Price. One of the best ways to attract clients to a new business with a competitive pricing strategy. Price is always a powerful buying factor for consumers because people love to save money.

One of your biggest challenges when you start a new business is attracting clients. By pricing your service below the competition you create a reason for the client/consumer to try you. This strategy works especially well for start-up entrepreneurs since they don't have the high expenses their established competitors have.

In many cases sharpening your pricing pencil will create a lot more business volume which will more than compensate for your reduced profit margin. In addition, you will "own" that customer, who will probably make repeat purchases of your services. Another hidden benefit is all of the referral business generated from the clients you attracted with price.

The key is to price your product or service just low enough to create buyer motivation. You do not want to underprice your service to a point that the client perceives you as inferior. If your prices are too low people become skeptical and you will be leaving too much money on the table.

Loss Leaders and Free Services. In marketing and merchandising you will become familiar with the term, "Loss Leader." This is the practice of pricing a highly visible product or service at or near cost and then advertising it prominently as a special or sale item. First, this strategy attracts attention from consumers. Next, it buys their mind by making them think all of your prices must be that good. Leader pricing also creates a lot of phone traffic to the business by folks inquiring about the advertised special. Another benefit is that it creates sales traffic, and a certain percentage of these clients can be up-sold into more profitable services or products. Lastly, it gets more clients to sample your services and in the future return to you if they believe you have treated them well.

Another clever technique is to create free services, samples, or trials so that the prospective client can get a taste of what you are offering. This again can create traffic and help initiate a long-term relationship so that you can provide other more profitable services. In the early 1930s my grandfather built a radio and appliance business using this technique. He went door to door offering people a free, one-week trial of radios and refrigerators with absolutely no obligation to purchase. Since these were brand new technologies, people loved hearing programs on the radio and not having to get ice for the icebox. His free trial conversion rate was high.

If you are new to a business you can stir up the market place by offering value prices combined with free services, trial offers, and loss leader offerings and see more business traffic. I have seen many businesses use sharp pricing as a tool to acquire market share and a client base. After a few years of building a client base they gradually raise their prices to market levels or higher. At that point the client/consumer is in their business pipeline and is "hooked."

Image IS Everything. It is amazing how we are influenced by image. In life many things are image based. For example, if you watched someone open their wallet and see it bursting with cash. You would perceive them to be financially secure, smart, high-income earner or something like that. For our example, let's say they have $900 in cash stuffed in that wallet.

Now what if you saw this same person's bank account statement and it said they had a $900 balance. You certainly wouldn't classify that as a high-income checking account would you? What if the person with the cash stuffed wallet only had $900 cash to their name? That would change your opinion wouldn't it? Yes. Smart businesses use tools, dress, props, and stationery to create image.

TIP: Uniforms or clothing embossed with your company name is an excellent way to create image. For instance, there are several companies that sell business clothing that they will embroider with your business name and logo. This looks especially professional and gives the image that your business is larger and well established than it actually is. This is a great idea for almost anyone in the services business (I think you will be surprised at how affordable this is). One catalog worth checking out is Lands' End at www.landsend.com or 800.338.2000.

Image is about creating assumptions in people's minds. People assume that if you are dressed cleaning and sharply, you are probably a responsible person. People assume that if your car is neat and detailed you are probably a respectable person. People assume if you're organized and detail oriented you are safe to do business with. People assume if you return phone calls within a few hours you are a reliable business person. (People make a lot of assumptions which may or may not be true.)

TIP: Here are almost "free" things you can do to improve your image. Work on polishing you (shined shoes, hair cuts, nice clothes, clean auto, clean teeth and breath, trimmed nails, clean language, politeness, graciousness).

TIP: One of the best ways to create a strong image is to have professional looking brochures, stationery, cards, and marketing documents that glow with quality and credibility. While I'm a big fan of desktop publishing programs, I think in many cases it pays to have a professional graphic designer create your marketing documents (with you providing the message and ad copy).

TIP: If you really are squeezed with your cash flow then I recommend creating your own marketing pieces with a program like Microsoft Publisher. Office supply houses sell premium cotton fiber stationery and envelopes that can be imprinted with your laser printer. Premium stationery has a rich feel like that used by expensive law firms. This will get you going for about $40 in office supplies while at the same time giving a classy look and feel.

Use 800, 888, and 877 Numbers. Toll free numbers will do several things for your business. They will add a degree of professionalism since the average person doesn't realize how easy and cheap it is to get a toll-free number. It helps give your business credibility since most "big" companies have these numbers. It also tends to increase customer response rates since they don't have to risk a toll call to get information.

Toll free numbers can typically be operated from your regular phone line without adding lines because the call rings on that line or even be forwarded into your cell phone. These numbers typically can be used on a per-use basis of around 7 to 10 cents per minute nationwide without other charges. It truly is a low-cost feature that can improve credibility and client response rates.

Remove Barriers Between You and Them. The companies that do best are those that remove all barriers between themselves and the consumer. This makes it easy for clients to reach you, buy from you, get information, and have their problems handled quickly.

You have probably had the experience of calling a large company and not being able to speak to a real person. You get shuffled from menu option to menu option, ultimately ending up in some voice mailbox. (In many cases there isn't even an operator option.)

And then, after waiting on hold for ten minutes, the computer disconnects you! Personally, I am surprised how many big companies make it hard for customers to reach them.

Removing barriers is all about making it easy for customers to: Call, get information, place an order, make payments, and get service in the event there is a problem—Don't make clients jump through hoops.

Favorite Marketing Colors.
When creating flyers, small signs, and various marketing coupons you will find certain colors will "pull" better than others. Here are my favorites: Fluorescent pink and yellow. I also like white stock with black ink and yellow and green highlighted areas.

Using Ethical Imitation and Knockoffs.
While I think it is important to create your own unique marketing niches, you also need to watch your competitors and industry to see what is working for them. If you learn about something your competitors are using that really works, you may need to adapt and implement their ideas yourself.

Copying ideas may not seem fair, but in business you must maintain your competitive advantage. I have been involved in several industries and have watched big companies copy each other all of the time. As soon as one company comes out with a successful new feature or selling advantage all of the rest follow suit with their own version. While this may seem distasteful and lacking in fairness, you must give consumers what they want. If someone discovers a consumer hot-button, you are smart to see if you can get in on the action.

Having been involved in the appliance industry I am amazed at how the big five companies each copy off each other's successful innovations and features. If one company increases its oven size, within a year the others will increase their oven size. If company X develops a stainless steel washtub, you can bet the others will come out with their own version, especially if company X gains market share with the new tub style. All of this is extremely common in the business world.

You can use your own spies and industry contacts to see what is working for your competitors. Also, watch for repeat ads and marketing gimmicks; companies don't keep using ads if they aren't working.

Signs as Advertising Tools. Signs can be one of the best advertising tools you can find. They provide perhaps the lowest cost per impression of any advertising medium. Signs are also fixed cost marketing. In most cases you pay only once for making the sign, exactly opposite to print advertising in newspapers or TV ads.

A good example of how signs are effective is the large changeable letter sign we use for one of our businesses. We bought it about fifteen years ago for around $500. We have used this sign every week from its location along the road for the past fifteen years. That brings a new meaning to the word low-budget. We change the message about every ten days, which keeps readers from losing interest. We get tens of thousands of impressions per month at almost no cost.

With the new vinyl lettering available you can go to an instant sign shop and have them create professional lettering for your vehicle. This lettering can be placed on your glass or the body of your vehicle. This works well if you have a service business or a business like buying properties. Like embroidered uniforms, this helps create a company image and professionalism along with an advertising effect.

Landlords should remember that signs work. Place for-rent signs on every available property. You'll pick up some good tenants with signs and they are cheaper than the newspaper. Be bold—use big signs.

Look for places where you can put small signs or banners at little or no cost. If you own real estate, check into the zoning restrictions for placing a sign on the side of your building or along the roadside. Another possibility is to make deals with other people to allow you to place a sign on their property for a small fee or barter of services. Be creative.

TIP: A friend of mine who experienced zoning problems with some of his wooden signs has found vinyl banners to be an acceptable alternative that seems to get around some zoning issues. It seems that banners strapped to buildings with cable ties may not get the sign police mad. Check into this yourself.

> **TIP: Sometimes banners or signs placed inside a building window facing out will effectively beat the zoning issues. Consider making a deal with a vacant storefront to hang a vinyl or paper banner in the window.**

Here's another idea that beats many of the zoning issues for signs. Paint your message on the side of an old truck and park the truck along a busy highway or on property you own. Whatever the case, see if you can advertise your business using signs. These signs can be placed on old buildings, along the road, on vehicles, in yards, on poles, or anywhere else people will see them.

Speed as Your Marketing Weapon. In today's business climate speed is one of the most powerful marketing weapons you can use.

Due to a multitude of economic and social reasons people need to make fast business transactions and decisions. If you are able to service your market by quickly responding to client phone calls, information requests, problems, and product or service orders, than you will have a competitive advantage.

At the risk of contradicting what I stated earlier about using price, speed of response and service can be your best strategy for charging a higher price and thus increasing profit margin. People will pay a price premium for speed of service. Look for unique ways to add a speed dimension to your business.

Coupons and Rebates. Over the years I have used coupons and rebates in my advertising and marketing documents. They are an effective way to increase ad response along with providing a way of measuring response.

Look for ways to work coupons and rebates into your marketing. Rebates can work well by enabling you to charge a higher price and then make the customer earn the discount by mailing the rebate in within a specified time period. If you use a rebate program consider having your accounting firm or outside bookkeeper handle its actual administration.

> **TIP: in coupons and rebates always use an expiration date along with some reasonably firm qualifying requirements.**

Appeasing Clients to Win More Business. In

business a natural friction develops every time people spend money with you. The source of the friction could be miscommunication, mistakes, late delivery of service or product, billing errors, poor service, or anything we could label as "Murphy's Law".

While a small portion of the complaints you receive will be from people "working" you (taking advantage of you) for a discount or concession, most will be legitimate complaints. From my experience it is best to not get into a battle of the wills, but to submit to their complaint and give the benefit of the doubt on these issues. It may cost you some money up front, but in many cases you'll make it up in future business or referrals you will get from them. Try to be gracious even though many times you will be right and the client is clearly wrong.

> **Tip: In your marketing documents and ads consider using the word specialist to describe yourself. For instance, a landlord's brochures or cards might say— Affordable Housing Specialist.**

Marketing Resources and Closing Thoughts.

Every business owner or manager should master marketing since marketing is the art and science of getting customers to buy from us. Take away all of the inner office stuff like accounting, bill paying, and legal issues and what you have remaining is marketing. The guts of any business is marketing.

While I have learned a lot from various books, my advice is to open your eyes to what totally unrelated businesses are doing to market their business. Become curious and ask a lot of questions. In many cases you can use the same concepts these other people are doing by applying your own unique twist to them.

I recommend several authors in your study of marketing. Jay Conrad Levinson has written an arsenal of marketing books with his trademark guerilla marketing titles. Most of them are a good read where you will find some gold nuggets. His web site is **www.gmarketing.com.**

Al Ries and Jack Trout have produced readable gems on the topic of business positioning and marketing strategy. Their book, *The 22 Immutable Laws of Marketing,* is worthy of your dollars (in fact, all their books are good).

Don't forget Jay Abraham. Over the years he has produced a number of tape courses and reports for business owners. His recent book, *How to Get Everything You Can from All You've Got,* is a superb synopsis of his marketing philosophy and well worth the price.

Dan Kennedy is another great marketing author. He is contrary in his approach and opinionated as well, which makes him fun and refreshing to read. He has a number of smaller books that are price-less for the small entrepreneur. Try various on-line book sellers for his titles.

10 Stupid Things Business Owners Do to Mess Up Their Businesses

In this chapter I will explain the most common business mistakes, blunders, and misjudgments that business owners make. I have accumulated this list from nearly twenty years of observing entrepreneurs, successful and non-successful. It should also be noted that many smart people make these mistakes.

Although business people often have a simplistic outlook about being in business, we need to realize that being a success can be far more difficult than it appears—especially in maintaining success over ten or twenty years. Novice entrepreneurs often become overconfident with early success in their business. They hit a few home runs and begin to think they are financial geniuses. The reality is they got lucky. I have seen my share of this in the business world. If you think you're clever about making money this is the time to watch out. Making money as an entrepreneur takes skill, hard work, focus, persistence, and a certain amount of boldness.

If you have been successful, don't rest on your laurels. In business it is folly to develop a sense of security or complacency about your business. Business is not easy. In fact, like many others, I have searched for "easy" "fast" and "no-risk" ways of making money and to my disappointment came up empty handed. As one of my favorite speakers, Brian Tracy, says, "The words easy and money don't go together in the same sentence except when you say—easy to lose."

One of the most irritating things for me to watch are infomercials with a slick sales guy telling you that you can be rich by next year in whatever business plan he is selling. Not to say that all of these programs are worthless or invalid, but it is the hype and silly testimonials that irk me. The reality of many of those testimonials is they are either totally bogus or given by folks who haven't fully experienced all of the normal storms of business life. I always say, talk to me in three years. If you're still in business and paying your bills I'll listen. So at the risk of sounding like a party-pooping cynic let me give you the 10 big mistakes you need to avoid to keep your business from crashing and burning. While there are far more than 10 stupid things we do as business owners, these are some of the most common.

1. The Absentee Management Problem.

Business owners often become tired of their business and turn over day-to-day operations to an employee manager or outside management firm. While this doesn't always produce disaster, many times it does. The old jingle is true, "While the cat's away the mice will play."

Good business owners are often fussy and demanding about customer service and quality. Many are control freaks to some degree or another. The truth is this is how they became so successful in the first place. There's a saying that no one cares as much about your money as you do. This is especially accurate when it comes to employees and managers—they frequently will do the expedient thing rather than the right thing.

Unless you're in one of those rare businesses that runs on autopilot, avoid absentee management. In absentee management situations you often see businesses being run into the ground over a slow period of time. Absentee management usually brings with it worker theft, sloppy service, and runaway waste.

Most of the good business owners I have met are people who are detail oriented and operate under a tight-ship mentality—very little slips unnoticed. Running a business takes a lot of time and energy. Stop thinking you can be off in the Caribbean seven months of the year. I like what Martin Edelston, founder of Boardroom Books says in his book titled *I-Power*. "Delegation is a very high-risk alternative to hands-on management. Only mediocrity can be delegated. High performance cannot be. High performance requires constant vigilance."

2. The Problem of Protecting Your Ego.

Business owners often try to protect their ego by not admitting something is failing and trying to keep a struggling investment or business alive. The principle is you have got to cut loses early.

Small businesses are more likely to have this problem. Major corporations tend to act quickly at shedding business losers or divisions of their business that are not pulling their weight. Several times in my town I have seen large chain stores open restaurants or stores only to close them a year or two later. Big businesses often work solely by the numbers while small entrepreneurs rely on their feelings and emotions.

A related problem area is not letting the marketplace determine your product or services. Instead, as obstinate entrepreneurs, we often try to force our opinions and ideas on the market. If, after substantial testing and experimenting, you can't get the market to buy what you are selling, abandon the course. So what if you were wrong. The truth of the matter is most business ideas are losers. If you're in business and have one or two successful ideas out of ten you will be successful. Folks get tripped up when they have a few false starts and ideas that don't work and think they are idiots. They just haven't worked enough ideas that's all!

3. The Uncontrolled Growth Problem. Many
viable and prosperous businesses have gone broke by growing too fast. Believe it or not, many good business models have failed because of their success.

Entrepreneurs make the faulty assumption that if I can do this well with one store (or apartment complex, restaurant, hotel, etc.) I can really make money if I open up five more locations. The problem is your risk levels and problems grow geometrically. If you're working 50 hours per week with one business you'll be working 80 hours a week with five. Furthermore, rapid growth is almost always done with high levels of debt, which create cash flow problems.

Business growth is a worthy goal, but only when it can be achieved with prudence and measured judgment. You need to be prepared for economic downturns and the unexpected pitfalls and blind spots that always arise. Take the Biblical advice of Solomon, the wisest person who ever lived—

"Those who seek fast riches will not go unpunished."
Develop a business plan with growth goals but try to have
as much cash and credit available to hedge the risk.
Businesses that develop a flush bank account have staying
power during the tough times.

4. The Boredom Syndrome. Entrepreneurs are

often idea people but weak in the area of management.
Because of this tendency, entrepreneurs become bored with
their businesses. The temptation to over-diversify and
venture into unknown business is great.

You see this with successful entrepreneurs who are at the
top of their field and move their efforts into a totally
unrelated business. In most cases this happens because they
are bored. The problem is that person has left their primary
field of expertise. In addition this type of moving away
from your core skills ends up diluting your efforts and
focus, and that usually results in hurting the original
business.

5. Employee Embezzlement and Theft. I

have cautioned you earlier in this book about having
employees, but eventually you will need some outside help
whether it be independent contractor or employees.

Never turn check writing responsibilities over to an
employee. Over the years I have seen a number of
businesses get robbed from the inside by so-called trusted
employees. In most cases it happens when employees get
control of check writing privileges.

As much as you want to trust people who work with you,
make sure you put safeguards and controls over workers
who have access to cash, check writing or product stock.

6. Accounts Receivable Problems. In business

you must make sure that you don't let your A-R get too
large. Your A-R is your accounts receivable, those open
accounts on your books where people owe you money.

You may also get into trouble if you don't keep a tight hold
and limit on how much outstanding debt you have on the
books. In some cases a major customer/client owing you

money will file bankruptcy, causing a chain reaction that puts your business in jeopardy.

This problem of uncollectable debts is very common when dealing with builders, contractors and especially *tenants.* As business people and landlords, we must take every precaution to collect what is owed us. Landlords are credit grantors just like banks. Collect those rents firmly and aggressively.

7. Spending and Lifestyle Problems. Another

common problem occurs with new entrepreneurs who find success early in the game. They begin making money and expand their lifestyle too quickly, gobbling up precious cash that should have been used to pay off debts, build cash reserves, and grow their business.

Make every attempt not to live off of debt. Also, remember business has cycles that flow just like the seasons. The summer you are experiencing could change into a winter. Even if business is excellent, don't spend like it always will be excellent. I recently heard a hugely successful landlord (1,000 units) tell our investment club that he lived on around $1,000 per month from his rental business for the first ten years and all of the rest was plowed back into his business. (It's worth noting his income was quite substantial during several of those ten years.)

8. Loafing and Other Related Challenges.

Being self-employed, you don't have anyone making you work. If you want to stay home and watch TV all day you can. While this is one beauty of working for yourself, it can be hazardous to your financial health. Some people find it enticing to wake up and loaf the day away. Occasionally this probably okay. But, if a pattern develops it can be hard to break. Eventually you develop a work debt. Here's how it works.

Every day you have an opportunity to do things that will make you money, even if it is a small amount. Let's say your time is worth a modest $15 per hour. Okay, we take today off. We are now about $100 to $150 in the hole. Not life threatening. Next week we don't take an entire day off just half a day. We are only $60 in the hole that day. Repeat this process over a year and you will develop a work deficit of around $4,000. Over five years it grows to $20,000.

We all need time to recharge and rest. Taking time for rest and recreations is not the issue. In fact, I'm totally opposed to working seven days a week because it is counter productive. What I am saying is you must use discipline and force yourself to work against all of your mind's longing for leisure. This problem plagues self-employed people. Work through the boredom and pain.

I love what financial writer Gary North says about this. He says the easiest way to increase your income by 20 percent is to simply work 20 percent longer. Sounds too obvious, but he's right. The truth is whenever you study the giants of business and entrepreneuring you find people who work long and hard. You must burn some midnight oil to become successful. As a general rule, the most successful folks are the hardest workers, whether they are students, athletes, entrepreneurs, scientists, politicians, or artists!

9. The Tax Payment Pitfall. Now here's a dragon I have seen slay many a good entrepreneur. In business there are a variety of taxes that need to be paid: estimated income taxes, business taxes, sales taxes, and property taxes.

Business people *frequently* get into problems in this area and if not dealt with soon enough tax problems can quickly force you into a cash flow crisis. In many cases the penalties and interest are more than the original tax bill. I know of one successful business that sold 10 million dollars per year of products and then fell into this trap. This is a real problem that can ruin your business!

Here's what happens. Business people get so busy running their day-to-day business with all of its problems and challenges that they spend money that should be used for tax payments. Often it is used as a short-term loan source, but eventually it bites them. Probably the number one problem for self-employed people is federal income taxes. It's so easy to spend this money, but after getting behind in a year or two's worth of tax monies it's hard to catch up.

You must create a separate account for your taxes and make disciplined payments into this set-aside fund. Do *not* use this money as cash flow. Don't even borrow from it. Hire a private bookkeeper or accounting firm to administer your tax bills on a monthly basis. Not doing this can be lethal.

10. The Loaning Money Error. Now here is another giant trap awaiting the good-hearted business person who's trying to help out a friend or employee.

Cash is the life force of a business. It must be treated as something close to sacred. You cannot get into the position of being a bank. Banks loan money—entrepreneurs sell products and services. You are not a bank.

Over the years I have seen several individuals and businesses get into a problem that was caused from loaning money. As much as people plead and beg you to loan them money, don't do it. For a business to loan money is like a mountain climber loaning his ropes and boots. Your survival depends on you having use of the money. Besides, in most cases the person needing the money want to use it for some dopey purpose like buying a big screen TV or some other questionable purpose.

As an addendum to this concept you must also never co-sign or borrow money for the benefit of someone else. Three times in ten years I met people who actually borrowed money against their home to loan the money to a "friend" who supposedly needed it. In all three cases the friend quickly changed into a deceitful and thankless thief who skipped with the money leaving the well-intentioned victim holding the proverbial bag. It is amazing how nice and sweet people are when they want you to loan them money, but they will often turn on you when they get in a jam. This can't be stressed enough—never, ever loan money or co-sign a debt.

The Main Principle of the Chapter. The consistent theme of this chapter is control your own money and assets as much as possible. Good business managers are very attentive to their business and customers. The business world is full of surprises and hardship for those folks who don't seriously guard their finances and exercise self-discipline in their business.

Conclusion and Information About the Author

If you've made it this far through the book you probably are serious about starting your own real estate business or investment career. This is great because the real estate industry offers the ambitious person dozens of opportunities.

I can honestly say that I am more excited today about real estate than I was in 1984 when I got started. This is rare. Most folks burn out. But to me, real estate is so interesting and stimulating that it gets better with time. It is a terrific field, especially for the patient ones who are willing to learn the craft. Time is on your side in this business, especially the investment side of residential housing.

My main advice is look before you leap and investigate before you invest. If you lose a real estate deal or two in the beginning because you don't understand it or aren't totally comfortable, that's okay—another one will come your way. Good business people are thoughtful and not impulsive.

I don't know what level of business or investing experience that you have, but I did my best to make this book as informative as possible. Most readers, even experienced real estate entrepreneurs, should be able to mine several sizable nuggets of gold from this work. I again encourage you, if you have skipped over any of the chapters try to find the time to read them. Buried within each chapter are ideas that might be usable in your real estate business or investments.

As you have seen real estate offers opportunities in service businesses, consulting, sales, rental investing, buying and selling, management, and publishing. Few industries offer this broad of a selection. Carefully and thoughtfully research and study your specialty before getting involved. You don't want to waste several years of your life learning you hate what you are doing. There are countless ways to make a living in this world. Real estate may or may not be for you. If you don't get excited, shop elsewhere until you find something that sparks some excitement.

Within real estate circles there is a natural tendency for many folks to quit their existing job and go full-time into real estate. While this works for some folks, you shouldn't feel pressured to do this. Real estate is unique in that it can effectively be worked as a second-job or parallel business. My father has been in real estate investing for three decades, and it has been done as a sideline opportunity that compliments his other businesses.

For Those Who Find Success Elusive. I think the starting point for those who have found success elusive is to begin with being honest with yourself. If you are not realistically analyzing your life—successes and failures—to come up with some sort of accounting of yourself, you are ducking truth.

Success is within your grasp yet elusive. So if you have found success elusive I guess we can say you are on the right track. Some folks won't even mentally concede that success is hard. They either give a list of excuses or are still looking for easy ways to make money. Either way, they are on the wrong road. It seems to me that the beginning of wisdom is truth. You have to be truthful with yourself as to what the sum total of your life is.

We all have the tendency to look for excuses as to why we haven't achieved what we want. This is self-delusion. You are not being honest with yourself. While a small percentage of us have had extreme and unexpected hardships that have totally devastated our lives, the vast majority of us have had reasonably average or normal lives mixed with a few crises along the way.

The starting point needs to begin by being frank with yourself. If you haven't been successful, you need to realize it's most likely your fault. Hear me out, please. You have let yourself down. Again, using my life as my reference I can say the vast majority of my failings have been caused by me. The primary culprit for most people (myself included) is self-discipline problems. If you can't make yourself perform the work or duties that need to be handled when you don't feel like doing them, you will have a rough time becoming successful.

The other contributory factor to many of us not finding success is a lack of persistent determination. You may be talented and educated, but without a dogged persistence you again will find long-term success elusive. Think of anything highly commendable and ask yourself if it would be possible without a high degree of persistence. If you analyze your life I think you will find many times again you have let yourself down by not being persistent. I'll bet at least once or twice you had success in your fingertips but let her go. She wasn't even putting up a fight, you just loosened your grip and quit holding her. She was ready to give her worthy treasure to you if you would have only held on a little longer. You didn't see any light at the end of the tunnel; little did you know the manhole cover was just a few feet away.

What is the answer? The answer is tough love. You have got to get tough on yourself. Get angry about it. You have let yourself down. But it's not going to happen anymore. From here on out you will be honest with yourself. No more rationalization or excuse making. You are responsible. Today and every day you will exercise an iron grip on your emotions and feelings. You will do what needs to be done even when you don't feel like it. There is not other way. When the going gets tough and you lose your confidence you will keep on persisting and take every setback as an education experience, not to be repeated again. You must realize that every successful person has had countless setbacks and difficulties like you have. The answer, my friend, is not quitting. Adjust course? Yes. Abandon your dreams? Never!

Along with following the above points you need to keep reading and studying to find breakthrough ideas. Books and people you meet can provide terrific ideas. A "breakthrough idea" is a new insight and idea that will help you become successful. Breakthrough ideas come in two forms. The first are totally new ideas, hidden opportunities that others don't recognize. The second, and more common, type of breakthrough ideas involve new ways of looking at old problems and seemingly "stale" opportunities. These have been especially helpful to me because they reveal dormant opportunities that I have missed in the past. Frequently, they are just attitude adjustments which show me that I have looked at a certain problem or opportunity in a nonproductive way. A great resource is the free weekly electronic newsletter called "The Slight Edge" which you can sign up for at **www.yoursuccessstore.com**. This e-zine is loaded with a weekly dose of high performance philosophy and tips to get and keep you on the right success track.

I want your feedback. If I have missed any real estate opportunities that you would like to share with me I would love to hear what you are doing. Also, if you know of ways this book can be improved I want these too. I am open to your criticism and comments at bwitt@nni.com.

About Bryan Wittenmyer. Bryan has been a real estate investor and entrepreneur since he was twenty years old. Although his formal education consists of the highly coveted HSD (High

School Diploma) he has more than made up for his lack of advanced degrees with nearly twenty years of in-depth personal study of real estate, business, marketing, and theology. His personal library exceeds a thousand books. He is an unabashed, conservative Christian who believes the Bible to be the complete word of God. His wish is that all of his readers would at the minimum think about eternity in light of the claims of the Scriptures.

Bryan has been a writer for several publications and newsletters including *Creative Real Estate, Mr. Landlord Newsletter, The Real Estate Entrepreneur,* and has authored two other books, *Perpetual Income,* and *The Hidden Secrets of a Real Estate Technician.* Along with his real estate investing and writing, Bryan served on the board of directors for Berk's County Real Estate Investors Association.

Along with his experience in the real estate industry, Bryan has been involved in the retail appliance business along with a few other businesses along the way. Bryan likes hanging around with other entrepreneurs who enjoy talking shop. In fact, a good part of his thinking has been shaped by the many real estate investors who have exchanged business and investing ideas with him. To them he says, "Thank You." You can contact him at: PO Box 13246, Reading, PA 19612 or 610.326.9800.

Appendix

Real Estate Business and Investment Resources

The following resources are as accurate and current as we can make them, but in this rapidly changing word, both author and publisher hereby disclaim all responsibility for the reliability, accuracy or trustworthiness of any web site or site content resource company listed. We also do not necessarily agree or endorse various views or content provided by these resources.

www.drudgereport.com Updated hourly with hot breaking news

www.hellodirect.com High-tech telephone and communication devices. HelloDirect, 5893 Rue Ferrari St., San Jose, CA 95138. 800.444.3556

www.stamps.com Source for buying postage on-line.

www.onesuite.com Incredibly cheap long distance rates

www.vistaprint.com Free business card offer

www.z-law.com Real estate software (business and investing), Z-Law Software Inc., 15 Westminster St. Suite 637, PO Box 40602, Providence, RI 02940. 800.526.5588. Good catalog

www.NaREIA.com Source for locating local investment clubs. National Real Estate Investors Association. PO Box 1759, Pittsburgh, PA 15230-1759. 888.7Na.REIA

www.nolo.com Self-help legal books and on-line legal helps.

Nolo Press, 950 Parker Street, Berkeley, CA 94710-2524. 800.728.3555

www.equifax.com National Credit Bureau. Equifax Credit Bureau, PO Box 740241, Atlanta, GA 30374-0241. 800.685.1111

www.experian.com National Credit Bureau. Experian, PO Box 949, Allen, TX 75013-0949. 800.397.3742

www.tuc.com National Credit Bureau. 800.916.8800

www.knowx.com Public records research

www.pacer.psc.uscourts.gov Credit/persons investigation 800.676.6856

www.IRS.gov Forms and on-line publications

www.1031.org Exchange Facilitators Association, Federation of Exchange Accommodators, 1127 11th Street, suite 1003, Sacramento, CA 95814, 916.388.1031 www.dealmakerscafe.com In-depth site for real estate investors

www.hud.gov Entry site for government repo's and Section-8

Creative Real Estate Magazine. Premier publication for investors. Drawer L, Rancho Santa Fe, CA 92067. 858.756.1441

www.infoleverage.com Generating Cash Flow from rental and contracts. Bryan Wittenmyer, PO Box 13246, Reading, PA 19612. 610.670.9900 bwitt@nni.com.

www.notesmith.com Software for serious note and income stream investors, Princeton Investments, Inc., 6225 Eagle Ridge Ct., Fort Collins, CO 80525 800.526.5588

HomePro Services, Inc. Affordable Home Inspection Business System. Michael Lennon owner/trainer 800.966.4555

www.professionalequipment.com Specialized tools and equipment for the home inspection industry 800.334.9291. Good catalog

www.ashi.com American Society of Home Inspectors

www.sanzospecialties.com Books, tools, supplies for real estate agents

Sanzo Specialties, Inc., PO Box 68, Endicott, NY 13761. 800.222.4041. Good catalog

www.housepad.com Great example of a cutting edge real estate broker

www.inman.com On-line news for the real estate and mortgage industry 510.658.9252

www.parapublishing.com On-line resource for non-fiction writers. Dan Poynter 800.727.2782

www.namb.com National Association of Mortgage Brokers. 703.610.9009. Membership packet

The Loan Officers Store by Hark and Associates. Great resource for those in mortgage brokering. 225 S. Brady, Claremore, OK 74017. 800.456.1001 good catalog

www.wholesaleaccess.com Mortgage industry directory of lenders. Wholesale Access, 6140 Jerrys Drive, Columbia MD 21044. 410.772.1161

American Collectors Association, Inc. Credit and Collections Resource. 952.926.6547

www.jjca.org Judicial Judgment Collectors' Association (JJCA). If you get into buying judgments this group will educate you

www.midoh.com Setting up self-directed IRAs for property and paper. Mid Ohio Securities 36 Lake Avenue, PO Box 1529, Elyria, OH 44036. 440.323.5491

Make Money Trading Mortgages: Starter Manual on Debt Instruments. Del Ashby, The Wellington Company 2579 Rutland Rd., Davidsonville, MD 21035 moneyman@moneypatch.com

www.metmtg.com Large institutional note buyer— wholesale dept. Metropolitan Mortgage, 601 W. 1st Ave., Spokane, WA 99201-5012, 800.268.9184

www.settlementcapital.com Large buyer of unusual debt instruments. 800.959.0006 www.noteworthyusa.com Newsletter and helpful site on paper investing. Noteworthy Newsletter, PO Box 31451, San Francisco, CA 94131. 800.487.1864

www.papersourceonline.com Newsletter and helpful site on paper investing. The Paper Source, 250 W. Main St., Suite 220, Kerrville, TX 78028. 800.542.2270

www.alta.org   Group servicing the title industry needs. American Land Title Association, 1828 L. St., NW, Washington, DC 20036

Perpetual Income, How to Generate Cash Flow from Low-end House Investments, by Bryan C. Wittenmyer 610.670.9900 bwitt@nni.com

The Hidden Secrets of a Real Estate Technician, by Bryan C. Wittenmyer. 610.670.9900 bwitt@nni.com

www.mrlandlord.com   Largest landlording newsletter and on-line site. Mr. Landlord Inc., Box 64442, Virginia Beach, VA 23467.

www.familyhandyman.com Magazine helpful to landlords and rehabbers. The Family Handyman, 2915 Commers Dr. Suite 700, Eagan, MN 55121

www.constructionbook.com Giant selection of construction books. 800.253.0541. Good catalogcatalog

The Society of American Foresters Contacts for those interested in selling timber. 301.897.8720

www.landsend.com Business clothing logo embroidery. Lands' End, Inc., 6 Lands End Lane, Dodgeville, WI 53595 800.338.2000. Good catalog.

www.gmarketing.com   Enormous marketing business site, Jay Conrad Levinson, author of Guerilla Marketing series

www.yoursuccessstore.com Free e-zine for high-performance people

Index

We Want Your Real Estate Business and Investing Ideas

Are you using a real estate investment or business technique that we haven't covered in this book? Do you know of any real estate businesses that we have not explained in this book? If so, we would love to hear about what you're doing.

If you email or mail us any new, clever, or unique ideas not covered in this book, we will email (or snail mail) you our Free Report, THE ULTIMATE BUSINESS SECRET, which will explain an awesome concept for making money and building profitable business relationships!

Send your ideas to—

Bwitt@nni.com

or

Infoleverage
PO BOX 13246
Reading, PA 19612

How to Generate Cash Flow from Low-end House Investments

Perpetual Income is an exciting book on income property investments by Bryan Wittenmyer. It covers in detail how to build an income stream from lower-income housing investments. Best of all, the concepts work with virtually any type of rental housing.

Perpetual Income is a system that works for you day and night, 365 days per year. It's like having annuity checks come in the mail every month. The great news is the income doesn't "wear out" like it does in many other investments. You can spend the "checks" without spending the principal from the asset.

When you study any investment program you must ask yourself if the system is easily duplicated or repeated. Many programs or systems are not easily replicated; therefore, they are not of much value. This book is different. The principles and practices explained are being used by elite investors all across the country.

There are litarally tens of thousands of people whoWANT and NEED the services you will be offering. Let's face it, housing is BIG BUSINESS!

Perhaps the greatest advantage of the perpetual income system is the personal freedom that can result as you get your housing investments up and running. Very few jobs or businesses provide long-term residual income like owning income property investments.

I'm the first to admit this area of investing isn't for everyone. Many folks just aren't cut out to be landlords. For others the normal problems are caused by improper investment strategy and technique. It's no fun to overpay for properties and have a bunch of nonpaying tenants. A lot of mistakes are made in the rehab, repair, and maintenance area, too! About 80 percent of this "hassle" can be eliminated with the right knowledge. The other 20 percent? Well, that's good ol' Murphy's Law and normal business friction, which ALL businesses encounter.

If you are involved in rental properties of any kind, you need this 185-page gem of a book. Again, this book doesn't lightly gloss over the concepts. It goes in detail few investment books go into.

Here are just a few of the topics explained in this book:

$ How to get houses free and clear in 60 months

$ Finding bargain properties from $3,000 to $25,000

$ Secrets of obtaining owner financing

$ Dozens of money-stretching fix-up and repair tips

$ Specific cash-flow rules and guidelines

$ Finding dirt-cheap or free rehab materials

$ 7 Secrets to personal freedom

$ How to sell and carry paper safely

$ Safe tenant profiles and high risk tenants

$ The $10,000 chapter

$ City codes solutions

$ Tax Sale Secrets

$ Finding salvage or almost "free" houses

If you want real estate that keeps paying dividends over and over at prices that allow tremendous equity and cash flow, then you should discover this book!

Call to Order with Visa Or MasterCard: 610-670-9900 or email bwitt@nni.com

Price is $39.95 plus $4.00 shipping and handling

Infoleverage
PO BOX 13246
Reading, PA 19612

Unconditional Money-Back Guarantee if after a 90-day review the book doesn't meet your expectations.

Real Estate Answers
Business Answers
Marketing Answers

Get your own personal coach and advisor for motivation, guidance, and answers to your real estate and business questions. Bryan will be your personal coach and answer man to help you start and operate your own small business and real estate investment program.

You can shave years off the frustration and learning curve by allowing entrepreneur, author, and real estate investor, Bryan Wittenmyer to share his nearly twenty years of real estate and business experience with you. Consult one-on-one with Bryan, personally via telephone and email.

Not only do you gain his experience, but you also gain the experience of his numerous business associates within the real estate field. If this weren't enough, remember, this guy reads books the way some folks watch TV. The guy is a book junkie (business and investment books mostly).

The investment for this valuable consultation program is only $45 per month. Remember, what old Ben Franklin said, "An investment in knowledge pays the best interest." For a small investment of only $45 monthly, you get fast and insightful answers to your real estate, marketing, and small-business questions. Plus, he will push, prod, and scold you (nicely) to get going and become agressive, so you can make your business and investing goals and dreams come true!

We are so sure you will benefit from his personal consultations and advisory service that we offer a complete money-back guarentee on the service. You have no long-term commitment. Use it only as long as you want it.

We are easy to work with. The only commitment on your part is a minimum of a 3-month term. After that you can stop or start on a will-call basis. And, if you're not completely delighted that your getting giant results on your coaching, then let us know, and you'll get a refund on the unused portion of the consultation.

For full details email us at bwitt@nni.com or call us at 610.670.9900.

Infoleverage
PO BOX 13246
Reading, PA 19612
www.INFOLEVERAGE.com